"The Incarnation of the eternal Word as a male did not result from a divine flip of the coin. There are Trinitarian, Christological, and metaphysical reasons for Christ's maleness and for His choice to call only men to be Apostles and to share in His priestly ministry. These reasons are closely intertwined with the Catholic Church's infallible teaching on a male-only ordained priesthood. But what about the diaconate and the minor liturgical orders or ministries? This book defends the Church's traditional practice of restricting sanctuary service to men, arguing that the complementarity of the sexes and Christ's identity as Head and Bridegroom of the Church have implications for all offices of liturgical ministry. In doing so, it presents a positive vision of the crucial vocation of the lay faithful while highlighting the contribution only women can make to the Church and the world. Readers will be enlightened as to the sacramental and liturgical significance of sexual differences, which grounds a proper understanding of the roles of the clergy and laity. At stake is the nuptial relation that forms the very order of the New Covenant of salvation."

— Fr. Thomas Kocik
Author, *The Reform of the Reform? A Liturgical Debate*

"These timely reflections on Holy Orders will encourage the laity to pray for priests and will help clerics in their configuration to Christ, the Sovereign High Priest."

— Fr. Armand de Malleray, FSSP
Author, *X-Ray of the Priest in a Field Hospital*

"The relation of man and woman is a profound and beautiful sign of the relation of Christ and His Church. In this challenging and brilliant book, Peter Kwasniewski explores the depths of this sign and shows the consequences that follow for the liturgical life of the Church."

— Pater Edmund Waldstein, O.Cist.
Monk of Stift Heiligenkreuz

"In *Ministers of Christ*, Peter Kwasniewski remains true to form and takes on squarely what amounts to nearly a half century of cultural drift in the Catholic Church. May the professor's energy, determination, and clarity of thought in this book provide men and women of good will with clear indicators on the way to that 'out of the way place' where our loving Lord can refresh us for mission in the service of the truth!"

— The Most Reverend Thomas E. Gullickson, JCD
Archbishop of Bomarzo, Apostolic Nuncio (retired)

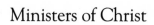

Ministers of Christ

Other books written or edited by Peter A. Kwasniewski:

Wisdom's Apprentice

On Love and Charity

Sacred Choral Works

Resurgent in the Midst of Crisis

Noble Beauty, Transcendent Holiness

Tradition and Sanity

Reclaiming Our Roman Catholic Birthright

The Holy Bread of Eternal Life

A Reader in Catholic Social Teaching

Newman on Worship, Reverence, and Ritual

And Rightly So: Selected Letters and Articles of Neil McCaffrey

The Ecstasy of Love in the Thought of Thomas Aquinas

Are Canonizations Infallible?

Peter A. Kwasniewski

Ministers of Christ
Recovering the Roles of Clergy and Laity
in an Age of Confusion

with
Bishop Athanasius Schneider

Foreword by
Leila Marie Lawler

Manchester, New Hampshire

Crisis Publications
Box 5284, Manchester, NH 03108
1-800-888-9344

www.CrisisMagazine.com

Sophia Institute Press® is a registered trademark of Sophia Institute.

paperback ISBN 978-1-64413-536-5

ebook ISBN 978-1-64413-537-2

Library of Congress Control Number: 2021945167

First printing

To Our Lord Jesus Christ, Eternal High Priest,
Exemplar of major and minor Orders

To Our Lady, virgin handmaid, wife and mother,
Queen of Heaven and Mediatrix of All Graces

To St. Joseph, just man and paragon of religion,
non-priest, non-Levite, humble father, exalted patriarch

To the Holy Family, Model of the Paradoxes
of Heavenly and Ecclesiastical Hierarchy

Let us preserve the precepts of our ancestors and not violate the stamp of tradition in a mood of reckless and daring boldness.

—*St. Ambrose of Milan*

The principle of piety admits of only one attitude: namely, that everything be transferred to the sons in the same spirit of faith in which it was accepted by the fathers; that religion should not lead us whither we want to go, but that we must follow whither it leads; and that it is proper to Christian modesty and earnestness not to transfer to posterity one's own ideas, but to preserve those received from one's ancestors.

—*St. Vincent of Lérins*

Contents

Foreword

The Nuptial Mystery Will Always Be True

[The Church] is called the spouse of Christ: "I have espoused you to one husband," says the Apostle to the Corinthians, "that I may present you a chaste virgin to Christ"; and writing to the Ephesians, he says: "Husbands, love your wives, as Christ, also, loved the Church, and delivered himself up for it"; and, also, speaking of marriage, he says: "This is a great sacrament, but I speak in Christ and in the Church."[1]

Christianity is a love story. Like every love story, its beginning—with Adam and Eve in the Garden—offers the promise of marriage and is fulfilled in the glory of union at the end—when, at the wedding feast, we are assured that they live happily ever after: "Let us be glad and rejoice, and give glory to him; for the marriage of the Lamb is come, and his wife hath prepared herself" (Rev 19:7). And: "These words of God are true" (Rev 19:9).

God offers mankind a great romance that plays out on all levels of His creation: the first man and woman were given to each other with the promise of a fecund love, flourishing with

[1] *The Catechism of the Council of Trent for Parish Priests*, trans. John McHugh, O.P., and Charles J. Callan, O.P. (Rockford, IL: TAN Books and Publishers, 1982), pt. I, art. IX, 98–98.

children and the increase of all of the created world, all of which is His; and yet He allows it to be given back to Him. To rescue His wayward Bride, He offered the sacrifice of the Lover of Man, Jesus, on the Cross. To participate in this sacrifice, each of us, man and woman, must be receptive like the Blessed Virgin Mary. All creation is hurrying toward the final marriage of heaven and earth spoken of in Revelation.

In medieval times, men aroused the common imagination as they began to sing of the Lady, the apotheosis of womanhood, who represents the prize worth fighting for (against both the enemy and themselves), capable of calling forth the virtue of manhood.

> The medieval ideal brought together two things which have no natural tendency to gravitate towards one another. It brought them together for that very reason. It taught humility and forbearance to the great warrior because everyone knew by experience how much he usually needed that lesson. It demanded valour of the urbane and modest man because everyone knew that he was as likely as not to be a milksop.[2]

The name of this virtue is chivalry, the baptism of mere *thumos*;[3] it's the Christ-like notion that authority and hierarchy exist to protect the weak. The paradox of courage united with meekness remains unknown to other religions. No pagan could achieve the synthesis on his own, nor would he consider it worth pursuing.

[2] C.S. Lewis, "The Necessity of Chivalry," first published in *Time and Tide*, August 1940, reprinted in Walter Hooper, ed., *Present Concerns: Journalistic Essays* (New York: HarperCollins, 1986), 3.
[3] A Greek word meaning spiritedness, anger, the conquering drive.

The past sixty years in the Catholic Church have seen us deprived of this story and its promise for our souls. The bishops seem to have forgotten the virtue of chivalry. They appear uninterested in the generative and receptive principles of male and female as they are expressed in human terms. They speak of love all the time, but too many withhold its necessary grounding, replacing it with something else.

What is that "something else"? I would like to sketch with broad strokes the Church's self-understanding before and after the moment of change. Let the reader understand that this is not a *liturgical* comparison per se, as one normally encounters in a discussion of the pre– and post–Vatican II eras.

The ecclesiology of the past

From the time of the Acts of the Apostles, the Christian Church evinces hierarchical realities. Through the ages, the Church oversaw the growth of an organic institution that dwelt in the world by means of the parish, with the bishop governing and protecting the parishes in his diocese.

In parishes, families receive the sacraments. They raise and educate their children. Parishes also offer the sacraments to those who, without having families of their own, recognize the primacy of the family in God's plan. The parish offers no "programs" as we know them today, although there are sodalities and devotional groups offering various activities or services—only these are run by religious or laymen, not paid parish functionaries.

The majority of new Catholics come from within Catholic families. Even in missionary territory this is the goal: to raise up the church from within families once conversions are made. A natural evangelization takes place when Catholics marry converts. Non-Catholics observe Catholics living like them, and yet differently, and want to convert. Any catechetical materials come from clergy and consecrated religious, or from lay people they oversee closely.

As they raise their children to be Catholic, parents are assisted by schools run by active orders of sisters and brothers, consecrated religious living the evangelical counsels of poverty, chastity, and obedience. Bishops have a keen interest in their flourishing. Active orders also engage in works of mercy, supported by the families who give of their substance to keep the orders going. (Remember Blessed Solanus Casey and the Capuchins who opened soup kitchens during the Depression.) Families on their own cannot help the poor on a large scale, but they support the orders and, in this way, participate in these good works, including missions aimed at winning converts. All this interdependent work represents a real economy of grace, where the members of the Body of Christ have their own functions and spheres and support each other, as St. Paul writes in his first letter to the Corinthians. The salient fact about these orders is their austerity: children and the poor know that those serving them are poor by choice, for the sake of the Kingdom, and this witness is important.

Contemplative orders provide spiritual support for the whole Church with prayer, in a hidden way, as well as mysteriously relating to the Body of Christ by living apart from the world. The contemplative orders provide the fullness of worship in living the hours of the Divine Office; just as families cannot totally commit to taking care of the poor, they cannot pray as intensively as those behind monastic walls. Yet by this division of labor, so to speak, total coverage is achieved in the matter of worship.

Living simply is seen as a virtue for all, from the poverty of consecrated religious to the poverty of large families. Generosity in welcoming children builds up the Kingdom here on earth as well as in heaven, and bishops remind the people of this truth often. As Pope Pius XII once put it: "Wherever you find large families in great numbers, they point to the physical and moral health of a Christian people, a living faith in God and trust in His Providence, [and] the fruitful and joyful holiness of Catholic marriage."[4]

Today's ecclesiology

What I have described above is how most of us think of the Catholic Church. But my argument here is that it is not, in the main, *how the bishops think of the Catholic Church*, no matter how often they reference "the good sisters"—nor are its goals represented in their plans for the future. Instead, in the Western world,[5] if we judge by the model of the United States Conference of Catholic Bishops, they are guided by professional-managerial (albeit ecclesiastical) "experts." On the parish level, meanwhile, we find the following:

The parish is run by a pastor, sometimes assisted by a parochial vicar, along with permanent deacons. Until recently, I was unaware that this position in its current manifestation is a relatively new one. It was revived—and, perhaps one could say, re-invented—in 1967. The parish administration is populated by laywomen, Extraordinary Ministers of Holy Communion (meaning laypeople who distribute the Eucharist), the stray un-habited sister, professional program providers such as "youth ministers,"

---

4   Pope Pius XII, *Address to the Directors of the Associations for Large Families of Rome and of Italy*, January 20, 1958.

5   And the same is planned for the developing world: see Pope Francis's Apostolic Exhortation *Querida Amazonia*.

and many others keeping themselves busy with activities. But the bishop is probably remote and not easily communicated with. He too is surrounded by women.

We find churches attended by older people beyond their active years, having raised not-very-numerous offspring; and very young families, the majority contracepting. The latter group is relatively small when compared with its cohort in the past, but noticeably eager to do the right things in all spheres, religion being simply one of them. These families tend also to be involved in sports and other activities for their children. They aspire to be "upwardly mobile," and their contact with parish life reinforces a very tempered, service-oriented, and expertly managed sort of social justice carried out from a suitable distance and mainly political in expression.

The objective observer finds that the church is a sort of club. As time goes on, the younger families eventually direct their energy toward school, sports, and other secular activities; slowly, they drift away. We can conclude this because there are few older children attending Mass, and few families between the young and old categories. The arrival of new, young families obscures the drift, but we see that they are not the grown children of the previous generation.

Families living out the real teaching of the church (identifiable by their large sizes and big vans) find little welcome in most parishes, which strongly emphasize activity measurable by participation in programs. These larger families find the pace too exhausting when attempted alongside the pressures of raising children in a hostile society. Therefore, the stated goals of many bishops, to increase such programs, are incompatible with real family life. I include in parish programs the bishops' commitment to "safe environment" policies, which destroy the possibility of forming normal friendships in the parish due to restrictions imposed on gatherings and interactions. That's not to mention the difficulty of the logistics of complying when one has many small children.

This pattern of life in the church—one oriented by and toward a managerial process rather than a nuptial pattern centered on the Sacraments—creates a disruption as the older generation dies off and is not replaced from within. Continuity is broken. The parish's focus turns from bringing young people up into adulthood in the church ("the old ecclesiology") to converting them ("the new evangelization"). Bishops view those outside the Church as the main means of gaining parishioners—that is, financial contributors. Aimed at recapturing the large number of fallen-away or never-assimilated Catholics (or, as Bishop Barron calls them, "nones"), this new mode of so-called evangelization confirms the bishops' perceived need for professional (that is, trained) experts in evangelization, of whom there are legions, as institutions of higher learning recognize a marketing niche of their own certification capability. And it becomes a self-perpetuating idea, not coincidentally for those same experts. Lose the young; convert the old; repeat.

The most important evidence for this new ecclesiology is the absence of a plan for forming Christians to carry on evangelization from within. Few of even our most "conservative" bishops have much to offer families who wish to raise their children in a way that holds out the best hope for keeping them Catholic. In fact, many place obstacles in their way. I can think of one exception: the diocese of Lincoln, Nebraska. There may be others, but their scarcity emphasizes the departure from what had been a universal recognition of responsibility. Despite the procreation and education of children being the primary responsibility of parents, the new ecclesiology simply does not address it or offer help—though it often hinders it. The one incredibly successful evangelical tool the bishops used in the past, the Catholic school system, has virtually vanished except in countries, like Australia, where Catholic schools are subsidized by the government; there they don't retain members of the Church, but they are undeniably thriving.

As to specifically religious education for the dwindling numbers of young people, parishes offer token extracurricular catechesis and invest heavily in youth conferences, promoted by professionals within chanceries who aggregate entrepreneurs from without. These operatives in turn make their living providing the service, as a sort of gateway through which the youth will pass. The idea is that, in this manner, they will be exposed to whatever has been lacking previously, to capture young people whom the bishops have allowed to be exposed to the world (in the form of mostly public education) with a product: youth ministry. Whereas in the past bishops went on record to warn parents not to send children to public schools, today they tacitly accept that most children will attend them. Where there are parochial schools, they are run by professional educators and administrators, not religious, because there are no religious to run them. Again, there are exceptions, but broadly speaking, that is how things are. These private schools are too taxing on families with more than a few children because, not being run by those vowed to poverty, they must provide a competitive wage for the staff, requiring burdensome tuitions, fundraising, and supplemental activity on the part of parents. Most families who depend on only one income fall back on homeschooling, if only to conserve resources.

In the main, bishops fail to understand the way educational institutions indoctrinate children with progressive ideologies, perhaps because the bishops themselves are progressives. What the cultural Marxist thinker Antonio Gramsci called "the long march through the institutions" remains an enigma to them, as is the subsequent vitiating effect on the Church's dwindling population of young people. Of course, their own doctrinal, liturgical, and moral derelictions blind them. The bishops manifest no interest in combatting universal sex education: programs openly dedicated to grooming young people for contraception and abortion and indoctrinating them with gender ideology. They don't even acknowledge that these issues exist. (Pro-forma statements on diocesan websites don't count.) Our bishops don't seem to want to secure for our time what we had in the past: an uninterrupted and coherent education of Catholics from infancy to adulthood, sheltered from worldliness. When you task their appointed representatives with this failing, their response is, "We can't rely on the family because today's families are broken." Which raises the question of how families got that way — not to mention that God's original plan to fill the earth with believers by means of the family was never superseded, nor could it ever be.

The new ecclesiology that I am seeking to delineate here implicitly accepts or actively promotes a church that is administrative in nature while maintaining the optics of the older model of complete devotion to a vocation set apart. Referencing strict nuns or soup kitchens keeps up appearances, but the reality is far different. Most bishops train priests to be functionaries in a bureaucracy, not brave men nobly sacrificing a natural family for the supernatural family of the Kingdom of God. Seminaries forthrightly compete with secular institutions, maintaining a college atmosphere. In their "off hours" the men may wear casual dress rather than clerical garb. Students play video games just like normal undergrads; breakfast features designer coffees. Asceticism is unknown there because those bishops are not preparing men for ascetic lives. And this worldly culture in turn informs our idea of the Church.

Such bishops' vision of how works of mercy will be carried out has changed, with dioceses becoming auxiliary bureaucracies offering government assistance. We know that the USCCB receives or oversees funds, directly or indirectly, in the billions of dollars from the government for its "charitable" works, which in turn take the form of funneling their clients back into government entitlement programs.[6] And yet they seem to have little interest in reviving the old charitable institutions that changed the world. I have never heard a bishop mention restoring or supporting active religious orders, with the possible exception of the Sisters of Life or visiting missionaries seeking a collection. Not only does this serious privation harm society, it also harms the people who have vocations to that life.

Orphanages, hospitals, schools, soup kitchens: all changed or simply lost. To respond to the crisis of out-of-wedlock pregnancy, the Church is comfortable with the secular model of single moms raising their babies, but leaves the laity to organize it. The Ordinary in my state pulled the Church out of adoption services altogether rather than fight mandated placement with homosexuals, a fight he could have won on religious freedom grounds. Had he lost, however, at least he would have made a stand for babies needing good homes. When the Church acts as an arm of the government, it requires the faithful to cooperate with and promote taxation (already burdensome on families), illegal immigration, the corrupt foster care system, universal healthcare, daycare, and other harmful and meddlesome activities.

---

[6]   See my article "Is It Time to Abolish the USCCB?," *Crisis Magazine*, September 16, 2019.

Women are not honored for being wives and mothers; large families are not encouraged. Pope Francis's apostolic exhortation *Querida Amazonia* was completely misunderstood by naïve or exhausted commentators. Nowhere did it speak of the family (other than in progressive "family of the world" terms), nor of the mother's role in it. On the contrary, this document, which elicited a mistaken sigh of relief from conservatives when it did not call for women in Holy Orders, actually advanced the groundwork for administrative ecclesiology:

> In a synodal Church, those women who in fact have a central part to play in Amazonian communities should have access to positions, including ecclesial services, that do not entail Holy Orders and that can better signify the role that is theirs. Here it should be noted that these services entail stability, public recognition and a commission from the bishop. This would also allow women to have a real and effective impact on the organization, the most important decisions and the direction of communities, while continuing to do so in a way that reflects their womanhood.[7]

What is not said is sometimes more important than what is said. When the hierarchy speaks exclusively of women providing services and having roles in administration, the indispensable role of women as mothers vanishes from its sight and its priorities. The traditional framework of the three societies — Church, State, and Family — is replaced by one that is not fruitful. Having lost concentration on the centrality of the family, bishops then pull away from their role in fostering traditional religious orders,

---

[7] *Querida Amazonia* §103.

which, after all, do depend on generous families for vocations. In the words (once again) of Pius XII:

> With good reason, it has often been pointed out that large families have been in the forefront as the cradles of saints. We might cite, among others, the family of St. Louis, the King of France, made up of ten children, that of St. Catherine of Siena who came from a family of twenty-five, St. Robert Bellarmine from a family of twelve, and St. Pius X from a family of ten. Every vocation is a secret of Providence; but these cases prove that a large number of children does not prevent parents from giving them an outstanding and perfect upbringing; and they show that the number does not work out to the disadvantage of their quality, with regard to either physical or spiritual values.[8]

The new ecclesiology narrows sacramental life to the Sunday Mass hour, because it is not particularly interested in worship. For the new ecclesiology, faith does not matter. We can observe that the clergy in the prosperous parts of the world, on the whole, live comfortably, assisted or in many cases supplanted by women in many of what the ordinary Catholic would think of as the duties that go with the priestly vocation. As Dr. Phillipa Martyr reports of the Church in Australia, "We don't have a priest shortage; we're rapidly developing a laity shortage."

Confession is nearly forgotten. The Divine Office has receded from consciousness: few religious are dedicated to the *opus Dei* or liturgical worship of God in solemnity and beauty, while (as Professor Kwasniewski will show) most priests don't say their breviary, and Vespers with Benediction no longer forms a regular

---

[8] From the address cited above.

part of parish life. In the past, Sunday Mass, although the apex of the liturgy, was not the only expression of divine worship, and devotions flourished. Today's void has taken its toll on the Church's identity and its rootedness in people's everyday lives.

Recovering the perfections of man and woman to restore the Church

If these observations about ecclesiology are true, we must conclude that it would be a mistake to focus *solely* on liturgical changes since Vatican II in order to explain the mess we are in today. The Council opened the door to meddling with worship; after Paul VI's new missal was promulgated, the self-styled experts took a mile for every inch. But the effects of the "new directions" were soon felt throughout the whole ecclesial system, even when the causes went unremarked. Or, even if we notice and rail against them, we don't quite internalize that what we call defects are perceived by the clergy as *features*. Using the pretext of active participation in the liturgy to bring about a leveling of hierarchy, rendering every office a merely managerial one, was perhaps an outcome we did not anticipate—nor can we quite reconcile it with our deeply held vision of what the Church is and must be.

I have come to agree with Peter Kwasniewski that until the Traditional Latin Mass is universally restored, we will remain in the situation described above. Even those who seek a more reverent version of the Novus Ordo must acknowledge, as the passage of time produces no real "reform of the reform," that there is a bureaucratic machinery at work in the background that cranks all variants into a mold of its own devising. But make no mistake: ecclesiology drives liturgy and doctrine, because all incentives flow from the way an institution goes about its business. The machinery I speak of is willing to accommodate lovers of tradition, grudgingly allowing them a marginal position within the multi-level market that is this new Church. For the radicals have subsided. Instead, we are simply managed, and managers are a generally tolerant lot—as long as no one asks or claims too much or challenges what Fr. Paul Mankowski, S.J., called "the deal in place."

I don't know how to oppose this machinery. For most of us, the only realistic option is simply to join in worship with those who cleave to a vision of the Church that is both more eternal and transcendent and more grounded, however obscured this vision may be. Getting as close to Tradition as we can brings its own grace, but I do think that unless at least some people are aware of the new ecclesiology and strive against it with intelligence and fortitude, the restoration will be much longer in coming.

I received an assist in putting my observations on paper when Fr. Thomas Reese, S.J., wrote an article called "The Future of Catholic Liturgical Reform" for Religion News Service on April 13, 2021. With admirable clarity (for my purpose, at least), he says:

> Bishops' conferences should discuss whether new liturgical ministries are needed and who may be called to perform liturgy. Can the work of liturgy be separated from the work of administration? Do all liturgical leaders have to be celibate, male, full-time employees? Can a deacon or layperson anoint the sick or hear confessions? In an age of declining numbers of priests, such questions must be faced.

Let's read it again: "Can the work of liturgy be separated from the work of administration?... Do all liturgical leaders have to be ... male?"

There it is in a nutshell. The logic of the new ecclesiology ends with women in ministry. Administration is the ultimate equalizer. Welcome to the ring: in *that* corner, we have Fr. Reese representing progressives who seem willing, at least for now, to relinquish the *terminology* of women priests, but not the goal. As he says, does it matter what exactly we call them? He has a copy of *Querida Amazonia* tucked in his back pocket. The practitioners of the new ecclesiology opportunistically use their "home" advantage, their secure positions in the Vatican and chanceries, to blur the essential difference between the lay and priestly vocations. The Church's internal life and external mission require ordained clergy for divine worship. Attempting to flatten this distinction has caused incalculable damage to the Church's internal life and external mission. If we accept the premise that the Church is at bottom administrative, then we must admit that no, it does not matter — priest, layperson, man, woman: all can equally carry out a worldly agenda. But if we reject the premise, because we see the Church as a divine institution and living body, not a bureaucracy, then we have to make the case for *men only* to serve at the altar.

I maintain, however, that the case must be argued not only as it relates to the suitability of men (and men would naturally argue in this way), but also in terms of the original nuptial meaning of man and woman and the perfections of women as well — for everything and everyone created has its, his, or her perfections!

Fundamentally, God gives woman her own unique nature as mother. Eve is the mother of all the living; Mary is the new Eve and our mother (John 19:26–27). Significantly, the Blessed Virgin is Queen of Apostles without being a priest. We must liberate ourselves from the spurious and distracting question of why women can't receive Holy Orders or serve at the altar; the more important observation is that priests can't be mothers. Without mothers, including spiritual mothers, there would be no priests. Putting women in the sanctuary steals something precious from their sex. It diminishes them and makes the faithful orphans. Pretending to offer women even quasi-priestly duties denies the reality of complementarity, of fittingness according to our respective natures. When those searching for ways to affirm an all-male priesthood ignore complementarity for structure alone, they make the claim of authority and hierarchy into a power issue. Where power is at stake, women will never relinquish the fight for equality—why would they? But the paradigm is all wrong. When the vision is of complementarity, women's protectors see that the exercise of authority lies in being willing to fight for womanly perfections in their rightful place, for the sake of all.

Since in many cases this fight will be branded by feminists (male and female) precisely as domination, men must take care to demand sacrifice of themselves and to be known to do so. In this way, they will assure those of good will that they are motivated by love.

My challenge to the reader is this: to see that the Church is being attacked in her very nature and that the cause is effeminacy, the vice of men refusing their own nature as men; it is not primarily about a power grab by women (although I certainly acknowledge that some women seek to grab power). The first move, just as in the Garden of Eden, was men turning away from taking responsibility—essentially an effeminate, emasculated position. Remember that effeminacy can manifest in two ways: unbecoming softness or overweening macho pride. Chivalry is the answer to effeminacy. Christ was the ultimate knight when He expressed His authority by dying on the Cross.

No argument for hierarchy and patriarchy can succeed only by insisting that woman acknowledge her unfittingness for doing what men do and her disordered desire to do it. The defender of tradition must demonstrate the appropriateness of male service at the altar, as well as how it fits into the hierarchy of being. But he must do so with respect for the woman's true and necessary place, humbly keeping in mind that it is the great Mother of God, *a woman*, who is, in the words of the sacred liturgy, "the glory of Jerusalem, the joy of Israel, the highest honor of our race," "more honorable than the cherubim, and incomparably more glorious than the seraphim."[9]

So in *this* corner we have Peter Kwasniewski and the book you hold in your hands. In *his* back pocket he has all the resources necessary in history, Tradition, Scripture, the Magisterium, and common sense, to convince the honest inquirer that God intends men, and men only, to be priests and for males only to serve (note well the verb) at the altar of God. Dr. Kwasniewski convincingly demonstrates his thesis using the framework of the goodness of God's creation in all its dispositions: goodness for men, goodness for women, goodness for the Church in her identity and Great Commission, as we strive to fulfill God's will for us—be it as members of the laity who leaven the world or as ministers ordained for worship, governance, and teaching. Our deepest longing, whatever calling we have received and acted on, is to be with our Lover: we hope to be with Him in Heaven, where we will be invited to the *marriage* feast.

—Leila Marie Lawler
Lancaster, Massachusetts
Feast of St. George, April 23

---

[9] Texts from the Gradual of the Mass for December 8 in the Roman rite and from the Byzantine Divine Liturgy of St. John Chrysostom.

Preface

Pope Francis's decision, by means of his motu proprio *Spiritus Domini* (2021), to modify canon law so that the "ministries" of lector and acolyte are now to be conferred upon women raises more numerous and far deeper issues than may be apparent to many at first sight. For well over 1,700 years, the Roman Church knew the existence of four "minor orders" (porter, exorcist, acolyte, and lector) and three "major orders" (subdeacon, deacon, and priest).[10] These roles concern the execution of the liturgy and were, on that account, reserved to men. Pope Paul VI attempted to abolish the minor orders[11] and to replace them with what are commonly called the "instituted ministries" of acolyte and lector, but he maintained some semblance of continuity by limiting them to men. Indeed, initially only men—whether formally instituted or not—could enter the sanctuary to fulfill these tasks.[12] In practice, however, the same kind of disobedience

---

[10] On account of a widespread lack of familiarity with this aspect of Catholic tradition, a brief description of the minor orders and the subdiaconate will be found after this preface.

[11] On why I say "attempted," see chapter 12.

[12] The 1970 Instruction *Liturgicae Instaurationes* states: "In conformity with norms traditional in the Church, women (single,

that led to Communion in the hand[13] led also to the routine use
of women and girls as servers and readers (i.e., not instituted
acolytes and lectors). Pope John Paul II, in one of the most
criticized and regretted moves of his pontificate, recognized
the practice as allowable, albeit not mandatory. Prior to 2021,
women and girls were therefore permitted, in the sphere of the
Novus Ordo, to substitute for lectors and acolytes, but canon
law still said that only men (*viri*) were to be "installed," that
is, to hold them in a permanent and stable way as ministries.
As I will show in this book, the situation inherited from Paul
VI and John Paul II was already theologically and liturgically
incoherent and has been made only more so by Francis's motu
proprio, which continues the pattern of rupture from Catholic
tradition.[14] Our age is not known for deep or careful thought
about the implications of the steps we take in pursuit of what

---

married, religious), whether in churches, homes, convents,
schools, or institutions for women, are barred from serving the
priest at the altar" (§7); similarly, the 1975 *General Instruction of
the Roman Missal* assumes laymen as lectors, says that women may
perform ministries "outside the sanctuary," and asks episcopal
conferences to "designate a suitable [other] place for a woman
to proclaim the word of God."

[13] See Most Rev. Juan Rodolfo Laise, *Holy Communion. Communion in the Hand: Documents & History*, fifth rev. and enlarged
ed. (Boonville, NY: Preserving Christian Publications, 2020),
esp. 98–109.

[14] A similar rupture can be seen in the postconciliar extension, to
so-called "extraordinary ministers," of the privilege of distributing Holy Communion, of which the sacramentally ordained are
understood to be the "ordinary ministers." For a critique of this
novelty, see my book *The Holy Bread of Eternal Life: Restoring
Eucharistic Reverence in an Age of Impiety* (Manchester, NH:
Sophia Institute Press, 2020), 147–58.

is believed to be "a better world"—we tend to shoot before we look—and it is no secret that knowledge of history, theology, and liturgy, even among high-ranking prelates, is deplorable and has been for some time now.

Thus, while Pope Francis's motu proprio may look like a technicality (and surely will make no noticeable difference in places where the sanctuary is already a female-dominated space), it represents, in fact, a tectonic shift both in theology and in praxis. Francis is saying that the Catholic Church, for the first time ever, should officially institute women as liturgical ministers—not as substitutes for ministers, but as ministers simply speaking. While such a decision does not logically demand an opening to women deacons or women priests, it is intelligible only against the backdrop of the pervasive feminism that has equated the worth of women with their taking-on of roles traditionally reserved to men. In that sense, it continues to stoke the flames of a false egalitarianism that will never stop agitating for women deacons and priests. Moreover, it reflects a failure to understand why ministries were reserved to men in the first place, and why the inclusion of women in these roles is contrary to the very nature and structure of the Catholic liturgy. Yet that is not all. The Church suffers today from great confusion about the roles proper to the clergy and the roles proper to the laity. An oft-bemoaned but seldom corrected trend to "clericalize the laity," whether women or men, introduces a false dynamic into the life of the Church and distorts our relationship to the liturgy and to each other in the Mystical Body. A necessary and long-overdue course correction requires understanding anew the indispensable, positive, transformative, and fulfilling role of the Christian laity in the world, working in tandem with the clergy in a way that is analogous to the complementarity of the sexes and the complementarity of active and contemplative religious life.[15]

Considering the importance of this cluster of topics, it is a cause for concern that literature arguing for the traditional point of view is slim to non-existent. This book is an attempt to fill that lacuna. I wrote it for three categories of Catholics. First, for liberal or progressive Catholics, who are convinced that the tradition of limiting ministries to men (ideally ordained men) is simply a knot of misogynistic assumptions based on outmoded ancient philosophy and a pagan ritualism reliant on categories of sacred and profane that Christian revelation has exploded. These readers need to see that the tradition has a coherent and comprehensive account behind it—one that rests in no way on the denigration of women or of the laity, but on reasons that benefit and augment the dignity of all: ministers and non-ministers, men and women alike. Second, for traditional Catholics, who know by a kind of instinct or intuition what is right and what is wrong in regard to sanctuary ministry but, apart from uttering a few generalities, would be hard-pressed to give a reasoned explanation of why it is right. If we are going to carry the torch of tradition forward in the teeth of increasing resistance, we very much need to see that we are defending not merely a preference but an apostolic and

[15] As the Congregation for the Doctrine of the Faith's 1973 Instruction *Mysterium Ecclesiae* states: "Christ the Lord, the High Priest of the new and everlasting covenant, wished to associate with His perfect priesthood and to form in its likeness the people He had bought with His own blood (cf. Heb. 7:20–22, 26–28; 10:14, 21). He therefore granted His Church a share in His priesthood, which consists of the common priesthood of the faithful and the ministerial or hierarchical priesthood. These differ from each other not only in degree but also in essence; yet they are mutually complementary within the communion of the Church."

patristic inheritance resting on the deepest theological foundations. Third, for so-called "conservative Catholics," who may well
have their "preferences" for what is (more or less) traditional but
whose ultramontanism puts them in a bind: in order to keep their
preferences, they must agree to let others in the Church have
contrary preferences, and their criterion of right and wrong must
be dictated solely by positive legislation. I wish to demonstrate, at
least on the present topic, that the way they hold their position
in fact does amount to a form of prejudice, discrimination, or (at
best) aestheticism. Only the traditional account can rise above
subjectivism to an objective order emanating from the original
creation and reestablished in Christ, the New Adam.

The book's chapters are grouped into three parts. The first
part, "Foundations," looks at the most fundamental questions:
how sexuality and the body have personal significance and therefore moral, theological, and liturgical significance as well; the
connection between the Incarnation of Our Lord and the male
priesthood and male sanctuary service; the blessing on womanhood conferred in and through Our Lady, the Virgin Mother
of God; the Old Testament background and New Testament
roots of the diaconate, subdiaconate, and minor orders, seen as
radiating outward from the priesthood of Jesus Christ, and the
solemn tradition behind this ecclesiastical hierarchy; and the
proper role of the laity in the great world outside the churches,
where they exercise their primary responsibilities. The second
part, "Deviations," takes a critical look at practices that entered
the Church after the Second Vatican Council — above all, the
habitual use of female lectors and altar servers, whether filling in
as "substitutes" or, as Pope Francis would now have it, installed
as ministers. It explains how these novelties misconstrue and
muddle the callings of laity and clergy as well as their diverse

but complementary modes of participation in the liturgy. Here it is especially important to free the notion of "active participation" from its harsh captivity as a slogan trafficked by modern liturgists and to indicate its original meaning and the conditions for its realization. The third part, "Restoration," charts a path out of this mess into a healthier church life, making the case for several related proposals. First is the universal reestablishment of the subdiaconate and minor orders — which, contrary to popular belief, have never been abrogated and remain in use to this day. Second is a return to the traditional *lex orandi* of the classical Roman rite, which embodies true doctrine about states of life, ministries, and sexes. Third is the wearing of veils by women in church as a sign of their distinctive role in the Mystical Body. Fourth is the full acceptance of the supernatural and sacrificial vision of priesthood and consecrated life that attracts vocations today as it always did in the past, together with a firm repudiation of the "heresy of activism" that extinguishes the primacy of prayer and the ultimacy of contemplation. Fifth is a reversal of the mad race of *aggiornamento* (updating), to be replaced by the serene embrace of the essential changelessness of the Christian religion, which worships the immutable God in His eternal truth, reflected in the liturgical rites of Catholic tradition and the stable forms of life they call forth and bless.

Ministers of Christ concludes with three litanies for private devotional use, following the general format of the public litanies. The first is for the clergy in general. The second and third, based on the traditional *Roman Martyrology*, remind us that the history of the Church provides many examples of saintly subdeacons, lectors, acolytes, exorcists, and sacristans, whom we ought to invoke. (Though sacristan is not a minor order, it seems fitting to include the two sacristan saints Abundius and Constantius, as clerics frequently perform the work of sacristans.) Since there are, happily, institutes and communities that continue to make use of the ancient rites for the subdiaconate and minor orders, these litanies would be most appropriately prayed by those who are preparing to receive said orders, those who have received them and exercise their functions, and those who wish to pray on behalf of such candidates, either by name or in general. What could be better than to call upon the intercession of the glorious martyrs and confessors of the Faith who, in their own lifetimes, received the dignity of these offices in the Church and are forever remembered by her in that manner?

Lastly, there is a select bibliography for those who wish to read more.

In these pages, I never say that men are superior to women or that every kind of distinction that has ever been based on sexual difference is praiseworthy and should be retained or revived. What I believe, instead, is that God created the two sexes for a profound reason—really, a set of interlocking reasons—and that we will be diminished human beings and Christians to the extent that we lose sight of those reasons and cease to act in view of them. He speaks to us, He teaches us through the inherent symbolism of the sexes and their intended relationship of complementarity, of unity-in-distinction. The irreducible complexity and interdependence of the two sexes benefit both men and women by drawing forth certain perfections characteristic of masculinity and femininity, which in turn support the full development of personhood and Christian identity, as men learn from and rely on women, and vice versa. We learn who we are and we learn of God *through the other* with whom we are in relationship. This alterity includes not just any "other," but the *sexual* other—members of the opposite sex—in the manifold relations of the natural and supernatural family: St. Joseph and the Blessed Virgin Mary,

Reverend Father in the parish and Reverend Mother in the convent, religious brothers and sisters— not to mention the natural father, mother, brother, sister, uncle, aunt, nephew, niece.... This alterity reflects and displays the analogy between nature and grace, with the latter building on the former and carrying it to a level nature alone could not reach. To step as far back as we possibly can: creation's ultimate purpose is the manifestation of the Father's goodness, which is perfectly accomplished in the Incarnation of His Son, who is the revelation and mediation of the Father's love. With a view to that goal, God created the relationship of bridegroom and bride, where there are "two (spirits) in one (flesh)"—which was seen first of all in Adam and Eve and their descendants; then, by divine initiative, in Yahweh and Israel; and finally, in the fullness of time, in Christ and the Church.[16] The distinction between clergy and laity, and, within the clergy, between the various orders or degrees, furthers this revelation and mediation in the Body of Christ.

I thank Leila Marie Lawler for her foreword, which places my book in a larger context—namely, that of the institutional Church in recent decades, which has chosen to remake (and unmake) itself into a bureaucratic behemoth panting after fashionable causes, softening or diluting its once-clear doctrine, its once-demanding discipline, and its once-magnificent liturgy. Well-meaning Catholics who try to avoid "finding fault" with the direction in which popes and bishops have been taking us since the Second Vatican Council too easily forget that each modification, abbreviation, suppression, or innovation alters the face and voice of the Church as the Bride of Christ and Mother of believers—how she "presents"

---

[16] See, *inter alia*, Gen. 2:23–24, Tob. 8:8; Ezek. 16:8, Isa. 62:4–5; Eph. 5:25–33, Rev. 21:2.

herself to the faithful and to the world, how her witness is seen
and her message heard. Such changes will never be neutral, but
will be either for the better or for the worse, measured against the
Church's deepest nature and purpose. And when we take into account the innumerable changes made in pursuit of an ill-defined
and highly manipulable project of *aggiornamento* over the course of
many decades, we can see that the cumulative result will be either
very good or very bad. Those capable of interpreting "the signs of
the times" without flinching—among which can be mentioned
the unending bad news of clerical sexual abuse, the unchallenged
hegemony of progressivism (or its byproduct, mediocrity) in the
vast majority of chanceries and seminaries, the alarming break-
down of marriage and family, the paucity of priestly and religious
vocations, and the pitiful (when not sacrilegious) execution of
Catholic liturgy in the Western world—will not fail to draw the
conclusion that the single largest "makeover" in Church history has
culminated in precisely the "silent apostasy" of formerly Christian
peoples lamented by John Paul II.[17]

It is crucial to see, with Mrs. Lawler, that our beliefs, our
worship, our life, exist in an ecclesiological framework: what the
Church *is*, and what she is understood to be *for*. A true ecclesiology
sustains and prompts the correct forms of belief, worship, and life.
These, in turn, reinforce that framework and repel what is contrary
to it. A matter such as disbanding an immemorial tradition of
minor orders or directing that women should assume certain ministries hitherto reserved to men is not just an isolated bureaucratic
decision, an arbitrary determination floating in a vacuum. It is
bound up with a vision of the Church. It represents the Church

---

[17] See the Post-Synodal Apostolic Exhortation *Ecclesia in Europa*
(June 28, 2003), §9.

under a certain aspect. It affects how the Church will or will not serve Christ and achieve the good of His members. Beyond utility or aesthetics, it is a matter that concerns *truth*—adherence to the truth that sets us free, or a drifting away from the truth by enslavement to modernity's ideologies.

Some readers may have a methodological objection to my entire project. They might say that since popes of the post-conciliar era have taken action to reduce, rename, extend, or redefine liturgical ministries in various ways, Catholics have no business critiquing these decisions and arguing that they are for the worse and should be rescinded. Obviously, if I accepted that point of view, I would not have written this book.

However, while I believe as a Catholic that papal teachings and decisions deserve the benefit of the doubt and ready acceptance in normal circumstances, it is also true—and the theological and canonical tradition of the Church has never denied it—that such benefit and acceptance have limits imposed by natural and divine law, by reason and faith, and by respect for venerable ecclesiastical traditions. The reader looking for a full account of how I understand the nature and limits of papal authority and the corresponding possibility of a judicious and respectful critique will find it primarily in two lectures: "My Journey from Ultramontanism to Catholicism"[18] and, in the wake of the motu proprio *Traditionis Custodes*, "The Pope's Boundenness to Tradition as a Legislative Limit: Replying to Ultramontanist Apologetics."[19] Along the same

[18] First published in three parts in *Catholic Family News* (November 2020–January 2021), then published online on February 4, 2021: www.catholicfamilynews.com/blog/2021/02/04/my-journeyfrom-ultramontanism-to-catholicism.

[19] Published at *Rorate Caeli*, August 3, 2021: https://rorate-caeli.blogspot.com/2021/08/the-popes-boundenness-to-tradition-as.html.

lines I recommend the book *Defending the Faith Against Present Heresies*,[20] particularly the articles in it by Fr. John Hunwicke, Claudio Pierantoni, Michael Sirilla, and Pauper Peregrinus.[21] In my judgment, *Traditionis Custodes*, although it will unquestionably make the lives of many Catholics more difficult for a time, only confirms the rightness and indeed urgency of the arguments and proposals presented in this book.

The dedication to *Ministers of Christ* deserves a bit of unpacking. The Holy Family is an ever-provocative model of the paradoxes of heavenly and ecclesiastical hierarchy, in which rulers are servants and servants are rulers, sanctity and position are by no means convertible, and a new covenant destined to fill the earth and resound in countless churches until the end of time is inaugurated in silence, hiddenness, interiority, domesticity, and labor. The Holy Family teaches us again and again the right understanding of Christian states and duties. It gives us the ability to detect and denounce open and subtle forms of clericalism, secularism, and activism. The full meaning of the dedication, then, is as follows:

> To Our Lord Jesus Christ, the Eternal High Priest, who, though being in the form of God, did not count equality with God a thing to be grasped, but emptied Himself, taking the form of a slave for the salvation of mankind (cf. Phil. 2:6–8), and in so doing made Himself the exemplar of major and minor orders in the Church, which derive their efficacy from Him; to Our Lady, Queen of Heaven and Mediatrix of All Graces, who did not count equality

---

[20] Edited by John R. T. Lamont and Claudio Pierantoni (Waterloo, ON: Arouca Press, n.d.).

[21] These articles will be found on pp. 199–209, 235–51, 315–22, and 415–20.

with her husband a thing to be grasped, but humbled herself as wife, mother, intercessor, and co-redeemer, meriting through her sinless and selfless charity the highest place in the heavenly kingdom; to St. Joseph, the just man, paragon of the virtue of religion, who did not count equality with priests and Levites a thing to be grasped, but accepted his paternal authority and constructive mission in the world.

May Our Lord Jesus Christ have mercy on His faithful ones, may the Holy Theotokos and Ever-Virgin Mary intercede for the clergy, religious, and laity, and may St. Joseph, Patron of the Universal Church, pray for its ever-needed reform in truth and holiness.

In its entirety, this book mounts a serious defense of the Church's traditional understanding and practice of liturgical ministries, but I am under no illusion that it utters the final word. I am well aware that more can and should be said, and I fervently hope and pray that others will enter the fray with books and articles of their own. When error and malpractice are on the loose, we need all the more to articulate the rationale for Catholic tradition and work to make it known, respected, and followed. We must refuse to collaborate or support the abettors of dissolution and must lend our aid, in whatever forms it may take, to those who patiently and bravely carry forward an inheritance that will always remain "sacred and great" for all of us.[22]

—Peter A. Kwasniewski
May 1, 2021
Feast of SS. Philip and James, Apostles

---

[22] To use the words of Benedict XVI in *Con Grande Fiducia* of July 7, 2007.

Definitions

Minor ordinations are a fanning-out of the holy diaconate instituted by Our Lord Jesus Christ. They order the soul of the minor cleric gradually toward the eventual reception of the sacred priesthood itself, preparing him not merely at a natural level through the discharging of sacred duties but supernaturally through the spiritual conferral of priestly powers and hierarchical grade. The minor orders are of apostolic origin but were prefigured in the various sacred ministers of the Levites under the Old Law (Numbers 18; 1 Chronicles 23). By their institution, Holy Mother Church imitates the divine law of Holy Orders in grace and permanence. Once received, a minor order may be neither repeated nor repealed. The powers they confer will remain with the man for the rest of his life. The dignity of each order is reckoned according to its proximity to the Blessed Sacrament.

Porter

Porters receive custodial power over the church, which is entrusted to their care along with everything that lies within. They summon Christians to prayer by ringing the bells in the bell tower and guard God's temple against intruders. The porter is (as an old devotional book says) "so to live that his conduct and behavior will be as so many little bells calling, inviting, and impelling men to know God and serve Him with love."

Lector

Lectors are given the power to read the Lessons in the church, to catechize children and the uneducated, and to bless bread and new fruits. This power of blessing gives the lector priestly dominion over the elements that will become the matter for the Eucharistic Sacrifice. The lector should (as the same source puts it) "possess all the virtues in an eminent degree so that he may indeed be a guide and a model of the spiritual life to those who see and hear him."

Exorcist

Exorcists receive the power to expel demons from the possessed in the name of the Church. This power, however, is bound by Church law, which has for centuries reserved the public exorcism of the possessed to the diocesan bishop or to a priest delegated by him. Exorcists are exhorted, however, to pray more fervently for the delivery of all souls oppressed by evil influences, and they do so with a special efficacy. In the ancient Church, exorcists purified the priest's hands with water in preparation for the Sacrifice and were responsible for making way among the faithful for the communicants to approach for Holy Communion.

Acolyte

Acolytes are given the power to light and carry the candles at Holy Mass, which symbolize the doctrine of the New Testament, and to present the cruets of water and wine at the altar for the offering of the Holy Sacrifice. They thereby gain a nearer proximity to the Blessed Sacrament and closely collaborate with the ministry of the subdeacon. Acolytes are called to "cast off the works of darkness and put on the armor of light" (Rom. 13:12). They ought to "shine as lights in the world" (Phil. 2:15) through holiness of life, in imitation of their divine Savior.

Subdeacon

In the words of a devotional manual: "The office of the subdeacon is to serve God and the Church in the Sacrifice of the Altar and to assist the deacon.... Our Savior spent His life serving God and men.... When the bishop consecrates a subdeacon, the ordaining prelate begs God to bless, sanctify, and consecrate the ordinand. Holy Mother Church implores Him to constitute the subdeacon a tireless and watchful sentinel of the heavenly army."

Due to the subdeacon's immediate proximity to the Holy Sacrifice, the subdiaconate is reckoned among the "major" orders of the Church's sacred hierarchy. As such, the subdeacon has traditionally been bound to perpetual celibacy and to the daily recitation of the Divine Office. The liturgical vestments of the subdeacon are the amice, alb, cincture, tunicle, and maniple. His sacred duties include serving the deacon at Mass; preparing the bread, wine, and sacred vessels for the Holy Sacrifice; presenting the chalice and paten at the Offertory; mixing water into the wine in preparation for the offering made by the priest; and incensing the Host and Chalice during a Solemn High Requiem Mass. With the celebrant and deacon, he prays the Ordinary of the Mass; with the priest, he offers to God the solemn chanting of the Epistle and afterward is charged with the purification of the sacred linens. Proper to a subdeacon is carrying the crucifix (the banner of Christ) in solemn procession, which the sacred liturgy connects with the holy Archangel Michael.[23] Early

---

[23] In the Offertory antiphon of the Requiem Mass: "sed signifer sanctus Michael repraesentet eas in lucem sanctam." According

popes would also use subdeacons to convey important messages to distant prelates—another angelic duty in service of the Church.

The ordination of men to the subdiaconate is one of the most ancient practices of the Church. In a letter from Pope St. Cornelius to Bishop Fabius of Antioch written in the year 251, we learn that in his day there were seven subdeacons among the grades of clergy at Rome.[24] Both of these prelates—one Eastern, one Western—recognized the subdiaconate to be the constant tradition of the early Fathers. The Fathers of the Council of Trent likewise acknowledged the apostolic origins of the order of subdeacons. This acknowledgment corresponds with the received liturgical and canonical tradition of the Roman Church, which regards ordination to the subdiaconate as a major step in the reception of Holy Orders.

to Cornelius a Lapide, the "sign of the Son of Man" in Matt. 24:30 is the standard of the Cross: "SS. Chrysostom and Augustine and S. Cyril teach that this standard of the Cross will be borne by the angels before the face of Christ, coming to judgment, as a trophy of victory, and a royal banner of supreme power and dignity." Speaking more broadly, the Levites—members of the tribe of Levi in the Old Covenant, and deacons and subdeacons in the New Covenant—are the earthly equivalent of the angels ministering in the heavenly liturgy. It is no coincidence that the apostles ordained seven deacons initially, since they are like "the seven angels that stand before God" (Rev. 8:2; cf. Tob. 12:15) but who do not offer the sacrifice themselves, which only the priest can do as representative of the Lamb standing as though slain (Rev. 5:6).

[24] Indeed, all seven orders—the four minor orders and the three major orders—are mentioned in this letter of Cornelius. Individual minor orders are also mentioned by Tertullian (†c. 225) and St. Cyprian (†258), among other early Fathers.

Oremus et pro omnibus episcopis, presbyteris, diaconibus, subdiaconibus, acolythis, exorcistis, lectoribus, ostiariis, confessoribus, virginibus, viduis: et pro omni populo sancto Dei.

Oremus. Flectamus genua. Levate.

Omnipotens sempiterne Deus, cujus spiritu totum corpus Ecclesiae sanctificatur, et regitur: exaudi nos pro universis ordinibus supplicantes; ut gratiae tuae munere, ab omnibus tibi gradibus fideliter serviatur. Per Dominum ... ℟. Amen.

Let us pray also for all bishops, priests, deacons, subdeacons, acolytes, exorcists, lectors, porters, confessors, virgins, widows, and for all the holy people of God.

Let us pray. Let us kneel. Arise.

O almighty everlasting God, by whose Spirit the whole body of the Church is sanctified and ruled, hear our supplications for all the orders thereof; that by the assistance of Thy grace all in their several degrees may render Thee faithful service. Through our Lord ... ℟. Amen.

—Good Friday Mass of the Presanctified

I

Foundations

1

This, Too, Reveals God:
The Body and Sexuality in Catholic Theology

On January 6, the Church celebrates the great feast of the Epiphany of the Lord (or Theophany, as our Byzantine brethren call it): the revelation of God to the nations and peoples of the world. The nations are represented by the three wise men who, guided by divine Providence, walked from the darkness of paganism to the Light of the one and only Savior of mankind.[25] In this Epiphany scene, we see the diversity of the Church *in nucleo*: mother, father, baby, and their guests, the shepherds and the Magi; queen, guardian, infant king, and courtiers; Jews and Gentiles, princes and paupers, the lofty and the lowly. At the

---

[25] In my article "Don't Stop Celebrating: After Christmas Day, Christmas Continues," *LifeSiteNews*, December 24, 2019, I encourage celebrating Epiphany beginning on the twelfth night of Christmas (First Vespers of January 5) and running to January 6 — as has *always* been the case in Christian tradition, East and West — and criticize how the observance of this feast has been shuffled off to the nearest Sunday, in a manner incongruous with the very mystery it celebrates. (*N.B.* In this book, online articles will be cited or referenced simply with the following format: author, article title, source, and date.)

most basic level, we see human beings, men and women, whose identities and functions were not assigned at random and cannot be exchanged *ad libitum*.

Every aspect of the Nativity scene tells us something about God and His plan for salvation. Looking at this familiar scene of the Holy Family, we might ask ourselves: How does God reveal Himself to us in masculinity and femininity?

In recent years, Catholic and secular schools alike have hosted endless on-campus discussions of "gender expression" and the so-called "gender binary." These are not obscure institutions but big-name places like Notre Dame, Villanova, and the University of San Diego. The assumption behind such discussions is that "gender" is a fluid thing, capable of many different forms and even allowing a person to shift from one form to another. Since the whole concept of "fluid gender" is new, even faithful Catholics may feel at a loss for a response. What does a Catholic believe about the importance of masculinity and femininity? How do we speak to a secular world that has lost its bearings on sexuality?

The Catholic Church bases her view of masculinity and femininity on Scripture, which places man and woman at the center of every stage of Salvation History. A brief tour of the story, beginning at the very beginning, will make manifest the consistency and depth of its message as well as the reason its central protagonists could never be redefined without undermining the message in its entirety — something, I think, of which the more intelligent opponents of Christianity are perfectly aware. After that, I'll look at why the culture around us makes it hard to understand Scripture's teaching, and I'll offer a few thoughts about how to speak effectively to a secularized world. But first, a look at Salvation History.

Creation

In the story of Creation, the human body makes invisible things visible. When God created the first man, He said, "It is not good that the man should be alone; I will make him a helper fit for him" (Gen. 2:18). The Creator knows that He made human beings to live with other human beings; as the *Catechism of the Catholic Church* puts it, we were created to be a "communion of persons" (CCC 372). But as Genesis tells it, this "communion of persons" was written directly into our bodies through masculinity and femininity. The woman was made from the man as a "helper fit for him," and when the man sees her, he rejoices: "This at last is bone of my bones and flesh of my flesh" (Gen. 2:23). The male and the female are "fit" for one another. Their complementary bodies make outwardly visible what is true of their inmost being.

Together, the man and the woman are commanded, "Be fruitful and multiply, and fill the earth and subdue it" (Gen. 1:28). Just as their masculine and feminine bodies show that they are meant for one another, their bodies also show that they are meant to serve others — their children first, and eventually the worldwide society founded on their procreative love. The human spirit's calling to community is made visible through the sexed body.[26] But this is only the beginning.

Ultimately, we have a calling to community because we are made in the image of the Trinity, the communion-in-unity of

---

[26] It is true that nowadays most people would say "gendered body," but we must be very clear about this: sex is a biological and personal phenomenon, while gender is a grammatical one. Many languages have "masculine, feminine, and neuter" *genders* for nouns and adjectives, but animals come in only two *sexes*: male and female.

Father, Son, and Holy Spirit. Genesis may even hint at this deep source of our creation when it says, "Let us make man in *our* image, after *our* likeness.... So God created man in his own image, in the image of God he created him; male and female he created them" (1:26–27). What the human body makes visible, in its basic dimorphism, is ultimately a divine reality that transcends the body but is capable of being echoed in it. God, we know, is an artist—and this is one of His masterworks.

Redemption

Masculinity and femininity become even more important after the Fall of our first parents. Already in the Old Testament, the prophets speak of God as Israel's husband and of the Chosen People as His bride: "I will betroth you to me for ever; I will betroth you to me in righteousness and justice, in steadfast love, and in mercy. I will betroth you to me in faithfulness; and you shall know the Lord" (Hos. 2:19–20). In the New Testament, this "marriage" of God and man takes on a far deeper meaning because "the Word became flesh" (John 1:14), bringing God and humanity into a literal one-flesh union. In Genesis, the male and female bodies made the human person outwardly visible, but in the Gospels, the body of Jesus makes outwardly visible the very person of God!

For Catholics, the Incarnation fills the human body with meaning. We feel the significance of our union with God's own body every time we approach the Holy Eucharist, about which Jesus said: "This is my body which is given for you" (Luke 22:19). The body of Christ, crucified at Calvary and glorified in Heaven, is God's greatest work of art. *This* body is His definitive self-portrait! And the Incarnation also brings us Mary, the Mother of God, the most exalted human person in all the universe, who received her high calling precisely as a woman.

Life in Christ

After Christ's Ascension into Heaven, His Incarnation continues to give meaning to our bodies. Baptism sanctifies our souls and our bodies by the power of His Cross. Christ's mystical marriage to the Church means that *our* bodies are *His* members: speaking to Christians caught in fornication, St. Paul asks, "Do you not know that your bodies are members of Christ? Shall I therefore take the members of Christ and make them members of a prostitute?" (1 Cor. 6:15). He goes on to challenge them, "Do you not know that your body is a temple of the Holy Spirit within you, which you have from God?" (1 Cor. 6:19). It is a challenge to live up to the holiness of the Christian body!

By the same token, Christians' bodily actions are powerful. Because their bodies are members of Christ and temples of the Spirit, the bodily union of Christians in marriage is even a sacrament, a sign and cause of supernatural grace. St. Paul appeals to the Romans to "present your bodies as a living sacrifice, holy and acceptable to God, which is your spiritual worship" (Rom. 12:1). This is the most basic reason we are liturgical beings: God has given us not just a mind with which to think of Him but a body in and through which to adore and praise Him. Liturgy is thoroughly wrapped up with bodiliness — that is, our nature as fleshly beings and, specifically, the one-flesh communion of Christ the bridegroom and His bridal Church.[27]

Consummation

The story of Salvation History ends with a strong emphasis on the human body when all the dead rise for judgment. The resurrection demonstrates once and for all the eternal significance of

---

[27] The next chapter delves more deeply into this truth.

the body in God's plan, because without saving the body, God's victory would be incomplete. The book of Revelation describes that last day as the "marriage of the Lamb," in which Christ finally and forever takes His "Bride," the Church (19:7).

This way of describing the end unlocks a puzzle. Although men and women will rise in their masculine and feminine bodies, Jesus tells us that they no longer "marry nor are given in marriage" (Luke 20:35). Does this imply that masculinity and femininity are no longer important? No. Rather, it shows that the natural meaning of the human body will be entirely fulfilled when we see God "face to face" (1 Cor. 13:12) in a "marriage" to our Maker.[28] The fact that we were made for communion means not only that we are in the image of the Trinitarian communion but, ultimately, that we were made for communion *with* the Father, Son, and Holy Spirit. Even now, in this world, we see that ultimate meaning of the human body in those who have chosen virginity "for the sake of the kingdom of heaven" (Matt. 19:12).

A secular worldview

So we see that the story of our salvation is not just about the salvation of souls; it is about the human body, too—from beginning to end! But even though the Catholic faith has a lot to say about the human body, speaking to a secular world is not as easy as quoting a lot of Scripture. Bad philosophy has permeated our culture, creating a roadblock that prevents even people of goodwill from understanding what the Church has to offer.

According to the *Catechism*, "the unity of soul and body is so profound that one has to consider the soul to be the 'form'

---

[28] See Isa. 54:5.

of the body...; spirit and matter, in man, are not two natures united, but rather their union forms a single nature" (CCC 365). Moderns generally understand that human *beings* are free and have rights simply by being human; we can't just do whatever we want to a human being. The Catholic Church holds that human *bodies* are also human, so we can't just do whatever we want to human bodies, either.

But the modern age has come to see the world in mechanical terms. We tend to imagine that there is no more "nature" in the human body than there is "nature" in an automobile; each is a collection of parts that has no higher unity or purpose than whatever utility might be obtained from its use, in any way it can be operated. In keeping with that reductionistic way of thinking, people rebel at the idea that "mere" biology can decide how we should live, because they do not see the biological realm as inherently meaningful. Why should having a female body involve a calling to motherhood? Why should having a male body involve responsibility to a family? Consequently, our culture sees the human body not as God's masterwork of art but as a blank canvas on which to paint. "What shall I make of my body?" we ask ourselves. "Shall I make it male or female or something else? Shall I make my body fertile or sterile? What shall I do?"

Likewise, for some time now, our culture has promoted birth control as a way of separating the body from any sense of *vocation*. Abortion and contraception have been pushed as a woman's control over her body. They appear to divorce her nature—her biology—from motherhood. All of this springs from the same root: people speak of "expressing themselves" through their bodies because they have stopped believing that the body already naturally does express them. In the end, we have "fluid gender" and "gender expression."

As we saw above, the natural meaning of the body is that the human person was made for community. But when our culture abandoned the idea of any "nature" of the body, it also abandoned the idea that society is "natural."[29] Individuals are seen as absolute and autonomous, while society is something artificial that we create for the sake of convenience. Even the family, the most obviously natural society, goes out the window when the natural meaning of the body is lost. The result is a radically individualistic idea of human rights in which each person has a "right" to decide his own bodily and spiritual meaning, even if this decision is bad for society as a whole—even if, in fact, this decision is bad for the individual rebelling against his own personhood.

Speaking to a secular world

If we are going to speak successfully to the secular world, we need to remove the philosophical and emotional roadblocks as well as we can. There is no quick and easy way to fix a broken worldview, but three rules of thumb will prove useful.

First, stay positive and work on the fundamentals. Before we get to all the "Thou shalt not" business, we need to say again and again, in as many ways as we can, that the human body is a wonderful thing deserving of respect. We need to stress

[29] Here we can see the profound connection between the early modern revolt against Aristotelian natural philosophy, which emphasizes form and finality, and the subsequent development of "social contract" political philosophy, which also rejects the idea of society as having an inherent form and finality. Society is then seen as a material conglomerate of parts on which some order is extrinsically imposed for the private ends of the parts that compose it and/or of the orderer.

the basic truth that the human body is not just mechanical: it *means* something. As a living body, it has a *nature*, an intrinsic principle of identity and operation, that comes before any of our own notions and theories. This nature is not a result of the interplay of atoms or molecules but actually comes even *before* the particles and uses them to make itself visible. And it is part of a greater whole known as a person, who *is* this body (though also more than merely it) and communicates himself in and through this body.

Second, don't make thundering disapproval your primary *modus operandi*. Our nature is a fallen one, wounded as a result of sin. We all experience tendencies and desires that contradict the real meaning of our bodies, no matter our "orientation" or state in life. Often a young person inherits a broken situation from parents or other mentors, and confusion follows. Sometimes that confusion leads to "straight" sexual deviancy; sometimes it leads to "gay" or other deviancies. The point is that sexual confusion is part of that general brokenness of humanity we all experience to one degree or another. "If we say we have no sin, we deceive ourselves, and the truth is not in us" (1 John 1:8). The wound of disordered concupiscence of the flesh afflicts one and all. Our own experience of temptation or struggle should keep us humble, compassionate, and capable of offering good advice that we ourselves have tested before we give it.

Lastly, emphasize courage. The holiness Christ brought to the body through His own wounded and risen body is *for everyone*, no matter what tendencies they experience. But it takes courage and conviction to live up to our high calling. Sexual morality is not about following a list of rules. It's about the arduous path to becoming *what* we are and *who* we are called to be in Christ. Pretending it's easy for "good" people helps no one. If we focus on the true nature of chastity, which is not about staying in a safe box but winning a battle to wholeness, self-mastery, and the ability to love, I think we will see a response from that innate hunger for greatness buried in every human soul and waiting to be awakened.

2

Incarnate Realism and the Catholic Priesthood

In discussions of the Catholic priesthood, one rarely hears a genuinely *theological* account of what makes a priest a priest. This defect rests, at least in part, upon a failure to consider the *metaphysical nature* of the priesthood as it can be defined from rational reflection on the data of revelation. Instead, one generally finds a parading of the supposed results of historical, biblical, psychological, or sociological "research," most of which is pressed into the service of revolutionary proposals at odds with orthodox Christian dogma and tradition. Yet if we are to make any sense out of our doctrine and practice, the theological or metaphysical account cannot be left aside. We have to go back to the basic truths that occupied the minds and hearts of the great theologians of the past, focusing our attention on the permanent and perennial, the fundamentals of what our Faith teaches us about Our Lord.

This chapter will give the outlines of an approach that might be called "incarnate realism" — that is, a consideration of the link between the *truth* that Jesus Christ, as true God and true Man, is the one Mediator between God and man, the Eternal High Priest after whom all priests must be modeled, and the *truth* that the Word became flesh not by assuming human nature in the abstract but by assuming a concrete or individualized human nature—namely, as male, as a member of one of the sexes.[30] By holding these two elements together, one can clarify the *intrinsic* rationale of our traditional teaching, making it easier in turn to assess the relative worth of other theories or of specialized research.

Priesthood in itself and by participation

St. Thomas Aquinas teaches that any creature is a being (*ens*) by receiving its act of being (*esse*) from, and thus in total dependency upon, the God who is His own being (*ipsum esse per se subsistens*). God is wholly "in act," of whom the participant is a likeness or imitation.[31] If one takes this term "participation" in its precise metaphysical meaning, it is clear, by extension, that Jesus Christ is the one High Priest in whom all other priests participate. Their priesthood is purely a gift of sharing in that priesthood which Christ possesses in Himself and not through another. This fundamental truth does not deny that each priest is *truly* a priest. It simply denies that he can be considered such "in or of himself" (*a se*)—just as all creatures are truly beings and causes but none is the First Cause who *is* self-subsistent being. None can exist or bring about effects save by the indwelling presence and causality of that First Cause working intimately within them, sustaining

---

[30] St. Thomas, *Summa theologiae* [hereafter *ST*] III, Q. 4, art. 4 and 5; Q. 5, art. 1 and 2. See Q. 18, art. 2: "The Son of God assumed human nature together with everything pertaining to the perfection of human nature. Now in human nature is included animal nature, as the genus in its species. Hence the Son of God must have assumed together with the human nature whatever belongs to animal nature."

[31] *ST* I, Q. 3, art. 4; Q. 4, art. 2–3; Q. 6, art. 3.

them at every moment.[32] The ministerial priest is a true minister precisely as participating in the priesthood of Christ.[33] His priesthood not only *makes* them to be His ministers, it is the only reality by which they *continue* to be and to function as "other Christs." As with any exemplar cause, the priesthood of Christ is the origin or principle as well as the goal or finality, the *terminus a quo* from which the form is taken and the *terminus ad quem* to which its activity tends. And as we name any motion both from its source and its end, so too the priest is called *sacerdos* because his state is at once derived from, and oriented to, Christ. Christ is the *summus sacerdos* foreshadowed by Melchisedek, of whom the Roman Canon solemnly reminds us after the miracle of transubstantiation effected by the priest. The failure to recognize this relationship between Christ and His minister engenders many serious errors in the theology of priesthood.

Since the fundamental role of a priest is to mediate between God and man, it follows that Jesus Christ — in whom the divine and human natures are hypostatically united in the Person of the Son of God — is the *ontological* Priest from the moment of His conception in the womb of the Virgin Mary. Thus the Fathers taught that Mary's womb was the temple of His priestly consecration. As St. Cyril of Alexandria teaches, "the Word of God ... when He became flesh and man like us, became High Priest and our Apostle."[34] St. Thomas clarifies: "Although Christ was not priest as God but as man, yet one and the same [Person] was priest and God."[35]

---

[32] *ST* I, Q. 8, art. 1; Q. 104, art. 1; Q. 105, art. 5.
[33] *ST* III, Q. 22.
[34] Third Letter to Nestorius (DS 261).
[35] *ST* III, Q. 22, art. 3, ad 1.

Christ not only mediates: He *is* the mediation between God and man, and that is why only His grace can justify, can sanctify, the soul.[36] All other priests are ministerial — that is, ingrafted through ordination into this eternal priesthood of Christ. They are ordained in order to channel His priestly blessings and graces to the people. They are not made into "other priests," independent sources of sanctifying grace, as though one could number them alongside Christ ("Jesus, the first priest of the New Covenant; St. Peter, the second; St. John, the third," and so on), just as it is impossible to number God alongside His creatures as though He were one thing among many.[37] Their dignity, their office, the origin and guarantor of their priestly *being*, is to conform to Christ, to offer the holy sacrifice *in persona Christi capitis*.[38] They cannot therefore claim any separate dignity, as though the office "belonged" to them. It belongs, *personaliter et essentialiter*, to Christ alone.

Therefore, when priests act in Christ's name — or, rather, when they act mysteriously in His place — they are not so many additional mediators. Rather, they are effaced and assimilated to Christ, their leader and archetype. They lose their personal distinctiveness. Individual priests differ *as individuals*, not *as priests*. Their distinctiveness is a function of their personality. In them there can be and certainly are varying degrees of intellectual power, moral strength, spiritual maturity, and artistic creativity. But there cannot be degrees in the power of confecting the Eucharist, a power corresponding to the sacramental character

[36] *ST* III, Q. 8 and 26; also, Q. 19, art. 4.
[37] See, e.g., *ST* I, Q. 30, art. 3.
[38] "In the person of Christ the Head": that is, acting in, by, and for Christ, the Head of the Mystical Body.

of Holy Orders. Either a man can act specifically and totally as Christ in offering the holy sacrifice, or he cannot.[39] There are not *many* priesthoods of the New Covenant, but one: Jesus Christ's. The powers, gifts, and activities of His priesthood flow through the many hands and mouths of His ordained servants, who are images, icons, and "personal sacraments" of the one High Priest.[40]

Saying Mass *in persona Christi*

It is Jesus who, mystically dwelling in His earthly minister, offers perfect worship to the Blessed Trinity during Holy Mass. This perfect worship, this act of total surrender in love and obedience, is the immolation of Christ Himself, Priest and Victim, upon the altar of the Cross. During Mass, and especially when the Canon shifts to the words of institution, the priest acts as Christ's living instrument. He does not speak in his own name or act from his personal powers, which are infinitely incommensurate

[39] This statement does not intend to deny that all of the baptized participate in some sense in the priesthood of Christ, nor that bishops receive the gifts and powers of the priestly office in a fuller way than priests. However, it must be borne in mind that the common priesthood of the laity is nothing other than receiving from the Lord the power and privilege to *offer oneself and the world* to God as a free and acceptable oblation, as a sacrifice of faith and love. It does not include the special power to reenact the Holy Sacrifice of Calvary, the one all-sufficient oblation through which all other offerings acquire eternal value. Nor does the increasing concentration of powers in deacon, priest, and bishop suffice to constitute three "grades" of priesthood. Strictly in terms of the power to offer the sacrifice at the altar, priest and bishop are equal; from the same point of view the deacon is radically *unequal* to either one.

[40] See John Saward, "The Priest as Icon of Christ," in *The Priest* 50.11 (November 1994): 37–48.

with the divine action and passion taking place in the sacred liturgy. Rather, he stands *as* Christ, *for* Christ. The priest works through Him, with Him, and in Him—conformed to the High Priest offering the one supreme and all-sufficient Sacrifice of the Cross. This is the heart of the mystery of the priesthood, and it explains two things: first, why Protestants are wrong to accuse Catholics of setting up "many mediators" between God and man, undermining the Savior's uniqueness; and second, why a woman could never be a priest.

Before returning to the latter point, I should mention that this analysis indicates one of the reasons why the priest offering the holy sacrifice should face *ad orientem* (toward the east, in the direction of the altar)—an "orientation" that symbolizes the unified longing of the People of God as it goes on pilgrimage, awaiting the Second Coming of the Lord.[41] When he faces *ad orientem*, the priest is no longer in a closed circle of earthly

[41] See Joseph Cardinal Ratzinger, *Feast of Faith*, trans. Graham Harrison (San Francisco: Ignatius Press, 1986), 139–45; idem, *The Spirit of the Liturgy*, trans. John Saward (San Francisco: Ignatius Press, 2000), pt. 2, ch. 3: "The Altar and the Direction of Liturgical Prayer." Assuming a liturgy celebrated according to the norms of the Church, the only time the priest should turn his face to the people for an extended period is when he is preaching the homily. Undoubtedly, the homilist is supposed to be teaching on behalf of the Church, but the homily is "paraliturgical"; it is a recommended practice, but not an integral part of—not *essentially* related to—the unbloody renewal of the sacrifice of Calvary and the faithful's participation in its fruits by receiving Holy Communion. It is fitting, therefore, that the time when the priest addresses the people in the vernacular should be the time when he is least hidden within, least plunged into, the dramatic action of the altar. See my article "The Homily Is Not Part of the Liturgy," *The Remnant*, January 15, 2021.

dialogue with the congregation. Instead, he is subsumed into the archetype of Christ. He merges silently into his office. His personality yields to the one overriding concern of the liturgy: that the sacrifice of Calvary be renewed for our salvation by the invisible Lord working through His visible ministers. In this way, each Mass commemorates the first advent of Christ in poverty and foreshadows His final advent in glory. The celebrant is hidden and momentarily forgotten in the liturgical action so that Jesus Christ may be all in all, Alpha and Omega. At the most solemn moment in the Mass, the celebrant should be disposed in such a way that his voice and his body and everything about him is assimilated to Christ, the High Priest.

Whether intended or not, the liturgical reforms enacted following the Second Vatican Council had the unfortunate practical effect of making it often seem as though the priest, in his strictly personal or individual aspects, is the one "doing" or enacting the divine mysteries. Nothing could be further from the truth.[42] If an icon draws attention to itself as a piece of painted wood, it ceases at that moment to function "iconically" and slips into the category of mere artifact—which could then, in turn, become an idol for the unwary.[43] Similarly, if a priest as "this man" becomes the object of attention, he ceases at that moment to represent mystically to the congregation the High Priest on the altar of the Cross, and he appears more as a minister in the Protestant sense, one who merely facilitates a ceremony.

---

[42] See my books *Resurgent in the Midst of Crisis: Sacred Liturgy, the Traditional Latin Mass, and Renewal in the Church* (Kettering, OH: Angelico Press, 2014), ch. 1, 2, 5, and 8, and *Noble Beauty, Transcendent Holiness: Why the Modern Age Needs the Mass of Ages* (Kettering, OH: Angelico Press, 2017), ch. 3 and 7.

[43] *ST* III, Q. 25, art. 3.

The same thoughts show, at least in part, the rich symbolic meaning of the sanctuary layout as it evolved in Western Christianity—why, namely, the altar is architecturally united with a tabernacle which acts as the base of a prominent crucifix. The Real Presence of Jesus in our midst follows from His gift of Himself in the Holy Eucharist, which in turn was given as a living memorial of the Passion, Resurrection, and Ascension, as the Roman Canon recalls immediately after the consecration. The Eucharist is the very Body of Christ offered upon the altar of Calvary and glorified on Easter morning. The sacrament of supreme love, through which man is united to God in the most intimate of all friendships, is identical with the sacrifice of supreme love by which sinners—enemies of God—are reconciled to Him in the Blood of the Lamb. The crucifix, to which all eyes are drawn, represents the act that unites altar and tabernacle, the death that gives life and the life that conquers death, reconciling the sinner and nourishing the saint: "And I, when I am lifted up from the earth, will draw all men to myself" (John 12:32). The integration of the altar of oblation, the tabernacle of presence, and the crucifix expresses the profound inner connection between suffering, love, and glorification. Each architectural element reinforces the other, voicelessly speaking the entire drama of salvation. The profusion of visual symbols, the overlapping layers of meaning, far from introducing confusion, are on the contrary just what makes it possible for us to come by small steps into the presence of Jesus—to begin to taste and see the infinite mystery of the Lord who is beyond all symbols and cannot be comprehended by reason alone.[44]

[44] To attempt to "clarify" or "simplify" the Mass by removing interwoven layers of symbolism is nothing other than to distort and

The scandal of particularity

The theological vision of priesthood traced out here lends powerful support to the dogma that the male sex is the only valid subject
or recipient of Holy Orders—with the necessary corollary that
women cannot be made ministerial priests.[45] As we have seen,
since ordination does not make a "new" priest but rather extends
into a new individual the hypostatic activity of Christ's incarnate
priesthood, the ordained individual himself must conform to
Christ's human nature, in and through which Christ is a priest
interceding with God for mankind; the ordained minister in his

---

dilute the sacred mysteries which are too bright for human eyes,
too strong for human ears. To put it somewhat provocatively,
the Mass should be celebrated in such a way that no one could
ever think he *fully* grasps what is taking place; the *structure* of
the sanctuary, the *rite* of the liturgy, should be fathomless, in-
exhaustible, in their symbolic meaning. The worshiper should
be able to attend Mass every day of his life and never reach an
end of new discovery and rediscovery. If everyone suddenly
"understood" everything, they would no longer be understanding
Christ but some finite human construct. They would, in fact,
be understanding themselves, their own small world, not the
Lord and His infinite wisdom. It is for this reason that much
of postconciliar worship is little more than self-worship; we
redesign churches and celebrate liturgies according to our own
time-bound, earth-bound ideas, failing to remember that even
the greatest mystics—or rather, *especially* the greatest mystics—bowed humbly before what they could not comprehend.

[45] It is not a question of "withholding" something from women;
if the thing is impossible, nothing is withheld, just as the fact
that men cannot carry a child inside of them is not properly
speaking a deprivation, a cosmic injustice, even though on the
natural plane there is no more perfect expression of incarnate
love than the conception and growth of a child in his mother's
womb.

own person must not *be* anything which conflicts with the iconic reality of the humanity of Jesus. Christ took on human nature as a man, as a male, by His eternal decree and choice.

Instead of divorcing "the Jesus of history" from "the Christ of faith," as many modern exegetes have done, we must see Jesus Christ as *one* reality, not two. He's not a contingent historical figure and then, over and above that, the archetypal Messiah or Savior. Everything essential to His humanity is part of His factual identity, part of the inmost being of the Incarnate Word. The Incarnation is the supreme "scandal of the particular": the Son of God becomes man—scandal enough for the abstruse metaphysical mind! More than that, however, Christ becomes the Son of Mary. His humanity, His human filiation, His sex, all pertain absolutely to who He is. If one of these is bracketed off, the others are implicitly negated.

"O the depth of the riches and wisdom and knowledge of God" (Rom. 11:33) displayed in the infinite mystery of Christ's particularity! The Son of God did not come to us as a sexless universal, an androgynous humanoid. He came as the Bridegroom. The human nature of Christ is the exemplar for all human beings and the means whereby we can imitate Him—but Christ *as man*, as male, is the exemplar for all individual men called to minister in His place as priests. They become sharers of His one eternal priesthood and ministers to His beloved Bride, the Church.

This is no mere matter of symbolism in the conventional sense, although that is important enough, as anyone who appreciates the nature of religious rituals can see. Nor is it merely a matter of Christ's example, since example is always based upon a prior principle, a commitment to some truth according to which one sets an example. Our Lord did not just "do things" for no good reason. He did everything with infinite wisdom and discernment.

God forbid we should say that He feared human custom or merely wanted to go along with the cultural practices of His time — He who broke conventions, who broke what the Jews took to be binding laws, whenever they impeded the accomplishment of His saving work! Nor, finally, could it be just a matter of ancient apostolic custom, nor even of unbroken ecclesial custom. After all, custom is valuable only to the extent that it is also founded upon a truth that cannot be gainsaid. This truth is the *facticity*, the scandalous and unforgettable facticity, of the Son of God incarnate in this individual human nature, at *this* time, in *this* place, with *this* way of life, with *these* words and signs and teachings, taking flesh *as a man* from the maiden Mary. The eternal deity, King of kings and Lord of lords, the infinitude of absolute perfection and holiness, irrevocably takes on flesh. He takes on flesh, and only *this* flesh. He takes it on in this way, and *only* in this way.

The Catholic Faith from its infancy has had to fight continually against the cheapening of this mystery. It fought against those who, holding that Christ was only divine, made of His humanity an illusion played upon our carnal senses. It fought against those who wanted Christ to be only human, a great prophet, a great moral teacher. To this day, it fights against the still more subtle heresy which, while seeming to admit that Christ is true God and true man, slides away from the silent worship of this overwhelming mystery and shifts all attention to ethics or social justice — as though the truth of the Incarnation could be acknowledged with a pious bow and then for all intents and purposes forgotten in the day-to-day life of the Christian community.

The Church fights against all these things, for they are all varieties of the ever-recurring disease of reductionism. Reductionists would have revelation on the cheap, tailored to our own ideas, our proprieties, our preferences, our sense of reasonableness and fairness. But God alone is truth. He alone is holy. If we or our theology are to have any truth, we must *conform totally* to the revelation He made, humbly embracing the word of God exactly as the Church has received it from her Founder.

The heresy of *contemptum carnis*

Because Jesus is the Eternal High Priest, sole Mediator and source of grace, it follows that Christian men who receive the privilege of acting at the altar *in persona Christi* are acting as His "separate and animated instruments"[46]—free and intelligent, but nonetheless instrumental, conduits of the priestly power which is His by nature and by right. The Incarnate Word is a priest *per se* and *in se*, while the ordained are priests *per ipsum et cum ipso et in ipso*, as participating in the historical and eternal reality of Christ's ontological priesthood.

Consequently, priests must not be *other* than Christ in His human identity. They can be drawn from every nation, race, and tongue, but they cannot be female, since sex is more fundamental to the constitution of the human being than skin color or height or weight or age or language. As Aristotle first noted, an animal generates, makes another like itself—the most prodigious power of animal life—in virtue of its sex, not in virtue of any other characteristic. An animal exists only in male and female modalities, which give rise to inclinations, behaviors, and capacities peculiar to each; there is no asexual or androgynous human person. Thus, while it is true that human beings cannot exist without a certain skin color, height, weight, and age, nor function unless they have language, none of these characteristics determines human nature as such in the way biological sex does. A human

---

[46] See, e.g., *ST* III, Q. 64, art. 1 & 5.

being may or may not be Asian, may or may not speak English, etc., but he *must* be a man or a woman before he is anything else, and as the foundation of anything else. All other traits, even if they are innate and immutable, are metaphysically posterior to sex: it is a *man* or a *woman* who belongs to a race and a family and who can then generate more members of that race or family.

At this point, a potential difficulty must be cleared up. In metaphysical strictness, the human *soul* cannot be male or female in itself, since it is a subsistent spiritual entity, and intellect as such is non-sexual. Sexuality is a property of animate body; only a living physical organism can be actually male or female. However, the soul alone does not constitute human nature. A human being is a rational animal composed of soul *and* body—one as form, the other as matter which receives being through form. The individual or concrete human being is *man* or *woman*, and the separated soul after death remains part of an incomplete nature until, at the resurrection of the dead, it is reunited with its body so that it may function again as the formal principle of an integral physical nature. As long as the human soul is considered *abstractly* and as a subsistent entity, it is non-sexed; but considering the soul abstracted from the body means that we are no longer speaking of a complete human nature but only of a detached and naturally incapacitated intellect—one which, moreover, is not fully *what it was*, since its history, its very life, was bodily, and all of its activities were founded in or assisted by the body. In other words, just as the soul never existed bodilessly, human nature in its fullness does not exist bodilessly either. As St. Thomas teaches, the soul is essentially *unibile*: unitable to a body and desirous of uniting to this body, which it needs for its activities and for the perfection of the person.

The dualist, on the other hand, who claims that sex (maleness and femaleness) is not really part of human nature—not on the "inside" of its being but instead some kind of supervening accident separable from and independent of human nature as such—denies any intrinsic connection between sexuality and the human soul, which is taken to be purely spiritual. Indeed, a consistent dualist has to maintain that sexuality is not only an extrinsic accidental feature but an imperfection, a lessening of human dignity—something to be overcome, thrown off, superseded. The condition of sexuality is a *fall* for the soul, an imprisonment in matter, matter being equated with, or viewed as the byproduct of, evil. On such an account, in Heaven everyone would be neuter(ed) human beings without any sexual characteristics.

But is it possible for someone who holds any version of this position to be in any meaningful way a follower of that revelation which at its beginning solemnly declares, "Male and female he created them," and toward the end, that husband and wife are a living image of the eternal nuptial bond between Christ the Bridegroom and the Church, His Bride? There are many "closet dualists" who would not overtly reject Scripture but who, perhaps ignorantly all the while, espouse positions that either *presuppose* or *lead to* anti-incarnational (anti-physical, anti-bodily, anti-sexual) heresy.

One begins to discern the subterranean connections between a seemingly theoretical heresy and the rampant sexual perversions of our day. These perversions are not rooted in an exaggerated opinion of the goodness of the flesh created by God. They are rooted precisely in a hatred of the flesh as an enemy to be conquered and subdued by detached calculation, in a rejection of the manifest *purposefulness* of sexuality which accounts for the polarity and harmony of the sexes, in a denial of the *sacredness* of the living body as the temple of the human soul and of the divine Spirit.

Since there is only one ontological Priest, Jesus Christ, ordained men are called priests *per posterius* (by extension or subordinate predication) owing to their sacramental connection to Him. A special bond to the full divine-human reality of Christ is bestowed on them. Hence the *de fide* doctrine that ordination confers an ineradicable sacramental character distinguishing the priest from all other believers, just as baptism confers a character distinguishing the baptized from the unbaptized. And this bond between High Priest and minister includes the mission, the imperative, to imitate Christ as Priest. As Christ is Priest in the totality of His incarnate reality, it follows that the one to be ordained must be male, since otherwise the ontological basis of conformity to the High Priest would be lacking in an element intrinsic to the constitution of human nature. In short, the ministerial priest would not reflect and could not act in the real, concrete Person of Christ.

"Woman, behold your son"

A reverse analogy to the priesthood may be found in the maternity of the Virgin Mary, who, whether nursing the newborn Christ-child or holding the crucified Savior in her arms, offers to our gaze the other pole of incarnate realism. The Virgin Mary in her femininity, in her womanhood, is the Mother of Christ and the Mother of God. In her historical individuality as the woman of faith, the first to believe, the one whose *fiat* caused the beginning of redemption in time, she is the Mother of all beloved disciples (cf. John 19:26–27) and the Mother of the Church (cf. Acts 1:14). Her vocation as the God-bearer, her role in Salvation History, is unique and unrepeatable: she is the most perfect created mirroring of the holiness of her Son, the most perfect recipient and conduit of His graces, the most perfect complement to His priesthood. The Word became flesh in her womb; the Incarnation of the Son and the Motherhood of Mary are correlative scandals of the particular. Considered in her metaphysical identity as a woman,

Mary's femininity, and all the more her maternity, cannot be shared by men. Nor can the priesthood of Christ, insofar as He is male, be shared in by women, who cannot be conformed to Him in this personal respect. All women have a special relation to Mary—namely, their common sexual identity and their virginity or their maternity; all men have a special relation to Christ the man, which makes them potential candidates for the priesthood. Just as it would be absurd for a man to complain that he can never be ontologically related to Mary in her womanhood and her motherhood, so too it would be absurd for a woman to complain that she cannot be assimilated to Christ as regards His sex.

One might object that this comparison illegitimately mixes together the natural and supernatural realms, for while there is only one Mary and only one Christ, there are many ordained priests who carry on His work, but no mothers who continue hers.

In response, one might say that just as the sacrifice of Christ is "once for all" and yet mystically renewed on the altar at the hands of His priests, so too the participation of the Mother of God in the mission of her Son, from His conception to her coronation in Heaven, is her special prerogative, and yet all who live for the sake of bearing Christ in their souls and delivering Him to the world—especially women who are consecrated virgins—mystically continue to participate in the same divine motherhood of Mary, extending its reach over time, *cum et sub Maria*, even as she herself co-mediates and co-redeems, *cum et sub Christo*, by participating in His singular mediation and redemption. But it should also be granted that the analogy is imperfect; it does not hold in every respect. There is an irreducible difference between the ordained priesthood that sacramentally participates in and effectively applies the mediation of Jesus Christ and the sexual likeness all women share with the Mother of God.

Yet we must not overlook the special link that women have to Mary, which parallels the special link that men have to Christ. By a likeness to Jesus her son, men have the capacity to exemplify Christ, High Priest and Bridegroom of the Church. In the Virgin Mother Mary, not only individual women but also the entire Church finds her highest archetype as Bride of Christ, and the believing soul — the *anima ecclesiastica* — bears Mary's imprint. The Virgin's divine maternity elevates the female sex to its greatest dignity and gives it a privileged ontological symbolism that the male sex cannot share. Mary's motherhood is a supernatural mystery encompassing her entire being, even as the Son of God assumes and encompasses integral human nature. It is arbitrary to say that Mary's womanhood matters less than Christ's manhood; that would be to miss the point of Salvation History. By His Providence, God enters His own creation not only thanks to Mary's free collaboration but also through her female sex. This singular privilege bestowed on womankind, by which the cosmos is forever altered and elevated, bears consequences for all women from the dawn of creation to the end of time.

> While it is true that God sent His Son to the whole world (cf. Jn 3:16), Christ was given first and most interiorly in the unrepeatable relationship of mother and child.... This gift is unique to the one woman who is truly the Mother of Jesus and hence the Mother of God (*Theotokos*); yet the gift has repercussions in all of feminine humanity. Since women are able to follow Mary either as consecrated virgins or as dedicated mothers, they share the glory with which God has blessed those states through their perfection in the Virgin Mother.

The Son of God could have come to us in many ways, for the power of God is no less infinite than His creativity. He could have formed a body for Himself out of the slime of the earth, as He did when creating Adam; He could have simply decreed that a fully mature body come to be *ex nihilo*. He chose, in His wisdom and love, to become man through the path of human birth; He chose to be the Son of Mary, *Filius Mariae*.[47]

Both men and women belong equally to the Church and receive through her the grace of Christ, who is Head of the Mystical Body; but this mutual belonging no more introduces sexual confusion than does the fact that husband and wife are equally spouses and equally participate in the same grace of matrimony. Indeed, they still have, and could not *not* have, their distinctive roles in the family as regards procreation, the rearing of children, and the regulation of the household. Equality of nature is not incompatible with distinction of office. All human beings benefit from and are called to participate in the redemptive work of Christ, even as all Christians are called to imitate, venerate, and turn lovingly to the Virgin Mary. In this respect, "there is neither male nor female" (Gal. 3:28), since the redemption of Christ is for all without distinction, and Mary's unconditional obedience and perfect trust stand as the everlasting model of the response all human beings should make to God. Here we find the encompassing spiritual framework that illuminates the Church's traditional theology and practice of holy orders, liturgical ministries, and ecclesiastical offices and prevents its distortion.

[47] From my article "The Son of God Made Flesh Can Never Be Separated from His Mother—Who Is Our Mother, Too," *LifeSiteNews*, May 4, 2021.

3

Doctrinal Foundations of
All-Male Sanctuary Service

In the Temple of Jerusalem, the Holy of Holies was a place solemnly set apart, separated from the rest of the temple and its surrounding courtyards, on account of the mystery contained within it: the presence of God above the mercy seat, in the midst of the physical reminder of the covenant in blood. Out of fear and reverence for the Lord, lay men and women, lower ranks of priests and Levites, would not dare to enter the Holy of Holies. Only the high priest could enter, under precise conditions, ready to offer the Lord his own prayers and the prayers of all the people.

Jesus Christ, our great High Priest, has pierced the veil and entered into the true tabernacle not made with human hands, preparing for us a way to follow Him into beatitude — even preparing for us, in this mortal life, a mystical banquet of His precious Body and Blood so that we may be made partakers of the food of immortality. Yet for all this intimacy of communion, He remains no less the Sovereign High Priest, crowned with glory, and we are no less His lowly servants. As we walk in pilgrimage toward the heavenly temple, there still remains the distinction between sacred and profane, baptized and unbaptized, the holy and the sinful, as well as the distinction of offices between ministers and laymen.

Far from being cut off from its ancient roots, worship in the New Covenant retains the spirit of chaste fear before the Lord, the awareness of stages of ascent into the holy presence of God, and a ministerial hierarchy that reflects the nature of the cosmos and the descent of grace from the Redeemer through the members of His Mystical Body. These truths are consummately expressed in the spaces and structures of classic church architecture, in furnishings, vestments, and vessels, and in poignant prayers and gestures of homage, adoration, and humility.

Traditionally, the sanctuary above all was seen as the symbolic domain of Christ the High Priest, and therefore was an area set apart from the rest of the Church, with all-male ministerial service. Roman Catholics kept this custom intact for nearly two thousand years, in continuity with the Israelites who went before us and with the Eastern Churches—both those united to Rome and those tragically separated from it—who have preserved to this day all-male liturgical ministry in its full integrity.

Let us recall the rationale behind the custom of limiting service in the sanctuary and at the altar to men only. Servers and lectors are in some way an extension of the ministry of the priesthood, to which it properly belongs to handle the divine mysteries and all that is associated with them. Only men can be priests; therefore only males are suited to priestly functions. Moreover, servers and lectors are a substitute for clerics in minor orders, who, in optimal conditions, are the ones called upon by the Church to fulfill these very offices.[48] Ministers are men set

[48] The formal ministries of acolyte and lector, even after Pope Paul VI's simplification and reconfiguration thereof, were open only

apart by the Church for a special function that is not equivalent to general lay participation in the liturgy.[49] Finally, serving as an altar boy was and still is a much-valued way to encourage vocations to the priesthood.

Not long after the Second Vatican Council, this hitherto unbroken practice was abandoned, and we saw the allowance of female lectors and, later, female altar servers. Now women and men freely mingle in the sanctuary and even at the very altar of sacrifice. Not only is this development contrary to the religious instincts of most cultures[50] and to well-known psychological requirements of boys,[51] it is also contrary to the common good of modern Christians who are living in an age of massive sexual

---

to men. The change made by Pope Francis is critiqued in this book in chapters 4, 6, and 11.

[49] The question of who should or may sing in a choir or schola differs, in my opinion, from the question of who should or may perform ministerial tasks in the sanctuary of a church. For arguments in defense of the permissibility of a schola of women (outside of the sanctuary), see my article "Are Women Permitted to Sing the Propers of the Mass?," *New Liturgical Movement*, March 8, 2021.

[50] See Manfred Hauke, *Women and the Priesthood: A Systematic Analysis in Light of the Order of Creation and Redemption*, trans. David Kipp (San Francisco: Ignatius Press, 1988), esp. 85–194; cf. idem, *God or Goddess? Feminist Theology: What Is It? Where Does It Lead?*, trans. David Kipp (San Francisco: Ignatius Press, 1995).

[51] I am referring here to the oft-noted phenomenon of altar boys dropping away and recruits drying up when girls flow into the ranks, and the opposite phenomenon of boys and young men volunteering in large numbers to serve when the ministry is all-male, exacting in its duties and running along the lines of a disciplined band of soldiers.

confusion, in which distinctions are blurred and the combination of democratic egalitarianism and reductive feminism treats men and women as if they were interchangeable.

While Christian anthropology is sufficiently different from that of other cultures and religions to allow St. Paul to say that "there is neither Jew nor Greek, there is neither slave nor free, there is neither male nor female; for you are all one in Christ Jesus" (Gal. 3:28), the context itself and the exegesis of the Church Fathers show us that the Apostle is referring to the dignity of baptism and the goal of salvation: the grace of eternal life is freely available to all, with no distinction of race, class, or sex. Heroic charity is in the reach of every baptized man, woman, and child, and the hierarchy of Heaven is established according to charity. This fundamental truth simply does not touch on how the Christian religion, visibly and socially embodied in this world, makes use of the God-authored order of creation (and, in particular, the permanent features of human nature) for the hierarchical form of its organization and worship.

The ideological shotgun wedding of feminism and egalitarianism strikes at the fundamental language of revelation, wherein God/Christ is the Bridegroom who acts and fertilizes, becoming the father and head of the family, and humankind/Israel/the Church becomes the Bride who receives as wife and bears fruit as a mother.[52] At the very least, it is not beneficial to the faithful to allow traditional practices to be canceled out as if they were arbitrary exercises of power, mistaken to begin with—particularly when these practices have sound anthropological and dogmatic foundations. In the case at hand, the gradual breaking down of correlative distinctions such as those between sanctuary and

[52] Chapter 7 develops this symbolism and its basis.

nave, ordained and non-ordained, ministers and recipients, has been able to feed into and feed upon the larger societal dissolving of distinctions between men and women, creating a perfect storm of confusion for the faithful and furnishing them with no effective countersign or alternative model.

A failure to see how the natural distinction of sexes is ordered to the common good of mankind and of the Church has, without a doubt, led to many abuses of power on the part of pastors and laity who take it upon themselves to create, abolish, or innovatively redefine offices, functions, symbols, and rites. Pastors concerned with communicating and reinforcing authentic Catholic doctrine should become more concerned with the many ways, open and subtle, in which our liturgical practices symbolize the truths of creation and redemption summarized in chapter 1, or, on the contrary, obfuscate that symbolism and undermine the transmission of those truths.

At this point the pragmatist chimes in: Can we *do* anything about the problem of female altar servers? Is it a problem worth solving—a problem capable of being solved, rather than a fateful mistake about which nothing can be done?

Imagine you are a bishop, thinking about what a wreckage feminism has made of the Church in the Western world as men continue to feel alienated, women no longer offer themselves to Jesus in religious life, and a pathetic number of priestly vocations dribble in. You are planning to send a letter to your presbyterate, explaining why you are abrogating the use of female altar servers in your diocese. What might such a letter look like? How would you make the case? You ask a young, orthodox, straight-shooting priest in your diocese, known for his traditional convictions, to compose a text for your consideration. A week later, you receive the following draft.

Ministers of Christ

✠

Dear Priests and Deacons,

Praised be Jesus Christ! With this letter I announce, after careful consideration and prayerful reflection, an important change in the liturgical praxis of the Diocese of Anytown.

As you know, some time ago the Vatican allowed local ordinaries to permit female altar servers because, due to Pope Paul VI's setting aside of the major order of subdiaconate and the minor order of acolyte and the reassignment of their duties to the office of instituted acolyte, this type of service appeared to be no longer directly connected with the path to priestly ordination. Indeed, in the old days, laymen — particularly boys — substituted for acolytes in most situations (hence the familiar term "altar boys"). At the same time, the Vatican made it clear that female altar servers are not required, may not be imposed against the will of a celebrant of any Mass, and do not cancel out the good of retaining the traditional practice of male-only service at the altar.

With the wisdom of hindsight, we can now see that this experiment of admitting females to the service of the altar has proved problematic, for several reasons. First, altar servers are visibly dedicated, both by their responsibilities and by their vestments, to ministering in the sanctuary at the altar. Theirs is a role that appears to be intimately associated with the offering of the Holy Sacrifice of the Mass. It was for this very reason that the discipline of training and working with altar servers was traditionally regarded as — and, in truth, still remains — a means of fostering vocations to the priesthood. To serve at the altar is to be involved in priestlike activities. Operative here is a language of symbols that is more powerful than mere words.

Experience has shown that the now widespread presence of female altar servers in the sanctuary continues to create confusion among the faithful about the roles that women may legitimately play in the liturgical life of the Church. Again, the symbolism of a vested altar server ministering at the altar speaks more decisively than any catechesis. It is therefore no surprise that many Catholics, despite the definitive judgment of the Church expressed in Pope John Paul II's *Ordinatio Sacerdotalis*, feel that "altar girls" are a first step toward the eventual allowance of "women priests." Such confusion on matters contained in the deposit of faith is not healthy for our faithful people.

More profoundly, John Paul II's "theology of the body" helps us to understand that a whole realm of cosmic and metaphysical symbolism is literally embodied in man and woman. Even if we are not always consciously aware of this symbolism, it has a steady formative effect on our thoughts and attitudes at worship. It should not be simply ignored in the assignment and execution of liturgical roles. Modern society has shown a remarkable ability to ignore the obvious natural and God-given differences between the sexes, differences that support their complementarity. As grace builds on nature, so does Christian liturgy build on natural anthropology. Introducing confusion at so basic a level prevents the liturgy from exhibiting clearly the spousal relationship of Christ and the Church, in which Christ is represented primarily by the celebrant offering sacrifice at the altar in the sanctuary, and the Church is represented primarily by the assembly of believers gathered in the nave to do Him homage and to receive His gifts.

Finally, on a practical note, the placing together of boys and girls has had the effect, consistent with human nature, of driving away boys who might otherwise have been interested in serving or who might otherwise have been persuaded to serve. Boys and girls of certain ages either do not wish to be together or find one another's company distracting. A similar distraction is caused for laymen by older girls or fully grown women in the sanctuary. If the "theology of the body" is true, and surely it is, we could have foreseen these problems and avoided them altogether by not having departed from the constant and universal custom of the Church in regard to altar servers. Moreover, boys enjoy the challenge of a demanding and regimented approach to serving, characterized by a manly *esprit de corps*. Mixed service cancels out this psychological advantage.

Even beyond these concerns, the expansion of ministries to more and more lay people is characteristic of the "clericalization of the laity" and the "laicization of the clergy," against which John Paul II warned many times. The role of the laity is to sanctify the vast world outside the Church, not to take care of the sanctuary and its tasks. The holiness proper to the laity is best expressed when they participate in the liturgical rites by the responses and gestures appointed for them. This is the "spiritual worship" (Rom. 12:1) that corresponds harmoniously to the sacerdotal and diaconal ministries exercised at the altar.

Recognizing that the novelty of female altar servers was never to be required but only to be allowed at the discretion of the diocesan bishop, and that male altar servers remain normative for the Roman rite, the Vatican left the decision in this matter in the hands of the diocesan bishop. Accordingly, exercising my right to legislate, I decree that, as of the Solemnity of the Assumption this coming August, the use of female altar servers is altogether abrogated in this Diocese and is to be discontinued without exception, all customs to the contrary notwithstanding.

I shall send you a brief pastoral letter on this subject to be read from the pulpit early in June; it will also be published in the *Anytown Catholic Register*. When and as necessary, please prepare your parishioners for the change, emphasizing that it has nothing to do with a lack of appreciation of the countless gifts that women bring to each parish and to the Church. As John Paul II frequently emphasized, the Church is feminine, indeed motherly, in her deepest identity as Bride of Christ and Mother of the faithful, and this is why the Virgin Mary is the supreme model of the Christian disciple. Those who minister at the altar, on the other hand, do so not merely as disciples but as representatives of Our Lord Jesus Christ, who is Eternal High Priest and Servant (Deacon). This role of representation is symbolically shared by other liturgical ministries, especially that of altar server. That is the fundamental basis of my decision, and I am sure that further reflection on it will show the wisdom of the hitherto unbroken Catholic tradition.

I count on your understanding and support in this important step for the renewal of our diocesan liturgical

worship, and I ask that you speak with me personally if
you have any concerns.

Cordially yours in Christ,

Etc. etc.

✠

So that is how it might be done. One can only hope that, as the
years go on, bishops will become more and more aware of the
harm that has resulted from shortsighted innovations in the Roman Rite and will take the necessary steps to restore liturgical
tradition, such as all-male service in the sanctuary.

Although in the letter it is mentioned only in passing, I am
convinced that part of the crisis of vocations to the priesthood
stems from the lack of real "vocational training" in the form of a
more demanding ministry for boys and young men in the sanctuary, connected with a richness of public worship that feeds the
imagination and the intellect. When the liturgy is celebrated in
a more traditional way, that is, with a certain solemnity, ritual
beauty, and complexity, it exercises a mysterious and powerful
fascination over the minds of youths. This experience of the
sacred and its inherent worthiness has drawn more than a few
men into the seminary. In that sense, it is not rocket science to
hold the view that moving the liturgical experience of Catholics
toward greater solemnity and continuity with tradition, while
curtailing female altar servers, will prove over time to be a sound
way to clear obstacles to and optimize conditions for the awaken-
ing of priestly and religious vocations.[53]

---

[53] See chapter 17.

4

The Significance of Minor Ministries in the Sacred Liturgy

Bishop Athanasius Schneider

The principle of divine law in the liturgy

Regarding the nature of the sacred liturgy — that is, of divine worship — God Himself has spoken to us in His Holy Word, and the Church has explained it in her solemn Magisterium. The first basic aspect of the liturgy is this: God Himself tells men how they must honor Him. In other words, it is God who gives concrete norms and laws for the development, even exterior, of the worship of His divine Majesty.

Man, we know, is wounded by Original Sin. For this reason, he is profoundly marked by pride and ignorance and, even more profoundly, by the temptation and tendency to put himself in the place of God at the center of worship, that is, to practice self-worship in its various implicit and explicit forms. Liturgical law and norms are therefore necessary for authentic divine worship. These laws and norms must be found in divine revelation, in the Word of God both written and transmitted by tradition.

Divine revelation transmits to us a rich and detailed liturgical legislation. An entire book of the Old Testament is dedicated to liturgical law, the Book of Leviticus, with additional guidelines set out in the Book of Exodus. The individual liturgical norms of divine worship in the Old Testament had only a transitory value, since their purpose was to be a figure looking to the divine worship that would reach its fullness in the New Testament. However, there are some elements of perennial validity. First is the very fact of the need for liturgical legislation. Second, that there is a detailed and rich legislation of divine worship. And, finally, divine worship must take place according to a hierarchical order. This hierarchical order presents itself as concretely tripartite: high priest–priest–Levite; in the New Testament: bishop–presbyter (priest)–deacon/minister.

Jesus came not to abolish the Law but to bring it to its fullness (cf. Matt. 5:17). He said: "Till heaven and earth pass away, not an iota, not a dot, will pass from the law, until all is accomplished" (Matt. 5:18). This is particularly valid for divine worship, since the adoration of God constitutes the first commandment of the Decalogue (cf. Exod. 20:3–5). The purpose of all creation is this: angels and men and even irrational creatures must praise and worship the divine Majesty, as the revealed prayer of the Sanctus says: "The heavens and the earth are full of Thy glory" (cf. Isa. 6:3).

Jesus Christ, the supreme worshiper of the Father and the supreme liturgical minister

The first and most perfect worshiper of the Father is Jesus Christ, the incarnate Son of God. His work of salvation had as its main purpose to give honor and glory to the Father in place of sinful humanity, who were unable to give a worthy and acceptable worship to God. The re-establishment of true divine worship and the making of atonement for sins before the divine Majesty, who was outraged due to the innumerable forms of perversion of worship, constituted the primary purpose of the Incarnation and the work of Redemption.

By constituting His apostles as true priests of the New Covenant, Jesus left His priesthood to His Church and, with it, the public worship of the New Testament, which has for its ritual culmination the offering of the Eucharistic sacrifice. He taught His apostles through the Holy Spirit that the worship of the New Covenant was to be the fulfillment of the worship of the Old Covenant. Thus the apostles transmitted their power and their liturgical service in three degrees — that is, in three hierarchical orders — in analogy with the three degrees of the ministers of the cult of the Old Covenant.

The supreme performer of the liturgy is Christ (in Greek: *hó liturgós*). He contains in Himself and exercises all the divine worship, even in the smallest functions. The following words of Christ can be referred to this fact: "I am among you as one who serves" (Luke 22:27). Christ is the minister; He is also the "deacon" or servant par excellence. The bishop, for his part, is the supreme possessor of the liturgical service of Christ, and for that reason, the episcopate contains all the ministries and services of public worship: the ministry of the presbyterate, the ministry of the diaconate, and the ministry of the minor orders, that is, the service of ministers such as acolytes and "altar boys." In the pontifical Mass according to the most ancient form of the Roman Rite, the bishop dresses in all the robes, even of the lower orders. In the absence of lower ministers, the bishop himself performs the liturgical functions of the presbyter, the deacon, the subdeacon, and even the minor orders. In the absence of the deacon, the presbyter himself performs all the liturgical functions of the deacon, the subdeacon, and the minor orders. In the absence of the deacon, the subdeacon, the holders of minor orders, or the altar servers can perform some of the functions of the deacon.

The tradition of the apostles

The apostolic tradition has seen in the triple hierarchical order of the Church the fulfillment of the typology of the triple hier- archical order of divine worship in the Old Covenant. This is what Pope St. Clement I, the disciple of the apostles and third successor of the apostle Peter, testifies to us. In his letter to the Corinthians, St. Clement presents the liturgical order divinely established in the Old Covenant as an exemplar for the right order of the hierarchy and worship of every Christian community. Speaking of divine worship, he states:

> We must do everything in order with regard to what the Lord has ordered [us] to do according to the appointed times. He ordered the oblations and worship services to be performed not by chance or without order. By His sovereign decision, He Himself has determined where and by whom these services are to be performed, so that all things will be done in a holy manner according to His good pleasure and pleasing to His will. For the high priest has been assigned liturgical services [*liturghíai*] reserved for him, priests have been given their own proper place, on the Levites devolve special ministrations [*diakoníai*], and the layman [*ho laikòs ànthropos*] is bound by the laws that pertain to laymen [*laikóis prostágmasin*].[54]

Pope Clement understands that the principles of the order di- vinely established in the Old Covenant must continue to operate

[54] 1 Clem. 40:1–3.5.

in the life of the Church. The most evident reflection of this order should be found in the Church's liturgical life, in her public worship. Thus the Holy Pontiff draws this conclusion, applied to the life and worship of Christians: "May each of you, brothers, in the position that is proper to him, be pleasing to God in good conscience and with reverence, without transgressing the established rule of liturgical services [*kanón tes leiturghías*]."[55]

Later, Pope Clement describes the hierarchy of the New Covenant, contained in the Lord Jesus Christ Himself and concretized in the mission of the apostles.[56] This reality corresponds to the order (*táxis*) willed by God. Here St. Clement uses the same terms with which he had previously described the liturgical and hierarchical order of the Old Covenant.

From the first centuries, the Church was aware that divine worship had to take place according to an order established by God in keeping with the example of the divine order established in the Old Covenant. In order to carry out a task in public worship, it was necessary to belong to a hierarchical order. Consequently, Christian worship, that is, the Eucharistic liturgy, was carried out in a hierarchically ordered manner by persons officially appointed for this purpose. As we said, these agents of worship constituted a sacred order divided into three degrees (episcopate, presbyterate, and diaconate) as they were in the Old Covenant worship (high priest, priests, and Levites). Pope St. Clement in the first century designated the service of the Old Testament Levites with the word "*diakonia*" (1 Clem. 40:5). We can therefore identify here the foundation of the ancient ecclesiastical tradition of designating the Christian deacon with the

---

[55] 1 Clem. 41:1.
[56] 1 Clem. 42:1ff.

word "Levite," for example in the *Constitutiones Apostolicae* (2, 26:3) and in the writings of Pope St. Leo the Great.[57]

The diaconate

A clear and important testimony of this parallelism between the hierarchical degrees of the Old and New Covenants is found in the ordination rites. The texts of the ordination rites date back to very ancient times, as seen in the *Traditio Apostolica* and then the *Sacramentaries* of the Roman Church. These texts and rites have remained almost unchanged in their essential formulas for many centuries, up to our days. The prefaces or consecratory prayers of all three sacramental orders refer to the hierarchical and liturgical order of the Old Covenant.

In the rite of episcopal consecration, the ancient Roman Pontifical pronounced this affirmation "*Gloriae Tuae sacris famu-lantur ordinibus*": The glory of God must be served with sacred orders. The ancient Pontifical expressly establishes the parallelism between Aaron, the high priest, and the episcopal order. In the new Pontifical, there is only a generic reference to this. In the presbyteral ordination in both Pontificals, explicit reference is made to the seventy elders, helpers of Moses in the desert. With regard to the deacon, the ancient Pontifical expressly says that deacons have the name and office of the Old Testament Levites ("*quorum {levitarum} et nomen et officium tenetis*"). And again, "*Eligimini in levitico officio*": Be elected for the Levitical office. The new Pontifical in the oration of ordination also compares the diaconate with the Levites.

In the Old Testament cult, the Levites performed a whole variety of secondary liturgical services of assistance to the priests.

---

[57] See *Ep.* 6:6; *Ep.* 14:4; *Serm.* 59:7; 85:2.

The deacons had the same task, as the praying faith and liturgical practice of the Church testify from the first centuries. Anyone who had not received a solemn designation for divine worship could not perform *any* liturgical function, even if this function was secondary or merely one of assistance. These secondary and assistant functions were performed by deacons, the New Testament Levites who were not considered priests. This is how the Church has always believed and prayed, as the *Traditio Apostolica* of the second to the early third century states: the deacon is "not ordained to the priesthood, but to service" ("*non ad sacerdotium, sed ad ministerium*," no. 9). The same document says again: "The deacon does not receive the spirit in which the priest participates, but the spirit to be under the authority of the bishop" (no. 8).

With the motu proprio *Omnium in Mentem* of October 26, 2009, Pope Benedict XVI clarified the diaconate doctrinally and canonically when he corrected the text of canons 1008 and 1009 of the current *Code of Canon Law*. The previous text of canon 1008 said that all sacred ministers who receive the sacrament of orders fulfill the function of teaching, sanctifying, and governing *in persona Christi capitis*. In the new formulation of the same canon, the expression *in persona Christi capitis* and the mention of the *tria munera* (triple function) have been removed. A third paragraph has been added to canon 1009:

> Those who are constituted in the order of the episcopate or of the presbyterate receive the mission and the faculty to act in the person of Christ the Head, while deacons are enabled to serve the people of God [*vim populo Dei serviendi*] in the *diakonia* of the liturgy, of the word, and of charity.

With this necessary clarification, the diaconate is understood both doctrinally and liturgically in a way that is more in conformity with the apostolic tradition and the great tradition of the Church. In fact, St. Thomas Aquinas said that the deacon does not have the power to teach, that is, he does not have the *munus docendi* in the strict sense. There is a difference between the nature of the bishop's or priest's sermon on the one hand and that of the deacon on the other. The deacon can only preach *per modum catechizantis* (in the manner of one catechizing). Instead, the *modus docendi*—the doctrinal exposition of the Gospel and of the Faith—belongs to the bishop and to the presbyter, said St. Thomas.[58]

With regard to the hierarchical order of the Church, the Council of Trent made a clear distinction between priests and those who are called ministers. The Council thus affirms: "In addition to the priesthood, there are other major and minor orders in the Catholic Church" (Session XXIII, canon 2). "In the Catholic Church there is a hierarchy established by divine disposition, and made up of bishops, priests, and ministers" (ibid., canon 6). The word "ministers" certainly includes deacons in the first place, and it can be deduced from the cited canon 2 that minor orders are also included in the hierarchy, although they do not belong to the ministerial priesthood as do the episcopate and the presbyterate. Deacons are not *sacrificatores*; they are not priests. For this reason, the great tradition of the Church has not considered deacons *ordinary* ministers of the sacrament of Baptism and of the distribution of Holy Communion.

---

[58] *ST* III, Q. 67, art. 1, ad 1. It is interesting to note that St. Thomas explains that while women are not permitted to teach publicly in church (that is, to perform the work of a deacon), any believer is permitted to instruct in the Faith privately (see *ST* III, Q. 55, art. 1, ad 3; Q. 71, art. 4, ad 3).

The whole tradition of the Church, both Eastern and Western, has always reiterated the following principle: the deacon prepares, assists, and lends his aid to the liturgical action of the bishop or the presbyter (see, for example, *Didascalia Apostolorum*, 11). Already the first Ecumenical Council of Nicaea in 325 unequivocally affirmed this truth and this practice received from tradition, saying:

> This great and holy Council has learned that in some places and cities deacons administer the grace of Holy Communion to priests [*gratiam sacrae communionis*]. Neither canonical norms [*regula, kanòn*] nor custom allow those who do not have the power to offer the sacrifice [*potestatem offerendi*] to give the body of Christ to those who have the power to offer the sacrifice.[59]

The deacon serves, in the bishop and in the presbyters, the one and indivisible priesthood in the same way as the Levites served the high priest and the Mosaic priests.

The diaconate and minor orders

Without actually being a priest, the deacon nevertheless belongs to the sacramental and hierarchical order. This fact expresses the truth that the subordinate or inferior liturgical functions also belong to the only true priest, Jesus Christ, since He, in the exercise of His priesthood, through the sacrifice of the Cross, became a servant, minister, a "deacon." In fact, during the Last Supper, Christ said to His apostles, to the priests of the New Covenant: "I am among you as one who serves [*ho diakonòn*]" (Luke 22:27). For the performing of services of assistance during

---

[59] Canon 18.

the liturgy—that is, functions that do not require proper priestly power—the apostles established a sacramental ordination to the diaconate. The liturgical services of the diaconate, with the exception of proclaiming the Gospel, were over time distributed to other servers of the altar for which the Church created non-sacramental ordinations, especially the subdiaconate, the lectorate, and the acolytate.

So we see that these other assisting roles are simply delegations of diaconal service; they belong properly to the clergy. Therefore, the principle according to which it is said that all liturgical functions which do not require proper priestly power belong, by law and nature, to the common priesthood of the faithful *is not valid*. This novel principle contradicts the principle established by divine revelation in the Old Covenant, in which God instituted through Moses the order of the Levites for the lower, non-priestly functions, and in the New Covenant, in which He instituted through the apostles the order of deacons for the same purpose. The liturgical service of the deacon also contains in itself the lower or the humblest liturgical functions, since they express the true nature of his order and his name: servant, *diákonos*. These lower or humbler liturgical functions can be, for example, bringing candles, water, and wine to the altar (subdeacon, acolyte), reading lessons (subdeacon, lector), attending exorcisms and uttering exorcistic prayers (exorcist), and keeping watch at the church doors and ringing the bells (porter).

In the times of the apostles, it was the deacons who performed all these inferior services during divine worship. Already in the second century, the Church, by a wise disposition, began to reserve to the deacons the higher non-priestly liturgical functions. She opened the treasury of the diaconate, distributing its riches, partitioning out the diaconate itself, and thus creating the minor orders.[60] St. Thomas Aquinas recognized this development when he wrote:

> In the early Church, all the lower ministries were committed to deacons because of the scarcity of ministers, as is evident from what Dionysius says: "other ministers stand at the closed gates of the temple; others work something else of their proper order; others set out the sacred bread and the chalice of blessing upon the altar with the priests." Nevertheless, all the powers mentioned were there, but implicitly in the one power of the diaconate. But later the divine worship was more widespread, and what the Church implicitly had in one order, she distributed [*tradidit*] explicitly over many; and according to this, the Master says in the text that "the Church instituted for herself other orders."[61]

For a long time, a small number of deacons could thus be preserved by multiplying the other lower ministers. In the first centuries, the Church of Rome, out of reverence for the tradition of the apostles, did not want to exceed the number seven for deacons. In third-century Rome, Pope St. Cornelius wrote that the Roman Church had seven deacons.[62] Still in the fourth century, the provincial Synod of Neocaesarea (between 314 and 325)

---

[60] See Dom Adrien Gréa, *L'Église et sa divine constitution*, with a preface by Louis Bouyer (Montréal: Casterman, 1965), 326.

[61] *Scriptum super Sententiis*, lib. 4, d. 24, q. 2, a. 1, qa. 2, ad 2; see *Commentary on the Sentences*, Book IV, Distinctions 14–25, trans. Beth Mortensen (Steubenville, OH: Emmaus Academic, 2018), 614.

[62] See Eusebius, *Ecclesiastical History*, I, 6:43.

established the same norm.[63] Dom Adrien Gréa gave this spiritually and theologically profound explanation for the organic link between the diaconate and the other lower or minor orders: "As the tree of the Church grew, this main branch of the diaconate, obeying the laws of a divine expansion, opened up and divided into several branches, which were the subdiaconate order and the other minor orders."[64]

What can be the reason for the admirable fruitfulness of the diaconate, from and for which the lower orders were born? The answer, according to Dom Gréa, lies in the essential difference between the priesthood and the ministry. We see this essential difference in the fact that only the priesthood acts *in persona Christi capitis*; the ministry of the diaconate, on the other hand, cannot do this, as Pope Benedict XVI reiterated in the motu proprio *Omnium in Mentem*. The priesthood is simple and by its nature indivisible. The priesthood cannot be partially communicated, although it can be possessed at various degrees. The priesthood is possessed by the bishop as head and by the presbyter as participant. In its essence, the priesthood cannot be dismembered.[65] The ministry, on the other hand, is fully possessed by the diaconate and is indefinitely open to sharing, since the multiple functions of ministers are all directed to the priesthood, which they must serve. Divine wisdom has imprinted the character of divisibility in liturgical *service*, which is not strictly priestly, and founded it in the sacramental diaconate, leaving however to the Church the freedom to distribute, according to needs and circumstances, in a non-sacramental way, the different parts of the diaconate which

---

[63] See Mansi II, 544.
[64] Gréa, *L'Église*, 326.
[65] Ibid., 327.

are found in the lower or minor orders, especially the ministries of the lectorate and acolytate.

Dogmatically defining the divinely established structure of the hierarchy, the Council of Trent chose the term "ministers" alongside the terms "bishop" and "priests," avoiding the term "deacons." Most likely, the Council wanted to include the diaconate, the subdiaconate, and the minor orders in the term "ministers" in order to say implicitly that these others are part of the diaconate. This is the formulation of canon six of session XXIII: "If anyone says that in the Catholic Church there is no hierarchy established by a divine arrangement, which is made up of bishops, priests, and ministers, let him be anathema." It can therefore be said that the major order of subdiaconate and the lower orders, such as the lectorate and acolytate, have their root in the diaconate by the divine institution, but they have been formed and distributed in several degrees by ecclesiastical institution.[66]

The historical development of the minor orders

Already in the second century, the distinct office of the reader or lector is found in liturgical celebrations as a stable category of liturgical ministers, as Tertullian testifies.[67] Before Tertullian, St. Justin mentions those who have the office of reading Sacred Scripture in the Eucharistic liturgy.[68] Already in the third century in the Roman Church, all the minor and major orders of the later tradition of the Church existed, as evidenced by a letter from Pope Cornelius of the year 251: "In the Roman Church there are

---

[66] See ibid.
[67] *Praescr.* 41.
[68] *1 Apol.* 67:3.

forty-six presbyters, seven deacons, seven subdeacons, forty-two acolytes, fifty-two exorcists, lectors, and porters."[69]

It must be taken into account that this hierarchical structure with its various degrees could not be an innovation but reflected a tradition, since three years later, Pope St. Stephen I wrote to St. Cyprian of Carthage that in the Roman Church there are no innovations, formulating the famous expression: "*nihil innovetur nisi quod traditum est.*"[70] Eusebius of Caesarea described the attitude of Pope Stephen I, which certainly also characterized his predecessors, the Roman Pontiffs, with these words: "*Stephanus nihil adversus traditionem, quae iam inde ab ultimis temporibus obtinuerat, innovandum ratus est*" (Stephen decided not to approve any innovations against the tradition, which he received from the previous times).[71]

In a matter of such great weight as the Church's hierarchical structure, the existence of the five degrees of ministers lower than the diaconate could not have been an innovation against tradition in the middle of the third century. The peaceful existence of these degrees below the diaconate therefore presupposed a more or less long tradition and had to go back in the Roman Church at least to the second century—that is, to the immediate postapostolic time. According to the testimony of all the liturgical documents and of the Fathers of the Church from the second century onward, the reader, and then also the other lower liturgical ministries (porter, exorcist, acolyte, subdeacon), belonged

[69] Eusebius of Caesarea, *Ecclesiastical History*, VI, 43, 11.
[70] In Cyprian, *Ep.* 74: the meaning is "Let them innovate nothing, but keep the traditions" or, as Fr. Hunwicke renders it, "We must not innovate anything, but stick to what has been handed down."
[71] *Ecclesiastical History*, VII, 3:1.

to the clergy, and the office was conferred on them through an ordination, although without the laying on of hands. The Eastern Church used and still uses two different expressions. For the sacramental ordinations of the episcopate, presbyterate, and diaconate, the word *cheirotenia* is used, while for the ordinations of minor clerics (subdeacons, acolytes, readers) the word *cheirotesia* is used. In order to designate that the functions of ministers inferior to the deacon are, in a certain way, contained in the ministry of the deacon itself and originate from it, the Church has also attributed to the lower liturgical ministers the term *ordo*, the same term with which the hierarchical ministers of the sacramental order are designated, albeit with the specification "minor orders" to distinguish them from the three "major orders" (subdiaconate, diaconate, and presbyterate) and from those that have a sacramental character, including the episcopate.[72]

The current situation of minor orders

Since the first centuries, for almost 1,700 years, the Church has uninterruptedly designated the liturgical ministries lower than the diaconate with the term *ordines* in both the liturgical and canonical books. This tradition lasted until the motu proprio of Pope Paul VI, *Ministeria Quaedam*, of the year 1972, with which the minor orders and the subdiaconate were transitioned

---

[72] The three degrees of the sacrament of Order, as solemnly defined by Pope Pius XII in 1947 in his Apostolic Constitution *Sacramentum Ordinis*, are diaconate, priesthood, and episcopate. These degrees should not, however, be confused with the traditional terminology of "major orders" as comprising subdiaconate, diaconate, and priesthood, with the episcopate being considered more a position of apostolically derived headship than a separate order from the rest.

or subsumed into the "ministries" of reader and acolyte, which were created to promote the active participation of the lay faithful in the liturgy—notwithstanding that such an opinion finds no concrete support in the texts of the Second Vatican Council. These services of reader and acolyte then received the qualification of "lay ministries." Furthermore, the liturgical service of lector and acolyte are often thought to be an expression proper to the common priesthood of the laity. On the basis of this argument, no convincing reason can be given for excluding women from the official service of lectors and acolytes.

This argument, however, does not correspond to the *sensus perennis Ecclesiae*, since until Pope Paul VI, the Church never taught that the liturgical service of the lector and the acolyte would be an expression proper to the common priesthood of the laity. Not only did the unbroken tradition of the universal Church exclude women from carrying out the liturgical service of the lector and acolyte, but the canon law of the Church in fact prohibited women from receiving minor orders.

By a gesture of great and clear rupture with the uninterrupted and universal tradition of both the Eastern and the Western Church, Pope Francis with the motu proprio *Spiritus Domini* of January 10, 2021 modified canon 230 §1 of the *Code of the Canon Law*, allowing access for women to the instituted ministry of the lectorate and acolytate. However, this break with the uninterrupted and universal tradition of the Church enacted by Pope Francis at the level of law was already being carried out or tolerated at the level of practice by his predecessors Popes Paul VI, John Paul II, and Benedict XVI.

A further consequence may be the proposal to ask for the sacramental diaconate for women. The fact that Pope Benedict XVI has reiterated the traditional doctrine according to which the deacon does not have the power to act *in persona Christi capitis*, not being ordained to the priesthood but to the ministry, has provided some theologians with the opportunity to request that women, on the basis of this argument, be granted access to the sacramental diaconate. They argue that since the deacon does not have the ministerial priesthood in him, the prohibition of priestly ordination — definitively confirmed by Pope John Paul II in the document *Ordinatio Sacerdotalis* from the year 1994 — would, according to them, not apply to the diaconate.

It must be said that a sacramental diaconal ordination of women would contradict the whole tradition of the universal Church, both Eastern and Western, and would be against the divinely established order of the Church, since the Council of Trent dogmatically defined the following truth: the divinely established hierarchy is made up of bishops, priests, and ministers, that is, *at least* also of deacons.[73] Furthermore, the famous liturgist Aimé Georges Martimort refuted with convincing historical and theological evidence the theory and claim of the existence of a female sacramental diaconate.[74]

The theological argument according to which the service of reader and acolyte is proper to the common priesthood of the laity contradicts the principle divinely established already in the Old Testament that says: to carry out any service in public worship, even a more humble one, it is necessary that the minister receive a stable or sacred designation. The apostles preserved this

---

[73] See Session XXIII, canon 6.

[74] See *Deaconesses: An Historical Study* (San Francisco: Ignatius Press, 1986); cf. Gerhard Ludwig Müller, "Können Frauen die sakramentale Diakonenweihe gültig empfangen?," in Leo Cardinal Scheffczyk, ed., *Diakonat und Diakonissen* (St. Ottilien: Editions Sankt Ottilien, 2002), 67–106.

principle by establishing the order of deacons by divine revelation in analogy with the Old Testament Levites. This fact is also evident from the aforementioned allusions of Pope Clement I, disciple of the apostles. The Church of the first centuries and then the uninterrupted tradition have preserved this theological principle of divine worship: to perform any service at the altar or in public worship, it is necessary to belong to the order of ministers designated for such functions with a special rite called "ordination."

For this reason, the Church, as early as the second century, began to distribute the various liturgical duties of the deacon — the New Testament Levite — to various ministers or lower orders. Admission to liturgical service without having received a minor order was always considered as an exception. As substitutes for the minor orders, adult men or boys could serve at the altar. In these cases, the male sex replaced in a certain way minor non-sacramental ordination, since the diaconal service and all other lower services, which were included in the diaconate, were not priestly services. The male sex, however, was necessary because in the absence of the minor ordination, it is the last link that linked the inferior "deputy" or "substitute" liturgical ministers with the diaconate at the level of symbol. In other words, the male sex of the inferior liturgical ministers was linked with the principle of the Levitical liturgical service, which in turn was strictly ordered to the priesthood and at the same time subordinate to it and reserved for the male sex by divine disposition in the Old Covenant.

Jesus Christ, properly the "deacon" and "minister" of all public worship services of the New Covenant, was male. For this reason, the universal and uninterrupted two-thousand-year tradition of the Church both in the East and in the West has reserved the ministry of public liturgical service to the male sex in the sacramental order of the episcopate, presbyterate, and diaconate *and also in the minor orders of the lower ministries* such as the lectorate and the acolytate. The female sex finds its model of ministry and service in the Blessed Virgin Mary, Mother of the Church, who designated herself with the word "handmaid," *ancilla* (Latin), *doúle* (Greek), the equivalent of the masculine *diákonos*. It is significant that Mary did not say "I am the *diacona* of the Lord," but "I am the handmaid of the Lord."

The liturgical service of women in the Eucharistic liturgy, as reader and as acolyte and servant at the altar, was altogether excluded in the theological reasoning of the whole Old Testament and New Testament traditions and of the two-thousand-year-old Eastern and Western tradition of the Church.[75] There were some exceptions in the cases of cloistered female monasteries, where the nuns could read the reading; yet they did not do the reading in the presbytery or sanctuary, but behind the enclosed grate, such as in some convents of Carthusian nuns.[76]

The proclamation of Sacred Scripture during the Eucharistic celebration was never entrusted by the Church to persons who were not constituted at least in the minor orders. The Second Ecumenical Council of Nicaea prohibited a contrary custom, saying:

> The order must be preserved in holy things and it is pleasing to God that the various tasks of the priesthood are observed with diligence. Since some, having received the clerical tonsure since childhood, without any other imposition of hands by the bishop, read from the ambo during

---

[75] See Martimort, *Deaconesses*.
[76] See ibid., 231ff.

the Eucharistic liturgy contrary to the sacred canons, we order that from this moment this is no longer permitted.[77]

This norm has always been preserved by the universal Church and especially by the Roman Church until the moment following the liturgical reform after the Second Vatican Council, when lay-men were allowed to read the readings publicly in solemn Masses. This allowance was gradually extended even to laywomen. Wish-ing to preserve the principle of the great tradition, which required that liturgical services be performed by the ministers of minor orders, the Council of Trent strongly recommended that the bishops ensure "that the functions of the holy orders, from the diaconate to the ostiariate [porter], in the Church since apostolic times, are to be exercised only by those who are constituted in such orders."[78] The Council allowed even married men to be ordained as minor clerics: "If there are no celibate clerics to exercise the ministry of the four minor orders, they can also be replaced with married clerics."[79] In the Roman liturgy according to the most ancient form (most commonly called "the traditional Latin Mass"), the proclamation of the reading in the Eucharistic liturgy can be made only by those who are constituted either in the minor orders or in the major orders; indeed, to this day, the minor orders are still pontifically conferred in communities that adhere to the *usus antiquior*.[80] This form of the Roman liturgy retains this principle transmitted from apostolic times and reaf-firmed by the Second Council of Nicaea in the eighth century and by the Council of Trent in the sixteenth century.

[77] Canon XIV.
[78] Session XXIII, Decree of Reform, canon 17.
[79] Ibid.
[80] See chapter 12 below.

The service of minor orders and the priesthood of Christ

Jesus Christ, the only true High Priest of God, is at the same time the supreme deacon. It could be said, in a certain way, that Christ is also the supreme subdeacon, the supreme acolyte and lector, the supreme exorcist and porter, even the supreme altar boy in the liturgy, since Christ's whole existence and saving operation was a very humble service. His priesthood in the ministerial priesthood of the Church must therefore also include the lower liturgical functions or the humblest liturgical services, such as that of the reader or acolyte. For this reason, the diaconate with its functions is part of the sacrament of Holy Orders, and implicitly also the lower liturgical degrees with their functions, which have always been rightly called *ordines*, although formally not sacramental, are part of this sacrament.

Here is a further theological reason for why the universal Church never admitted women to the liturgical public service, not even in the lower grades of lector or acolyte. In the life of Christ one can see how He fulfilled the function of reader when He read Sacred Scripture in synagogue worship (Luke 4:16). It can be said that Christ exercised the function of the porter when He chased the merchants from the temple of God (cf. John 2:15). Christ often performed the functions of an exorcist, driving out unclean spirits. The function of subdeacon or deacon was exercised by Christ, for example, during the Last Supper when He girded Himself with a servant's apron and washed the feet of the apostles who, during the same Supper, were constituted by Him true priests of the New Covenant.[81]

Humble and inferior liturgical services also belong to the greatness and nature of the ministerial priesthood and the sacrament

---

[81] See Council of Trent, Session XXII, ch. 1.

of Holy Orders. It would be an error, and a human and worldly thought, to affirm that only the *higher* liturgical functions (proclaiming the Gospel, uttering the words of consecration) are proper to the ministerial priesthood while the lower and humbler liturgical functions (uttering the other scriptural readings and serving at the altar) are proper to the common priesthood of the lay faithful. In the kingdom of Christ, there is no discrimination, there is no competition to have more powers in the exercise of divine worship; rather, everything is concentrated in the reality of and in the need for humility, conforming to the model of Christ the Eternal High Priest. Dom Gréa left us the following admirable reflections:

> When a bishop or priest performs some function of simple ministry, he exercises it with all the grandeur that his priesthood gives to his action. The divine head of bishops, Jesus Christ Himself, did not disdain to perform the actions of the lower ministers, raising them all up by the sublimity of His high-priesthood.... As a priest in the fullness of the priesthood that He received from His Father (Ps 109:4; Heb 5:1–10), He wanted to sanctify in His person the functions of the [lower] ministers. In exercising them, He raised them up by the dignity of His sovereign priesthood and descended to them without lowering or degrading it.[82]

All liturgical services within the sanctuary of the church represent Christ, the supreme "deacon," and therefore, according to the *perennis sensus* of the Church and its uninterrupted tradition, both the higher and lower liturgical services are performed by

[82]   Gréa, *L'Église*, 109.

male persons. The common priesthood, on the other hand, is represented by those persons who, during the liturgy, are gathered in the nave of the church, representing Mary, the "handmaid of the Lord," who receives the Word and makes it fruitful in the world. The Blessed Virgin Mary never would have liked to perform, and she never actually performed, the function of reader or acolyte in the liturgy of the primitive Church. And she would have been most worthy for such a service, being all-holy and immaculate. Participation in the liturgy according to the model of Mary is the most active and fruitful liturgical participation possible on the part of the common priesthood and especially on the part of women, since "the Church sees in Mary the highest expression of feminine genius."[83]

---

[83] Pope John Paul II, *Letter to Women*, 10. See "The Spirit of the Liturgy in the Words and Actions of Our Lady," in Kwasniewski, *Noble Beauty*, 53–87.

5

The Laity's Role in the World— and in the Church

What kind of presence are Christians supposed to have in the world around them? What kind of influence should they exercise within their families and upon the wider communities to which they belong? What is the basic relationship between "secular" society and the Christians who dwell in it as citizens, receiving certain goods from it, of course, but also—and one hopes more energetically—*giving* to it something that it would otherwise lack, to its own imperilment?

For Paul VI in his Apostolic Exhortation *Evangelii Nuntiandi*, the question of Christianity in the world comes down to this: the willingness of Christians, in spite of all opposition and setbacks, to bear witness patiently and courageously to Christ and to His Gospel, living according to His teaching and translating it as well as they can into the rhythms and structures of everyday life—not excluding, but neither being identified with or collapsed into, politics and political society.

We have seen errors emerge in our time that reject this teaching, albeit from opposite extremes. First is the error of the liberation theologians who, taking their inspiration from Karl Marx, reduce the Good News of salvation to the militant fight against the wealthy and powerful and the provision of adequate food and shelter. The other is the more subtle error of classical liberals, who speak as if the flourishing of markets and the extension of technological benefits to as many people as possible were an answer to the predicament of fallen humanity—a sort of secular Gospel that they believe has power to liberate man from ignorance and vice. Both are forms of reductionism that exchange the promise of the Kingdom of Heaven, which sustains man in hope despite all hardships, for abundant material bread, which by itself cannot drive away despair. It is a fool's bargain, for "man shall not live by bread alone, but by every word that proceedeth out of the mouth of God" (Matt. 4:4). It is nothing less than the Lord Jesus Christ, the eternal Word proceeding from the Father, who gives meaning to our life and purpose to our strivings and sufferings. Without His Resurrection, we are truly the most miserable of men (cf. 1 Cor. 15:12–19).

So, then, what is needed above all is the infusion of Christ's glorious life into our souls and bodies, our work and leisure, our families and friends, our city, society, and nation, so that it becomes the principle from which and for which we act. Thus Pope Paul VI writes: "What matters is to *evangelize* man's culture and cultures—not in a purely decorative way, as it were, by applying a thin veneer, but in a vital way, in depth and right to their very roots."[84] He continues:

> The kingdom which the Gospel proclaims is lived by men who are profoundly linked to a culture, and the building up of the kingdom cannot avoid borrowing the elements

---

[84] *Evangelii Nuntiandi* (1975), §20.

of human culture or cultures.... The split between the Gospel and culture is without a doubt the drama of our time, just as it was of other times. Therefore every effort must be made to ensure a full evangelization of culture, or more correctly of cultures. They have to be regenerated by an encounter with the Gospel.

It is a short step from here to the role of the laity in the world —a major theme of the Second Vatican Council, but still neglected in the contemporary Church, where "involvement" has been construed as parish busywork and clericalization rather than brave interventions and concerted efforts in the cultural spheres proper to the non-ordained. Whatever difficulties one may have with the documents or legacy of Vatican II, on this point there is no question of its soundness.

Paul VI understood what was demanded of the lay faithful:

Lay people, whose particular vocation places them in the midst of the world and in charge of the most varied temporal tasks, must for this very reason exercise a very special form of evangelization. Their primary and immediate task is not to establish and develop the ecclesial community—this is the specific role of the pastors—but to put to use every Christian and evangelical possibility latent but already present and active in the affairs of the world. Their own field of evangelizing activity is the vast and complicated world of politics, society and economics, but also the world of culture, of the sciences and the arts, of international life, of the mass media. It also includes other realities which are open to evangelization, such as human love, the family, the education of children and adolescents, professional work, suffering. The more

Gospel-inspired lay people there are engaged in these realities, clearly involved in them, competent to promote them and conscious that they must exercise to the full their Christian powers which are often buried and suffocated, the more these realities will be at the service of the kingdom of God and therefore of salvation in Jesus Christ, without in any way losing or sacrificing their human content but rather pointing to a transcendent dimension which is often disregarded.[85]

Paul VI echoes the Council's Decree on the Apostolate of the Laity, *Apostolicam Actuositatem* — which calls for an intensive involvement of lay Catholics in every sphere of social life — against the dominant modern conception, traceable to the Enlightenment, that religion is a private affair that should not make waves in the public square or even in any endeavor involving other people, rather like a coat one takes off and hangs in the foyer before going into the office to start the day's work. On the contrary, the specific vocation of a Christian living in the world is to seek to *transform* it by the energetic exercise of moral and theological virtues, not in pure solitude, as a hermit might do, but *in society*, and as a *public* activity and witness. The Council did not ask that the State be separated still further from the Church ("equivalent to the separation of human legislation from Christian and divine legislation," as Pope Leo XIII succinctly put it in his Encyclical Letter *Au Milieu des Sollicitudes*), but rather, that the laity infuse the spirit of the Gospel into *all temporal realities*. Thus, *Gaudium et Spes* §43 exhorts the laity to "impress the divine law on the affairs of the earthly city." *Apostolicam Actuositatem* is still more

---

[85] *Evangelii Nuntiandi*, §70.

precise. In §7, the Council Fathers, recognizing the "intrinsic value" of temporal realities, note how easily they can be perverted to the grave harm of mankind and issue a call to Christians, especially the laity, to *transform* the temporal order according to the Gospel.[86] Surely, modern Christians have tended toward the opposite extreme, that is, the divorcing of personal conviction from public life, which is a perilous attitude that results in dilution and eventual obliteration. The historian Todd Hartch writes:

> Vatican II emphasized the special vocation of lay Catholics, not to the ambo or the head of the communion line, but to the worlds of family, commerce, politics, culture, and all the many forms of human life *outside* of the doors of a church. They were supposed to transform their environments and to be witnesses of Christ to all those around them. After the Second Vatican Council this worldly lay vocation was exactly what American Catholics failed at most dramatically, with Catholics conforming to the culture of modernity much more than they transformed it. In fact, they did *much worse* in this area than the generations before Vatican II, who created vibrant Catholic subcultures.[87]

These "vibrant subcultures" were not (and were never intended to be) the ultimate goal, for that goal could only be claiming an

---

[86] Without, needless to say, aspiring to a simple fusion of temporal and spiritual societies, as occurred historically in a number of ways: the Caesaropapism of Byzantium, the Erastianism of some Western nation-states, the Gallicanism and Josephinism of the Enlightenment.

[87] Todd Hartch, *A Time to Build Anew: How to Find the True, Good, and Beautiful in America* (Brooklyn, NY: Angelico Press, 2021), 9.

entire country for Christ and His Church. Yet there is no winning of a nation without the winning of a neighborhood. There is no conversion of a people without the internal vitality of a parish. And without the support of good, consistent, and pervasive Catholic customs—which create, as it were, a microcosm or little world—it will be impossible to maintain one's spiritual identity over and against the dominant forces of a world that has lost its way and its wits. That is why the much-maligned "Catholic ghettoes" were, in fact, crucial to the flourishing of the Church in American to the extent that it flourished and why their loss coincided with the assimilation and absorption of Catholics into secularity. That this was not the wish, though it may well have been the byproduct, of the Second Vatican Council may be seen in the unequivocal words of *Apostolicam Actuositatem* §7:

> The whole Church must work vigorously in order that men may become capable of rectifying the distortion of the temporal order and directing it to God through Christ. Pastors must clearly state the principles concerning the purpose of creation and the use of temporal things and must offer the moral and spiritual aids by which the temporal order may be renewed in Christ [*ut ordo rerum temporalium in Christo instauretur*]. The laity must take up the renewal of the temporal order [*ordinis temporalis instaurationem*] as their own special obligation. Led by the light of the Gospel and the mind of the Church and motivated by Christian charity, they must act directly and in a definite way in the temporal sphere.

The same document defines the social apostolate as "the effort to infuse a Christian spirit into the mentality, customs, laws, and structures of the community in which one lives" (§13). Note, however, that it mentions not only mentality and customs, but *laws* and *structures*. The phrases "renewed in Christ" and "renewal of the temporal order" — though *instauratio* is better translated "restoration" — call to mind the mottoes of two outstanding popes of social engagement: St. Pius X's *Instaurare Omnia in Christo* ("to restore all things in Christ") and Pius XI's *Pax Christi in regno Christi* ("the peace of Christ in the kingdom of Christ").

These are our marching orders.[88] The fight is difficult, more difficult than ever, but we must be clear on what we are fighting *for*. We are not looking for tolerance. We will not settle for religious liberty. We are not expecting Heaven on earth, for Heaven is God's throne and earth is His footstool (Isa. 66:1). We are looking to restore creation in Christ, that all may know the peace of Christ in the kingdom of Christ — a wisdom, justice, mercy, and joy they would never know otherwise. This kingdom entered the world in the fullness of time; it permanently exists in the world through the Church, which will last until the end of time; in favored centuries it has penetrated and conquered the world, when her faithful children have prayed, suffered, and labored. Our task is no different.

Learning from Newman

The canonization of John Henry Newman elevated to the honors of the altar one of the greatest champions of dogmatic orthodoxy, anti-liberalism, and the primacy of the supernatural in Christianity. Newman once said that it would be better for the entire material universe to come to an end than for one soul

---

[88] For a complete introduction, see Peter A. Kwasniewski, ed., *A Reader in Catholic Social Teaching, from* Syllabus Errorum *to* Deus Caritas Est (Tacoma, WA: Cluny Media, 2017).

knowingly to commit a venial sin. That would be *his* version of Christian ecology![89]

Newman was a staunch defender of the central place of the laity in the life of the Church — *not* in the postconciliar vein of parish council populism and assignments in the sanctuary but in the noble and dignified calling proper to them in the Mystical Body of Christ, which cannot be conflated with that of the clergy and which, in its very "worldliness," permits them to do immense good in their own realm. The celebrated preacher Fr. Richard Cipolla expounds this point:

> It is obvious that the vision of the [Second Vatican] Council for the apostolate of the laity is mainly within

[89] Here are his exact words: "The Church aims, not at making a show, but at doing a work. She regards this world, and all that is in it, as a mere shadow, as dust and ashes, compared with the value of one single soul. She holds that, unless she can, in her own way, do good to souls, it is no use her doing anything; she holds that it were better for sun and moon to drop from heaven, for the earth to fail, and for all the many millions who are upon it to die of starvation in extremest agony, so far as temporal affliction goes, than that one soul, I will not say, should be lost, but should commit one single venial sin, should tell one wilful untruth, though it harmed no one, or steal one poor farthing without excuse. She considers the action of this world and the action of the soul simply incommensurate, viewed in their respective spheres; she would rather save the soul of one single wild bandit of Calabria, or whining beggar of Palermo, than draw a hundred lines of railroad through the length and breadth of Italy, or carry out a sanitary reform, in its fullest details, in every city of Sicily, except so far as these great national works tended to some spiritual good beyond them" (*Certain Difficulties Felt by Anglicans in Catholic Teaching*, vol. 1, lecture 8, §4).

the world in which the laity live: in their homes, at work, among their friends, in their many encounters with the world in their lives as laity. They must be witnesses in their marriage, to their children, to their friends, to the many and varied people they meet, in their political life, in their intellectual life. They must take their proper role not only in witnessing to the Catholic faith but also in combating those real forces in contemporary culture that are contrary to the Christian faith.

But notice there is no mention of the laity taking specific roles in the liturgy that Sacred Tradition never afforded them, Tradition here understood not as a song from *Fiddler on the Roof* but rather as what was passed down from the Apostles themselves to the Church and down to the Church of our own time. So what happened practically is that the laity after the Council became clericalized, they became, in a wonderful Italian word for altar boys, *chierichetti*, "little clerics," as lectors, Eucharistic ministers, members of liturgical committees, and so forth. The clericalization of the laity after the Council has been a disaster for the laity and the Church in general. And this is because their clericalization has prevented them from fulfilling their mission to the world as laity.[90]

Fr. Cipolla goes on to note that the laity whom Newman admired the most in Church history were the countless and

---

[90] "Saint John Henry Newman, at the Heart of Tradition," sermon for the Solemn Mass of Thanksgiving for the Canonization of John Henry Newman, October 9, 2019, published at *Rorate Caeli*, October 13, 2019.

nameless faithful in the fourth century who, simply on the basis of holding fast to the faith they had received in Baptism and at the hands of the Church, opposed the Arian heresy when most of their bishops had gone over to the side of error or simply kept their mouths shut for fear of imperial repercussions.

But there is a second and most important reason for an educated laity, especially educated in the Catholic faith. We live in a time in which the very nature of Tradition, what has been handed down to us from Jesus and the Apostles, in Scripture and through the Church Fathers and the ancient Creeds, is under attack. It is under attack not by the world of *The New York Times*, which is quite happy that there is dissension within the Church, for that makes the Church a much less formidable threat to the world of strident secularity. The attack is coming from those who are ordained by God to be true to the Tradition of the Church and to guide their flock during these times of tempests in the world. These men, mostly clerics, claim the right to change Tradition, including the witness of Scripture. They have taken the secular attitude that Tradition is relative and conditioned by its history. They do so in the name of mercy, but this understanding of mercy has little to do with the mercy of God. And it is here and now that an educated laity, educated both in the Faith and intellectually, must be a witness to the Faith handed down to the Church from the Apostles in Scripture and Tradition. Just as the laity were faithful to the Catholic faith at the terrible time of the Arian apostasy in the fourth century and beyond, when most bishops became heretics, so at this time the laity must be faithful to the Catholic faith in a way that is humble, firm, and full of joy.[91]

It is startling and sobering to read Newman's account of the Arian crisis, to which he devoted an entire book. He writes:

The episcopate, whose action was so prompt and concordant at Nicaea on the rise of Arianism, did not, as a class or order of men, play a good part in the troubles consequent upon the Council; and the laity did. The Catholic people, in the length and breadth of Christendom, were the obstinate champions of Catholic truth, and the bishops were not. Of course there were great and illustrious exceptions; first, Athanasius, Hilary, the Latin Eusebius, and Phoebadius; and after them, Basil, the two Gregories, and Ambrose.... But on the whole, taking a wide view of the history, we are obliged to say that the governing body of the Church came short, and the governed were pre-eminent in faith, zeal, courage, and constancy.[92]

Newman, ever the theologian as well as the historian, asks himself why the Lord permitted such a trial to beset the Church, why the shepherds were allowed to become wolves for a time, why good and saintly bishops were a small minority, and why the people were called upon to hold fast even against their "betters."

---

[91] Ibid.

[92] Appendix, Note V, in *The Arians of the Fourth Century*, with an introduction and notes by Rowan Williams (Notre Dame, IN: University of Notre Dame Press/Leominster: Gracewing, 2001), 445; also available online at www.newmanreader.org/ works/arians. A first version of this appendix was published in *The Rambler* in July 1859 as Newman's article "On Consulting the Faithful in Matters of Doctrine."

Perhaps it was permitted, in order to impress upon the Church at that very time passing out of her state of persecution to her long temporal ascendancy, the great evangelical lesson, that, not the wise and powerful, but the obscure, the unlearned, and the weak constitute her real strength. It was mainly by the faithful people that Paganism was overthrown; it was by the faithful people, under the lead of Athanasius and the Egyptian bishops, and in some places supported by their Bishops or priests, that the worst of heresies was withstood and stamped out of the sacred territory.[93]

In fact, Newman goes so far as to assert that

in that time of immense confusion the divine dogma of our Lord's divinity was proclaimed, enforced, maintained, and (humanly speaking) preserved, far more by the "Ecclesia docta" [i.e., the laity] than by the "Ecclesia docens" [i.e., the hierarchy]; that the body of the Episcopate was unfaithful to its commission, while the body of the laity was faithful to its baptism; that at one time the pope, at other times a patriarchal, metropolitan, or other great see, at other times general councils, said what they should not have said, or did what obscured and compromised revealed truth; while, on the other hand, it was the Christian people, who, under Providence, were the

---

[93] Newman, 445–46. For excellent commentary, see the lecture given by Cardinal Walter Brandmüller with the same title, April 7, 2018, the full text of which was published under the heading "Cardinal Brandmüller Warns Catholics Not to Heed 'Majority' but 'Minority Who Truly Live the Faith,'" *LifeSiteNews*, April 7, 2018.

ecclesiastical strength of Athanasius, Hilary, Eusebius of Vercellae, and other great solitary confessors, who would have failed without them.[94]

But how did the laity survive during the Arian crisis? What actions did they take to preserve the Faith and to resist the heterodox bishops? The short answer: it was exceedingly difficult, but with God's grace, they did whatever was necessary.

To start with, the orthodox faithful stopped their ears against the wheedling and threats of the Arian and Semi-Arian bishops, who no doubt tried to manipulate and "guilt" them, as bad bishops do today, into thinking that they were being "disobedient" by not following the lead of their shepherds. Since the liturgy was often in the hands of the heretics, the laity were forced at times to stop going to their local churches and to gather outdoors or in secret. Newman relates to us that St. Basil the Great, around the year 372, wrote these harrowing words: "Religious people keep silence, but every blaspheming tongue is let loose. Sacred things are profaned; those of the laity who are sound in faith avoid the places of worship as schools of impiety, and raise their hands in solitudes, with groans and tears to the Lord in heaven."[95] Four years later, Basil was to write:

Matters have come to this pass: the people have left their houses of prayer, and assemble in deserts,—a pitiable sight; women and children, old men, and men otherwise infirm, wretchedly faring in the open air, amid the most profuse rains and snow-storms and winds and frosts of winter; and again in summer under a scorching sun. To

94 Newman, *Arians*, 465–66.
95 *Epistle* 92, in Newman, *Arians*, 459.

this they submit, because they will have no part in the wicked Arian leaven.[96]

And in his next letter:

Only one offence is now vigorously punished, — an accurate observance of our fathers' traditions. For this cause the pious are driven from their countries, and transported into deserts. The people are in lamentation, in continual tears at home and abroad. There is a cry in the city, a cry in the country, in the roads, in the deserts. Joy and spiritual cheerfulness are no more; our feasts are turned into mourning; our houses of prayer are shut up, our altars deprived of the spiritual worship.[97]

One cannot help but be reminded by these words of the many Catholics who, over the past fifty years, have had to invite priests into their homes, seek out obscure chapels, or travel long distances in order to continue to practice the traditional Catholic faith that we receive from the Church. Although in some ways the situation has improved in parts of the world, what we are seeing under Pope Francis can only make us wonder if we are heading toward a time darker than the already Stygian 1970s. Priests who wish to remain faithful to Our Lord Jesus Christ should be mentally prepared for a day when, having been dismissed for refusing to collaborate with (or resigning in order not to collaborate with) the Lavender Mafia, the diocesan Liturgical Commission, a chancery directive to give Communion to adulterers, etc., they will have no choice but to leave their post and go underground.

---

[96] *Epistle* 242, in Newman, *Arians*, 459–60.
[97] *Epistle* 243, in Newman, *Arians*, 460.

They should have a complete set of vestments, altar missal, and other required paraphernalia at the ready.

All of us — laity, clergy, religious — desire to be at peace with the members of the hierarchy. We love their souls, redeemed by the Blood of Christ, and pray for their conversion as for our own, since no man alive is without sin. We will obey them in everything that pertains to their office and is required of us, but never if they oppose the Faith. There are times when bashful whispered misgivings must yield to open confrontation. At this point it is no longer possible to deny that we are living in an age of unprecedented conflict between the laity and the hierarchy. Eminent church historian Roberto de Mattei speaks of what is too often necessary in today's situation, as well as what will always remain true:

> It is not enough to denounce the pastors who demol-
> ish — or favor the demolition of — the Church. We must
> reduce to the indispensable minimum our ecclesiastical
> cohabitation with them, as happens in an agreement of
> matrimonial separation. If a father exercises physical or
> moral violence toward his wife and children, the wife,
> although recognizing the validity of the marriage itself,
> and without requesting an annulment, can request a sepa-
> ration to protect herself and her children. The Church
> permits it. In our case, giving up living habitually together
> means distancing oneself from the teachings and practices
> of the evil pastors, refusing to participate in the programs
> and activities promoted by them.
>
> But we must not forget that the Church cannot disap-
> pear. Therefore, it is necessary to support the apostolate of
> shepherds who remain faithful to the traditional teachings

of the Church, participating in their initiatives and encouraging them to speak, to act, and to guide the disoriented flock. It is time to separate ourselves from evil pastors, and to unite ourselves to the good ones, inside of the one Church in which both the wheat and the cockle live in the same field (Mt 13:24–30), remembering that the Church is visible, and cannot save herself apart from her legitimate pastors.[98]

St. John Henry Newman praised the laity in the time of the Arian heresy for supporting the true, traditional Church despite the many hardships they faced as a result. May he intercede for us as we pass through what Bishop Athanasius Schneider has described as the fourth and greatest crisis the Catholic Church has ever experienced.[99]

---

[98] *Love for the Papacy and Filial Resistance to the Pope in the History of the Church* (Brooklyn, NY: Angelico Press, 2019), 153–54.

[99] See Athanasius Schneider, with Diane Montagna, *Christus Vincit: Christ's Triumph Over the Darkness of the Age* (Brooklyn, NY: Angelico Press, 2019), ch. 11, "The Fourth Great Crisis."

II

Deviations

6

Lay Ministries Obscure Both
the Laity's Calling and the Clergy's

With the motu proprio *Spiritus Domini*, Pope Francis modified the *Code of Canon Law* to open the ministries of lector and acolyte to women. Those who think "it's not a big deal, it just formalizes what we've already been doing for decades!" underestimate the difference between custom (which can include bad custom) and legal formalization, and more to the point, between substitution (women filling in for certain functions) and institution (women being installed in ministry by episcopal action).

As I have noted elsewhere,[100] Pope Francis's documents often bear titles that suggest a parody of tradition. In the case

[100] "Christ's Universal Dominion and the Modern Tower of Babel," *OnePeterFive*, December 23, 2020. A still more recent example than *Spiritus Domini* is the motu proprio *Antiquum Ministerium* (May 10, 2021), the first sentence of which utters a simple untruth—for there was never any "ministry of catechist" in the ancient Church, in the properly theological sense of "ministry," which ancient ecclesiastical records always connect with the sacrament of Holy Orders, as Bishop Schneider discusses in chapter 4. St. Paul gently rebuked the Corinthians of his day for their obsession with obtaining charisms instead of focusing on the *unum necessarium* of charity. We could say the same

at hand, the phrase *Spiritus Domini* ("The Spirit of the Lord") calls to mind the centuries-old Introit of Pentecost (and of any Votive Mass of the Holy Spirit): *Spiritus Domini replevit orbem terrarum, alleluia: et hoc quod continet omnia, scientiam habet vocis. Alleluia, alleluia, alleluia,* "the Spirit of the Lord hath filled the whole world, alleluia; and that which containeth all things hath knowledge of the voice. Alleluia, alleluia, alleluia" (cf. Wisd. 1:7). The motu proprio's first two words bring us squarely to the mystery of Pentecost.

Now, what happened on the original day of Pentecost? The apostles were gathered around the Blessed Virgin Mary. She was indescribably holier than they, but after the descent of the Spirit, did *she* go out and preach the Gospel? No. It was the male apostles who did that, in imitation of, by the power of, and in the person of Christ. The Blessed Virgin Mary is the highest-ranking human person in the Church and the most powerful, but she was not and is not intermingled with the earthly ecclesiastical hierarchy. This is not how her Son set things up.

As the eminent Swiss Cardinal Charles Journet explains (echoing countless other theologians), the ultimate and only lasting hierarchy in the Church is that of charity and sanctity. In Heaven, everyone's "rank" is determined by this and by nothing else:

> The [ecclesiastical] hierarchy will no longer exist in heaven. The hierarchy was instituted in order to prolong the sensible contact by which Christ desired to touch our wounded nature in order to cure it. This is why the

---

today about the drive to multiply "charisms of ministry" in the Church.

84

Fathers and Doctors constantly present its mediation as a remedy for our sin. It would have had no reason for being in the state of original justice. It will have even less reason to exist in the state of glory: all our infirmities will have vanished. Therefore, Christ's action from a distance will equal that by contact; it will be able to penetrate us with the same ease and connaturality. At that point the visible hierarchy will no longer serve a purpose....

The hierarchy is for the Church, not the Church for the hierarchy. The hierarchy does not exist for itself. When the Church passes from time into eternity, the hierarchy will cease to be. Then a new hierarchy—one that is already being formed in time—will rise up from the heart of the Church of heaven in order to shed its light on all, with the saints and angels. This will not be a hierarchy of signs and symbols, a hierarchy of exile—such as the one here below. It will be a pure hierarchy of sanctity, a hierarchy of the beatific vision and love.[101]

On earth, however, the Mystical Body of Christ—which must represent to us the mediation of Jesus in a symbolic manner we can grasp—is differentiated into offices or roles; and among holders of these offices, the most important for the threefold ministry of ruling, teaching, and sanctifying are the successors of the apostles, the bishops. Taking part in their ministry are the presbyters and deacons they ordain, and, at a further remove but still in the same line, the ministers who assist them in the

---

[101] Charles Journet, *The Theology of the Church*, trans. Victor Szczurek, O.Praem. (San Francisco: Ignatius Press, 2004), 104–5, 166–67.

performance of their duties. These *viri*, or males, represent Christ in and to the Church.[102]

To clarify my meaning: in the face-to-face vision of God in Heaven, there is no need for a physical manifestation of the universal and necessary mediation of Christ our Redeemer, not because it is superseded but because it is patently obvious to the blessed: the one Mediator is resplendent in visible and intelligible glory. On earth, however, as we walk by faith in God and not by the sight of Him, we must walk by the sight of *signs* of Him that form and direct our faith. It would be not only misleading but false to set up, in the Church on earth, signs of ecclesial governance, magisterium, and sanctification that lacked explicit reference to the God-man. Thus, for example, a woman bishop or a woman priest would set up a competing signification that did not rest in and point to Christ. Such a "dis-incarnational" deviation could not be faithful to the Chalcedonian Definition or find its fulfillment in heavenly vision.

The Spirit of the Lord, to whom in the Creed we attribute the conception of the man Christ in the womb of the Virgin Mary, is the same Spirit who, at work in the ministry of the God-Man, raised up twelve *men* to bring the Gospel to the ends of the earth. At the same time, the holiest among His disciples by far—the all-holy Mother of God—never spoke a word in public. Had she done so, we can be sure that these words would have been cherished, gathered up like gold, and preserved for posterity, as occurred with the other precious words of Mary in the Gospels. Her role was superior to that of the male apostles. She received

---

[102] They are also, as baptized faithful, simultaneously members of the Church, and in this capacity, they receive gifts from God just like the laity.

the Son of God in the most sublime manner and lived her union with Him with a sinless perfection. None of the apostles could say that of themselves. Nevertheless, hers was an absolute perfection of receiving, embodying, nurturing, and following—the fundamental Christian vocation that belongs to all of us by virtue of our baptism.[103] It would not have added to her sanctity or her charity to busy herself, like Martha, by taking on "ministries" in the sanctuary of a church; in fact, *it would have detracted from it.* In like manner, it would not have added to the sanctity or charity of the apostles to offload or outsource their properly apostolic tasks to other competent individuals; again, it would have detracted from it.[104]

The motu proprio *Spiritus Domini* therefore commits a double categorical error by conflating the dignity of the baptized with the dignity of active liturgical ministry. On the one hand, it implies that only the baptized who take up instituted ministries are fulfilling their proper lay vocation as fully as they might: they become clerical, to the extent possible, in order to be fully lay. On the other hand, it implies that the laity who choose simply to receive the gifts of grace provided in the liturgy—to be, in other words, just like the Virgin Mary—are second-class citizens in the Church, men and women who have not embraced their

---

[103] See "The Spirit of the Liturgy in the Words and Actions of Our Lady," in Kwasniewski, *Noble Beauty*, 53–87.

[104] The apostles ordained deacons to assist them in lesser works so that they themselves could remain focused on prayer and preaching the Gospel, and as they built up local churches, they ordained successors who would receive their episcopal authority and tradition of sound doctrine. These are examples of "replicating" and "multiplying" powers through ordination, not of inviting extraneous individuals to emulate their work.

calling to be "engaged," to "exercise" their rights, to "participate" in a leadership role. In short, as Fr. Peter Stravinskas has pointed out, *Spiritus Domini* is a triumphant proclamation of clericalism, exactly contrary to the warning of Pope John Paul II in his Apostolic Exhortation *Christifideles Laici*.[105]

That *Spiritus Domini* is an intentional rupture is signaled clearly in the text of the letter to the Prefect of the Congregation of the Doctrine of the Faith that accompanied the motu proprio:

> For centuries the "venerable tradition of the Church" has considered those that were called "minor orders" — including, precisely, the Lector and the Acolyte — as steps on a path that was to lead to the "major orders" (Subdiaconate, Diaconate, Presbyterate). Being that the sacrament of Orders is reserved to men only, this was a valid fact for the minor orders as well. A clearer distinction between the responsibilities of *those that today are called* "non-ordained (or lay) ministries" and the "ordained ministries" allows a loosening of the reservation of the former to men only.[106]

---

[105] See Peter M. J. Stravinskas, "Confusion Twice Confounded: On the Motu Proprio *Spiritus Domini*," *Catholic World Report*, January 11, 2021. We have seen that the teaching contained in other documents of Pope John Paul II, such as *Veritatis Splendor* and *Familiaris Consortio*, has also not fared well under this pontificate of rupture. For detailed discussion, see Lamont and Pierantoni, *Defending the Faith Against Present Heresies*.

[106] "Letter of the Holy Father Francis to the Prefect of the Congregation for the Doctrine of the Faith on access of women to the ministries of Lector and Acolyte," January 11, 2021, https://press.vatican.va/content/salastampa/en/bollettino/pubblico/2021/01/11/210112b.html; emphasis added. The translation of this letter has undergone revisions since it first appeared.

Note how Francis openly acknowledges that there is a centuries-old (indeed, bimillennial) "venerable tradition of the Church" concerning the minor orders that reserved all of them to men only. Then, in the manner of a rabbit emerging from a hat on its own initiative, "a clearer distinction" somehow gets drawn between "lay ministries" and "ordained ministries." Where did this come from? Why was it done? What are the grounds for departing from the "venerable tradition of the Church"? On what basis do we have the right to "loosen" (or, as the Vatican's initial translation said, "dissolve") what the Church has always done, everywhere and by everyone, propounded and administered in the most solemn language? There has been no adequate explanation and there will not be, because any attempt at explanation would expose the latent confusion about baptismal dignity and the underlying clericalism, feminism, and activism of the project.

What we need to see, and see clearly, is this: the highest dignity of the baptized is to welcome Christ the Lord in Holy Communion. Period. Nothing else we do, no other function or service or activity, can compare to the Marian privilege of receiving God. When we elaborately multiply functions, services, and activities, we introduce distractions, invert priorities, build false hierarchies, and undermine simple faith, devotion, humility, and reverence. The *participatio actuosa*, or actual participation, of the faithful in the liturgy is not primarily about *doing* things but about *being* a good recipient of the Word so that this Word may be fruitful in us. It is not about being busy with much serving but about contemplation, the union of love.

In the initial publication, the last phrase read: "makes it possible to dissolve the reservation of the former to men alone."

Ministers of Christ

The proper role of the clergy, for its part, is *to serve actively*, bestowing divine gifts or assisting in their bestowal. This role embraces *all* ministers who assist the clergy in the sanctuary, as they collectively prepare and offer the sacrifice of Christ on behalf of all and for all. The purpose of this distinction, written into the Mystical Body of the Church no less than sexuality is written into the human body, is not to show off the better members or let them lord it over others or announce that they have powers, privileges, and perks that lesser mortals lack. No: it is a power to lead the people closer to the Lord Jesus, whom the clergy and liturgical ministers are to show forth not only in their official actions but also, importantly, in their very person. What we *do*, what we *see*, what we *hear*, what we *believe*: in traditional Catholic worship, these are and must be mutually consistent. The powerful, primal, sacramentally relevant and revealed symbolism of the sexes should not, and in the end cannot, be ignored.

If we are no longer able to recognize these luminous and fundamental truths of the Faith, then we are far indeed from the Spirit of the Lord, and well mired in the Spirit of the Age.

A long journey from busyness to abiding

The motu proprio *Spiritus Domini* has a personal resonance for me. Under the regime of progressive Catholicism in which I grew up, I recall hearing one message loud and clear: "Show your faith by signing up for XYZ ministry."[107] The underlying assumption was that merely assisting at Mass was not quite good enough. That was for the uncommitted, the uninterested, the unmotivated.

---

[107] See Dan Millette, "Pope Francis's Lesson on How to Make Female Ministers," *OnePeterFive*, January 15, 2021.

So I dutifully signed up to be first an altar boy, then a lector, and finally, an extraordinary minister of Holy Communion (this would have been in the 1980s). Throughout boyhood and adolescence, I didn't understand *at all* what the Mass was about; I hardly had a clue what the Eucharist was; I'm not even sure my views would have differed, in essence, from how Protestants view their services. Actually, that's not true — a Protestant would have had a much higher view of biblical inspiration and inerrancy than I would have had. I was serving at *something*, I knew not what; I was reading *something*, I knew not what; I was distributing *something*, I knew not what.

My attitude toward what I was doing began to shift when, in my senior year of high school, a teacher (who happened to be a convert to Catholicism) handed me a copy of Ludwig Ott's *Fundamentals of Catholic Dogma*. The teacher saw that I was trying to be a serious Catholic and that I was a voracious reader interested in theology. He thought I would benefit from a deep dogmatic dive. I can only say that my world was rocked by what I read, especially in the section on the Holy Eucharist.[108] Face to face with page after page of authoritative Church teachings of which I'd never heard in spite of so many years of education in Catholic schools, I began what would turn out to be a quest of many more years for an explanation of why solemn truths required for salvation — the most important truths one could ever know in this life, and the basis on which the Christian life should be built — were no longer being proclaimed, no longer passed on, no longer expressed in the way we worshiped. At first, I was

---

[108] See Ludwig Ott, *Fundamentals of Catholic Dogma*, trans. Patrick Lynch, ed. James Canon Bastible, rev. Robert Fastiggi (London: Baronius Press, 2018), 395–438.

naïve enough to think that it was only a problem of "misguided individuals" or "the wrong implementation" of a good plan. It would not be until a few years later that I first encountered the traditional Latin Mass, which rocked my world a second time. I discovered the form of worship that corresponded to the Church's dogmatic confession. For the first time, the two pieces—creed and liturgy—snapped together to form a single whole. At the time, I could not have belted out the Latin phrase *lex orandi, lex credendi*, but I was experientially confirming its truth.

It was for me a huge breakthrough, a profound liberation, to discover through more and more frequent attendance at the traditional Latin Mass that one can simply *be* at the liturgy and soak it in like a sponge, abiding in Him who abides. One can come to find this receptivity utterly fulfilling. It was not necessary or even desirable any more for me to volunteer, to sign up, to go up, to do stuff. I was giving myself as deeply as I could by internalizing the prayers and gestures of the sacrifice. I was uniting all of myself, body and soul, to the perfect oblation of Jesus Christ. Instead of seeing the priest as a functionary and the church as a place to be busy, I came to recognize the image of Christ offering Himself in the court of Heaven, before the throne of grace. External activity gave way to admiration and adoration. I learned for the first time that liturgy can be prayer, that it can open up a place of freedom, quiet unworldly joy, and inspiration.[109] I found a liturgy that is

---

[109] A friend of mine wrote to me this beautiful description of her own transition from new to old: "What I found hard before—that is, worship in the Novus Ordo—becomes almost effortless now because the right attitudes are fostered in us. We don't do the work. This being 'thrown headlong' takes the place of plodding along on foot. We go by leaps and bounds and marvel at the growth of our interior spirit of prayer the same way a mother

capable of being everything to everyone, because it is not closed in on itself but rides across the centuries and classes of mankind, indebted to all and beholden to none. Perhaps that is the saddest lesson of the motu proprio *Spiritus Domini*: its change to canon law makes sense only in the context of a liturgy that has lost its *raison d'être* and is struggling to be something to anyone.

The motu proprio once again raises the question of the vocation of the laity.[110] What *are* laypeople supposed to be doing? Have they a proper work of their own, or do they just collect the scraps that fall from the clergy's table — or, better yet, climb up and jostle elbows?

The Church's answer has always been consistent: the laity's work is to influence, purify, and elevate *temporal affairs*, bringing them as much as possible into harmony with the law of God and the Church's mission to glorify God and save souls. As discussed in the preceding chapter at greater length, the Second Vatican Council espoused this traditional point of view: *Gaudium et Spes* exhorts the laity "to impress the divine law on the affairs of the earthly city" (§43), while *Apostolicam Actuositatem* sets as our goal "rectifying the distortion of the temporal order and directing it to God through Christ" (§7). The latter document establishes a distinction between those who teach principles and those who

---

marvels at the rapid growth of her infant child. Maybe others will disagree and say the TLM [Traditional Latin Mass] is hard work and its own sort of plodding. I think people with that view are simply forgetting that the Holy Mass is a place of rest, poetry, sweetness, and immersion in the presence of God. They are trying to 'do it' like Martha when the one thing necessary is to simply 'be' like Mary."

[110] For more on this subject, see my article "May His Kingdom Come: Catholic Social Teaching, Part VI — Conversion of Culture," *Catholic Family News* online, September 25, 2020.

implement them: on the one hand, "Pastors must clearly state the principles concerning the purpose of creation and the use of temporal things and must offer the moral and spiritual aids by which the temporal order may be renewed in Christ" (ibid.); on the other hand, the "apostolate in the social milieu," which is *proper* to laity, involves "the effort to infuse a Christian spirit into the mentality, customs, laws, and structures of the community in which one lives" (§13). As John Paul II wrote in *Ecclesia in Oceania*: "It is the fundamental call of lay people to renew the temporal order in all its many elements. In this way, the Church becomes the yeast that leavens the entire loaf of the temporal order" (§43).

Thus, in spite of Pope Francis's talk about the "co-responsibility" of the ordained and the lay faithful, we may say that the true responsibility of the laity is not taking up tasks *inside* the church but taking on the world *outside* the church. Conversely, priests should not normally be significantly invested in secular affairs, even highly worthwhile ones. The horizontalist social-worker model of the priesthood — popular after the Second Vatican Council — leads to the worst kind of clericalism, in which the clergy have to get involved in everything (including what is more proper to the laity) and in which the laity, in turn, feel they must emulate the clergy and take on quasi-clerical functions in order to have worth or be contributing to the life of the parish. This terrible confusion, still rampant, puts a serious obstacle in the way of renewal in the Church's mission of glorifying God, saving souls, and sanctifying the world; these goals are achieved through worthy worship, which is the clergy's responsibility, and through the Christianization of the secular realm, which is the laity's primary and distinctive role. For laymen and laywomen to confront unbelief with Christian witness, defeat secular narrowness with the grandeur of the Gospel, leaven temporal occupations with a supernatural perspective and motivation, and do all this consistently and courageously is far more challenging—and far more urgent—than mounting an ambo to read a text or donning an alb to pass cruets. It is also more genuinely *priestly*, according to a right understanding of Catholic doctrine, as Church historian Henry Sire articulates:

> There is a legitimate Catholic doctrine of the priesthood of the laity, but it is one that will never diminish the sacramental priesthood. The neo-Protestant doctrine is a piece of the self-assertive ethos of modern times, one concerned with claims rather than duties. In the Christian understanding, no one is a priest for his own sake. The priesthood of the faithful, in the genuine sense, means the duty that the layman has to mediate the knowledge and grace of God to those around him, but that is the last thing that the Modernists mean by it. They turn it into a usurpation of the place of the clergy and the dereliction by priests of their proper role. One can truly say that at no time in the Church's history have the laity had less of a priestly spirit than now, in the sense of a love of the Church's doctrine and sacramental life and the desire to transmit them; in their place is the assertion of rights and the magnifying of self that are the mark of modern humanism.[111]

In fact, the more that laity see themselves as fulfilled in aping the clergy, the more they will be deceived into thinking that they

---

[111] *Phoenix from the Ashes: The Making, Unmaking, and Restoration of Catholic Tradition* (Kettering, OH: Angelico Press, 2015), 319.

have done what they were supposed to do as Catholics. They have, as it were, punched their religion ticket and can get back to secular life in its total secularity.[112]

In the sacred liturgy, the laity exercise the Marian role of receiving divine gifts, which is the creature's highest activity: "Be it done unto me according to Thy word," as Our Lady said at the moment before the Word became flesh in her womb (Luke 1:38). No charism can be more honorable or more important than this receptivity. The gifts bestowed upon the clergy and the various liturgical ministries are at the service of the charity and holiness of the Church; they exist not as ends in themselves but as instruments for the pilgrimage of mankind to the City of God, where there will be no sacraments and no temple, since God will be "all in all" (cf. Rev. 21:22–23; 1 Cor. 15:28). The Marian receptivity of laymen and laywomen opens them to the light and strength they need for their active, transformative mission in the family and in the world. Without drinking deeply from the wellspring, there can never be watered gardens. How ironic and how tragic that the laity's misplaced liturgical activism seems inversely proportional to their zeal for the irreplaceable mission that is theirs in the home, on the land, in the city! The

---

[112] I hasten to add that I am not at all averse to the recommendation—first found in the Council of Trent, no less—that a certain number of suitable and competent laymen (not excluding those who are married) should be ordained to minor orders for each parish so as to assist in the dignified celebration of the liturgy, in this way improving on the current custom in traditional communities of distributing non-priestly roles to altar boys who are, after all, substituting for clerics. The most eloquent appeal and thorough proposal is that of James Thomas More Griffin, "More Than Boys: Why Men Are Needed to Serve the Altar," *Modern Medievalism*, May 18, 2016.

laity are meant to offer themselves up in sacrificial love (cf. Rom. 12:1) so as to be a leaven in the world. *That* is their domain, *that* is their honorable and salvific "service."

At the time of the French Revolution, the Catholic peasants and aristocrats of the Vendée region lived a pure Marian faith during the Reign of Terror by fully assuming their role to defend the Faith, to protect Catholic cities and families, and to do battle against hostile forces. Never did they try to substitute for clergy when their priests went missing. They knew the teaching of St. Paul in 1 Corinthians 12. The Body of Christ has many diverse and unequal members that depend one upon another. The eye has to be the eye, the hand the hand—each part has to be just what it is, to the best of its ability, and not a poor substitute for some other one. The layman took up a musket to defend his family and nation against godless revolutionaries; the priest took up a maniple to offer the Most Holy Sacrifice. The "dignity" of the laity is in no way *augmented* by their taking on of quasi-clerical liturgical functions, just as neither is their dignity *diminished* by being spouses, parents, workers, citizens, or fighters.[113]

---

[113] Leila Marie Lawler noted: "Not one theologian or academic I'm aware of (please prove me wrong) read *Querida Amazonia* and reported on *what it does NOT say*. It does not mention the family and the woman's irreplaceable role in it, as every previous reflection on the Church in the world has done. It does not mention mothers and their role in forming children. It does not mention fathers as providers and protectors. But it *does* speak of women as sort of parallel apostolic agents who ought to be recognized as such. In other words, it speaks—very clearly for those who have ears—of a new ecclesiology in which traditional apostles, men who are priests, must give way to and work with, and often under, women in apostolic roles. This ecclesiological vision is what is behind Cardinal Ouellet's letter on women being given equal roles

Ministers of Christ

I wrote the above words around the time of the Second Sunday after Epiphany in the *usus antiquior*, and once again noticed the hand of God's "liturgical providence,"[114] which placed before me an Epistle and a Gospel that both referred expressly to "ministries." We can learn some important lessons from meditating on these readings. The Epistle of the day is Romans 12:6–16:

> Brethren: Having different gifts, according to the grace that is given us, either prophecy, to be used according to the rule of faith; or ministry, in ministering [*ministerium in ministrando*]; or he that teacheth, in doctrine; he that exhorteth, in exhorting; he that giveth, with simplicity; he that ruleth, with carefulness; he that sheweth mercy, with cheerfulness. Let love be without dissimulation. Hating that which is evil, cleaving to that which is good. Loving one another with the charity of brotherhood, with honour preventing one another. In carefulness not slothful. In spirit fervent. Serving the Lord. Rejoicing in hope. Patient in tribulation. Instant in prayer. Communicating

in seminaries. And it is behind this move (QA is referenced by Pope Francis in his letter to the CDF) to codify in canon law the long-established role of women as lectors and women and girls as acolytes. (As always with progressives, praxis precedes formal legislation.) So no, *Querida Amazonia* was not the anodyne letter proving that the orthodox needed to apologize for worrying about Pope Francis's destructive tendencies. In fact, it was one more wedge in the modern fissure threatening the bulwark of the Church. When women start to think of their 'baptismal dignity' as being proven in the sanctuary, the work of these corrupt shepherds will have been accomplished" (public comment on Facebook).

[114] On this notion, see my article "How God's Providence Is Sung in the Liturgy and Reappears in Our Daily Lives," *LifeSiteNews*, November 10, 2020.

to the necessities of the saints. Pursuing hospitality. Bless them that persecute you: bless, and curse not. Rejoice with them that rejoice; weep with them that weep. Being of one mind one towards another. Not minding high things, but consenting to the humble.

The Apostle gives us here a rich portrait of the true variety of gifts to be found in the Holy Church of God. There are gifts of ministry, but there are also gifts of prophecy, teaching, exhorting, ruling, and works of mercy. The passage then shifts from special charisms to the fundamental Christian vocation of loving: loving without dissimulation, with the charity of brotherhood; hating what is evil and cleaving to what is good; honoring, serving, praying, and offering hospitality.

When we read about *offering hospitality*, should we not be thinking of the baptized and confirmed laity? Hospitality has always been seen as one of the great duties and privileges of lay people: to open their homes, to share with the needy, to welcome friends and strangers. Indeed, what greater hospitality can husband and wife exercise than by giving food and shelter, love and education, to the children who are their common bond and the chief calling of their life? They own and manage property precisely for that reason: to share generously. Their primary calling is to bring Christian prayer, witness, and virtues into the home, and thence, into the workplace and marketplace, the political arena, the broad world of culture. The sanctuary is not their home, but their home can become an extension of the sanctuary. They do not "mind high things," as if seeking a rank or a task that does not belong to them; rather, they consent to be found among the humble (the English Standard Version translates this passage: "do not be haughty, but associate with the lowly").

Ministers of Christ

The clergy, stewards of the mysteries of Christ, are busy with their own proper work, according to the gifts bestowed on them in the Mystical Body. Their primary calling is within the temple of God, offering Him exalted praise and ministering to the people, and in this work they will find fulfillment and sanctity if—and this is a crucial *if*—they enjoy the freedom to be fully what they are and to utilize fully the armory and treasury of the Church's liturgical inheritance. In short, they must have the best wine, drink it freely, and give it to others to drink.

The Gospel appointed for the Second Sunday after Epiphany is John 2:1–11:

> At that time there was a marriage in Cana of Galilee: and the mother of Jesus was there. And Jesus also was invited, and His disciples, to the marriage. And the wine failing, the mother of Jesus saith to Him: They have no wine. And Jesus saith to her: Woman, what is that to Me and to thee? My hour is not yet come. His mother saith to the waiters [*ministris*]: Whatsoever He shall say to you, do ye. Now there were set there six water-pots of stone, according to the manner of the purifying of the Jews, containing two or three measures apiece. Jesus saith to them: Fill the water-pots with water. And they filled them up to the brim. And Jesus said to them: Draw out now, and carry to the chief steward of the feast. And they carried it. And when the chief steward had tasted the water made wine, and knew not whence it was, but the waiters [*ministri*] knew who had drawn the water, the chief steward calleth the bridegroom, and saith to him: Every man at first setteth forth good wine, and when men have well drunk, then that which is worse. But thou hast kept the good wine until now. This

beginning of miracles did Jesus in Cana of Galilee; and manifested His glory, and His disciples believed in Him.[115]

In this Gospel, Jesus is the Eternal High Priest who will offer the perfect sacrifice when "His hour" has come to glorify the Father (note how His Holy Name is mentioned seven times, which underlines His perfection as God and man — students of St. John will know that this is anything but accidental); wine will be the symbol of the sweetness and abundance of His redemption. The *architriclinus*, or chief steward, is like the deacon who ministers to the priest at Solemn Mass; the "waiters" (*ministri* in Latin) are like the subdeacon and the acolytes who minister, in turn, to their superiors.

The guests at the wedding feast are the congregation. They are not serving; they are not busy with providing the food and drink. They are simply taking it all in and feasting. Theirs, in a sense, is "the better part" of Mary of Bethany.

The Virgin Mary is neither a minister *nor* a simple guest. Like the ministers, she brings about results — more, indeed, than anyone else! — but in the mode of an intercessor. She joins the power of the priest to the needs of the people, even as she joined in her womb the supreme deity with the neediness of human nature. Like the guests, she gratefully and joyfully receives good things from the Lord.

---

[115] In the Bible the reading begins "On the third day," but in the liturgy this phrase is replaced with "At that time" (*in illo tempore*). This pivotal Gospel pericope, read every year in the traditional Roman rite, was reduced in the new lectionary to being read only once every three years. On the significance of this shift, see my article "Basking in the Glow of Epiphany: The Wedding Feast at Cana," *Rorate Caeli*, January 13, 2018.

Ministers of Christ

The Epistle and Gospel of the Second Sunday after Epiphany remind us of the wisdom of the Catholic Church in her traditional hierarchical and Christocentric liturgical praxis. Compared with the irrefutable coherence of the *usus antiquior* as it returns to more and more altars, the "polyesterdays" of liturgical experimentation are shown to have no staying power, no future—even on the artificial life support of canon law.

7

Should Women Be Lectors at Mass?

Given that Catholic churches throughout the world swarm with "lay liturgical ministers" of both sexes,[116] it may seem a bit late in the game to offer theological arguments against the practice of female readers, or lectors.[117] But there are several good and urgent reasons to do so at this time.

First, the sizable number of parishes and chapels in which the traditional Latin Mass is celebrated have reintroduced all over the world, to the relief of traditionally minded men *and*

[116] Note that I do not say "gender," which is a grammatical concept, but "sex," which is an anthropological reality. The almost universal shift away from speaking of the male and female *sex*, something present in the very body of a person, to male and female *gender*, something merely attributed as a convention, is a significant cultural indicator of the triumph of subjectivism over realism.

[117] A word about the use of the term "lector." Broadly speaking, this word has come to be synonymous with "reader." Traditionally, "lector" refers to a male officially ordained (or, in the postconciliar context, "instituted") so as to be appointed to the ministry of reading, as occurs in many seminaries at a certain point in the formation process. Here, I am asking a more basic question: Is it more appropriate for a man, as such, to give the readings at Mass, than for a woman, as such?

women, the custom of male-only service in the sanctuary. But the very experience of this once-universal practice necessarily prompts Catholics to raise the question of why it "had" to change at all, and the related question: Is the Church better off for the change or, as with Communion in the hand while standing or Communion under both kinds, *worse* off? Second, we are living in an age when many believers are revisiting and critically examining the blithe assumptions and hasty moves of the past half-century — and are finding, perhaps to their surprise, that the rationales behind many of the changes are shallow at best, ideological at worst. Third, now that the evil fruits of a disordered feminism are far more apparent in society and in the Church than ever before, Catholics who have their heads screwed on straight are more open than ever to a fundamental critique of the modern tendency to treat men and women as interchangeable entities.

To ignore the differences of sex or to pretend that such differences make (or should make) no difference in the fulfilling of liturgical roles is surely to ignore, or rather, to contradict, the "theology of the body" given to the Church by John Paul II.[118] Especially in our times, when confusion about sexuality is rampant, how we conceptualize and implement male and female roles in the Church cannot fail to have huge ramifications in our theological anthropology, moral theology, and even fundamental theology, extending all the way to the inerrancy of Scripture and the trustworthiness of apostolic Tradition.

---

[118] On the psychological ramifications of exchanging a woman for a man at the altar, see Gintautas Vaitoska's "Nonverbal Interaction: Another Take on Why Women Can't Be Priests," *OnePeterFive*, July 31, 2017. Dr. Vaitoska's argument would extend beyond priests to other ministers as well, including lectors.

The question I shall pose is not whether female lectors are *permitted* at this time (since it is obvious that they are permitted in the sphere of the modern rite of Paul VI) but whether the practice *makes theological sense* and to what extent it may have introduced confusion into the minds of the faithful. Moreover, we cannot avoid asking why there *was* an unbroken practice for nearly two thousand years — or more than three thousand years, if we include the worship of the Israelites as preparatory to the New Covenant. Were our predecessors unreconstructed chauvinists who didn't understand the "genius of women" and the contributions they could make to the life of the Church? That seems really unbelievable when one looks at the facts.[119]

In the form of a Thomistic question, I will present arguments on both sides, resolve the question in favor of the Church's Tradition, and respond to the initial objections.

Whether Women Should Read the Readings at Mass

Objection 1. It would seem that it is most appropriate for women to read the readings at Mass. For a woman is capable of representing more perfectly the Church as our Mother, to whom the Word of God has been entrusted. But it belongs to a mother to instruct her children in the ways of God. Therefore a woman appropriately delivers the Word of God to the faithful.

Objection 2. To read Scripture is proper to every member of the Church, for the Roman pontiffs have constantly recommended that *all* Catholics read Scripture and have even enriched this

---

[119] Historian Régine Pernoud demonstrates that women were, if anything, more appreciated, more influential, and more capable in the Middle Ages than in the more "enlightened" centuries that followed. See her book *Women in the Days of the Cathedrals*, trans. Anne Coté-Harriss (San Francisco: Ignatius Press, 1998).

activity with indulgences. Reading Scripture at Mass is nothing more than doing what is proper and recommended for all. Therefore it is indifferent whether men or women serve as readers.

Objection 3. In the traditional liturgy, the lectorate is a minor order for an auxiliary function. It is not equivalent to the major orders of subdiaconate, diaconate, and presbyterate. Now, it is only priestly and diaconal ordination that is reserved to males. Therefore, lectorship is not reserved to males. Much less, then, is the simple function of reading reserved only to males.

Objection 4. The Apostle says: "There is neither Jew nor Greek, there is neither bond nor free, there is neither male nor female. For you are all one in Christ Jesus" (Gal. 3:28). Hence it is irrelevant whether a reader is male or female, so long as he or she is a Christian.

Objection 5. The Church has allowed women to read the readings at Mass. Therefore, it must be good to do so.

On the contrary: The Apostle declares to the Corinthians: "As in all the churches of the saints, the women should keep silence in the churches. For they are not permitted to speak, but should be subordinate, as even the law says. If there is anything they desire to know, let them ask their husbands at home. For it is shameful for a woman to speak in church" (1 Cor. 14:33–35). Again, the same apostle says to St. Timothy: "Let a woman learn in silence with all submissiveness. I permit no woman to teach or to have authority over men; she is to keep silent" (1 Tim. 2:11–12).

Moreover, in accordance with this apostolic judgment, the Church, for nearly two thousand years, did not permit any woman to exercise a liturgical ministry in the sanctuary, a tradition epitomized in the words of canon 44 of the Council of Laodicea (AD 365): "Women may not approach near the altar." But the

Church, being guided by the Holy Spirit, cannot err in the pleasing worship of Almighty God. Therefore her constant customs indicate a divine disposition, and all discordant novelties are to be rejected.

I respond: It ought to be said that in Sacred Scripture, the Word of God is always compared to seed, and the preacher to the one who plants the seed in the soil. The one who *hears* the Word is the mother whose faith receives the seed—the womb in which the seed is implanted, begins to grow, and, with patience, bears fruit. For this reason, the congregation of the faithful is the image of the Virgin Mary, while the lector is the image of God the Father, implanting in their hearts the seed of the Word, Jesus Christ, even as He did in Mary through the instrumentality of the Archangel Gabriel at the Annunciation.

Hence, for a woman to be proclaiming the Word is self-contradictory: it makes the female who receives the seed the male who issues the seed. To deny this symbolic dissonance, one must maintain that being male or being female is metaphysically incidental and irrelevant and that no religious symbolism attaches to male or female characteristics. Such views suggest that the archetypes handed down in Scripture are conventional, changeable, and even false, rather than based on nature, permanent, and true. Such views also suggest the heresy of the Manichaeans, who denied that bodily realities were made by the good God as manifestations of His wisdom.

Consequently, the now nearly universal custom of women reading at Mass deserves to be abolished as the historical aberration and theological danger that it is. Such a restoration of ancient discipline would be one more way to celebrate and consolidate the authentic teaching of the Second Vatican Council, which did not breathe a word about opening up liturgical ministries to women and which expressly stipulated: "there must be no innovations unless the good of the Church genuinely and certainly requires them."[120]

To the first objection, therefore, it should be said that *all* of the sacraments have been entrusted to Holy Mother Church, and the Mass is her chief glory. If the proposed argument were true without qualification, it would be fitting, or more fitting, for all the sacraments to be performed by women. Indeed, there would be no metaphysical argument against female priests but only a positivistic argument: Jesus chose men, therefore the Church chooses men. At this point, we will have abandoned the enterprise of theology, faith seeking understanding (*fides quaerens intellectum*). While on earth, the Lord Jesus did not do things arbitrarily. If priests *ought* to be males, then lectors, servers, ministers of Communion, and so forth *ought* to be males, because all of these are roles of *giving*, of *acting upon*, while the response made by the faithful is always one of *receiving* and of *being acted upon*. This, of course, is the very point of the metaphor of planting or sowing the seed versus taking it into the womb of the ground where it germinates and bears fruit.

To the second objection, it should be said that Holy Mass is not a moment of private prayer or a Scripture study but a public liturgical act offered to the Father by Jesus Christ the Eternal High Priest, at the hands of ministers who are conformed, more or less perfectly, to the image of this High Priest. Hence, it is not proper to every member of the Church to be a public reader of Scripture, any more than it belongs to any member to preach the Word of God to a congregation, as the Apostle teaches in the aforementioned passages.

[120] *Sacrosanctum Concilium* §23.

To the third objection, it should be said that denying that ministers in the sanctuary need to be conformed to the Eternal High Priest as regards their human constitution amounts to a denial of the mystery of the Incarnation, in which the Son of God became not just human (*homo*), but a man (*vir*). Hence, even if one were to say that a reader need not be actually ordained in order to fulfill his function, it would remain fitting that the one reading be ordainable, that is, one who is of such a nature as to reflect the concrete personal identity of the Incarnate Son of God, Jesus of Nazareth.[121]

It may be said, in addition, that rationalism has played far too great a role in the liturgical reform and in the evils that have followed from it, as Joseph Ratzinger frequently observes. We are considering here a poignant example. Could anything be more rationalistic than ignoring the raw, earthy, elemental differences between man and woman? Could anything be more Cartesian than pretending they are the same, or indistinguishable, or interchangeable, or substitutable? Our age will surely go down in history, if there is much of history left, as the age in which common sense met its demise. Anyone with the slightest knowledge of human nature knows that when a child wants or needs its mother, no one else will do. When a situation demands the father, no one else will do. When the Church, for her part, needs a ruler, teacher, or sanctifier, she chooses and appoints a man, for no one else can *represent* the face, the voice, and the hands of Jesus Christ. It is not a matter of loving and suffering *as*

---

[121] For more background to this response and the next, see chapters 2 and 3. The argument offered here is more easily seen in the case of altar boys, who often substitute for ordained acolytes in the traditional Latin Mass.

Christ, for it seems that many more women are Christlike in that sense. It is strictly a matter of who may formally act in His person as Head of the Church (*in persona Christi capitis*) while making present His redemptive *action* upon us who receive its fruits.

To the fourth objection, the Apostle cannot be saying that sexuality no longer exists after baptism or no longer has any role to play in the Christian life, otherwise his comparison of the relationship of husband and wife to the relationship of Christ and the Church (Ephesians 5) would carry no force.

Moreover, grace does not destroy nature but elevates it. There-fore, while grace heals and elevates equally the souls of men and women, other things being equal, it never cancels out their sexual difference. Since only a woman can be a mother, it was the Blessed Virgin Mary who enjoyed the greatest privilege known to cre-ation—namely, to give the Son of God His body and nurture Him in her womb and on her breast. Since only a man can be the image of Christ in His total incarnational reality, Christ chose only males to exercise His priesthood at the altar of sacrifice, as foreshadowed by the priests of the Old Covenant.

To the fifth objection, the history of the Church furnishes nu-merous examples of permissions that were unwisely granted, and later, wisely taken away. For example, the Church has the author-ity to attach indulgences to donations, but this arrangement in practice was so susceptible to abuse ("the sale of indulgences") that the Church withdrew the permission.

Moreover, there is a crucial distinction between allowing and encouraging. When the Church *requires* her children to go to Confession and Communion only once a year, it is clear that she *allows* them to receive this pair of sacraments so rarely, which is a scenario manifestly not optimal for the spiritual life. That does not mean she *encourages* such minimalism. Similarly, moral theology allows married couples to have relations prompted by concupiscence so long as they remain open to life, but that motivation can hardly be considered the ideal for conjugal love. Thus, merely because something is allowed does not mean it is, or should be, encouraged. For, as the Apostle says in a similar context, "'All things are lawful for me,' but not all things are helpful" (1 Cor. 6:12).

Moreover, one must reject the minimalist mentality that asks: "What can I get away with, without disobeying the Church?" for the same reason that one should reject the minimalist mentality behind the question "What is the least I must do to get into Heaven?" To think that way indicates a deficiency in one's mentality. We should be striving to do what is most excellent, fitting, and appropriate.

Looking to Church Fathers and mystics

The argument given above is likely to attract a number of objections. For example, a man might say: "According to his logic, men should not be listening to the Word. If the congregation is like a mother, and the Word is like a seed planted in us, then I, as a man, shouldn't be listening — I'm not supposed to have the 'seed' implanted in me!" A more thoughtful critic might develop the objection this way: Let us agree for the sake of argument that being female aligns with the motherhood of the Church as Bride of Christ who "receives" in her womb the seed (Word of God) from the giver (male/man/God) and nurtures it to grow and bear fruit. Simple enough to understand and no arguments there. But then the claim is made that having women as lectors is self-contradictory: the congregation represents the Virgin Mary, the Church is female, we should be receiving the Word. But what about the *males* in the congregation? If sexual differences are to determine our respective roles, wouldn't all the males who are seated among the females in the pews be self-contradictory too?

These are (or can be) good questions to ask. In his book *Redeemer in the Womb: Jesus Living in Mary*, Fr. John Saward dedicates his sixth chapter to the theme "Christ in the Womb of the Heart." Here he quotes many Fathers and mystics of the Church who compare the Word of God to a seed implanted in the womb, first of the Virgin Mary, and then of every Christian believer who imitates her faith, such as these lines from St. Augustine:

> Mary is therefore blessed because she heard the Word of God and kept it. She kept the truth in her mind longer than the flesh in her womb. Christ-truth, Christ-flesh: Christ-truth in Mary's mind, Christ-flesh in Mary's womb.... The Mother carried Him in her womb; let us carry Him in our hearts. The Virgin was pregnant by Incarnation; let our breasts be pregnant with faith in Christ. The Virgin gave birth to the Saviour; let our souls give birth to salvation, let us give birth to praise. Let us not be barren. Let our souls be fruitful for God.[122]

Fr. Saward goes on to explain in his own words this classic teaching of the Faith:

> Both the Church as a whole and the individual Christian share in Mary's divine motherhood, her bearing of the divine Word.... In and through the Church, the believer is a "mother" to Christ. The individual Christian is called to become what the Church as a whole is, Christ's Bride and Mother, a truly "ecclesiastical soul." ... Mary is the model

[122] St. Augustine, *Sermo de Verbis Evang. Matt.* 12; *Sermo* 180.

of all the souls which form and give birth to the eternal Word in their hearts.... The tradition of the mystical carrying of Christ highlights the favoured status of womanhood as an image of the creature's proper attitude towards God. The soul is always analogically feminine — bridal towards the Bridegroom, motherly towards the Child. To quote the Holy Father [John Paul II] again, "'being the bride,' and thus the 'feminine' element, becomes a symbol of all that is human." Pregnancy in particular is dense with spiritual lessons; being "with child" is the model of being "with Christ" in faith, hope, love, in humble service and deepest prayer.[123]

To respond, then, to the objectors: as many saints and theologians have maintained, *all* Christians are, before God, symbolically in the role of bride and mother. Creatures are fundamentally receptive; and the Church is a bride, of which all of us are members (cf. Ephesians 5). Now, naturally, this symbolism is not going to be pressed into the faces of men in such a way that they are made to feel uncomfortable. Men need the language of being providers, builders, guardians, warriors, etc. But still, our *fundamental identity* as a Christian is that of one who receives grace and is made fruitful by it. This is why the Blessed Virgin Mary is a model not just for women but for all Christians as such.

In the liturgy, it is clear that the sanctuary and ministers around the altar represent Christ, while the nave of the church and the faithful worshiping there represent the Church upon whom He acts and who, by listening in faith and acting on the

---

[123] John Saward, *Redeemer in the Womb: Jesus Living in Mary* (San Francisco: Ignatius Press, 1993), 106, 108, 112, 116–17.

Word received, give back spiritual fruit to Him. When the word is proclaimed by those who represent Christ, the men sitting in the congregation are no less receptive than the women. This role of listener does not *require* that we be women, since all rational beings can listen and cleave to Christ in faith and love. Ministry in the sanctuary, on the other hand, is specifically tied to Christ the High Priest, who, in His ontological reality as Incarnate Word, is a man and *not* a woman. This is obviously pertinent to the question of why *only* men can be priests, when there is no such limitation on who can receive the other six sacraments.

In short, the argument is based on grasping that not all images are interchangeable: some comparisons do not function exactly the same way in both directions. Christ *is* a man, a priest, a bridegroom; this is no mere metaphor, but a fact of the natural and supernatural orders. The Christian is *like* a woman, a mother, a bride; this is a metaphor of a certain fundamental spiritual identity and vocation. The sacred liturgy must take into account facts as well as metaphors, in a coherent synthesis—and this is precisely what Catholics have had in their theological and liturgical tradition until the confusion of the last few decades.[124]

In the end, to sustain the appropriateness of female lectors, we would have to conclude that the People of God (Israel and the

---

[124] Some who agree with my conclusion nevertheless dispute this chapter's argument in support of it. The most honorable dissenter in that regard is Dr. Joseph Shaw of the Latin Mass Society of England and Wales, whose response is worth a read: see www. lmschairman.org/2015/08/1p5-on-female-lectors-response.html, published on August 14, 2015. On the other hand, some not only agree with my conclusion but take it further: see Jonas Alšėnas, "Female Lectors and the Parable of the Sower," *OnePeterFive*, March 12, 2020.

Church) were committing a serious error for three thousand years in their restrictive requirements for public worship, and that all of our forefathers — including the Church Fathers and Doctors and hundreds of popes — were wrong to limit these ministries to men, until the enlightened 1960s showed us a new and better way.[125] Given all the good things we got from the sixties and seventies, forgive me for thinking that the absurdity of these conclusions requires no further comment.

---

[125] One is reminded of the similar absurdity of Pope Francis teaching that capital punishment is "*per se* contrary to the Gospel," "inadmissible" and "immoral," and that it "abases human dignity" — in spite of a triple witness of Scripture, Tradition, and Magisterium to the contrary. With "development" like this, no reversal in Catholic teaching is impossible, because all can be justified by an evolutionary dialectic. See my lecture "What Good Is a Changing *Catechism*? Revisiting the Purpose and Limits of a Book," *Rorate Caeli*, June 15, 2019; cf. Thomas Heinrich Stark, "German Idealism and Cardinal Kasper's Theological Project," *Catholic World Report*, June 9, 2015.

8

Does God the Father Have "Sons and Daughters"?

When clergy today preach about our relationship to the Father in Christ, almost without exception they will refer to Christians as "God's sons and daughters." The Congregation for the Doctrine of the Faith's Letter *Placuit Deo* on Certain Aspects of Christian Salvation (2018) falls in line:

> The Christian faith has illustrated, throughout its centuries-long history, by means of multiple figures, this salvific work of the Son incarnate. It has done so without ever separating the healing dimension of salvation, by which Christ redeems us from sin, from the elevating dimension, by which he makes us sons and daughters of God, participants in his divine nature (cf. 2 Pet. 1:4).

You might be thinking: What could be wrong with this? Isn't it true that we are God's children? Yes, that is true—and thanks be to God for such a wondrous gift. The problem consists in the almost obligatory introduction of the term "daughters" rather than saying simply "sons" or "children" or "offspring." After explaining why this is a theological problem, I will come around to the revised (2011) ICEL translation of the *Roman Missal* and the dissonance it presents in the *lex orandi*.[126]

When speaking of our relationship to the Bridegroom Christ the Lord and to His Bride, Holy Mother Church, one could find room for speaking of *their* sons and daughters, taking Christ metaphorically as the father of the family and the Church as His fruitful wife (cf. Ps. 127). But when speaking of God the Father and of our insertion into the Father-Son relationship, there are *only* "sons in the Son," *filii in Filio*, which, indeed, is the way the New Testament consistently speaks:

> All who are led by the Spirit of God are sons of God. For you did not receive the spirit of slavery to fall back into fear, but you have received the spirit of sonship.... For those whom he foreknew he also predestined to be conformed to the image of his Son, in order that he might be the first-born among many brethren. (Rom. 8:14–15, 29)

> In Christ Jesus *you are all sons of God*, through faith. (Gal. 3:26)

> But when the time had fully come, God sent forth his Son, born of woman, born under the law, to redeem those who were under the law, *so that we might receive adoption as sons*. And *because* you are sons, God has sent the Spirit of his Son into our hearts, crying, "Abba! Father!" So through God you are no longer a slave but a son, and if a son then an heir. (Gal. 4:4–7)

---

[126] This is not, to be sure, its only or its most serious dissonance with the corpus of Roman rite liturgical books, but our focus here is narrower: the question of liturgical ministries and sexual difference.

He destined us in love to be his sons through Jesus Christ, according to the purpose of his will, to the praise of his glorious grace which he freely bestowed on us in the Beloved. (Eph. 1:5–6)

It was fitting that he, for whom and by whom all things exist, in bringing many sons to glory, should make the pioneer of their salvation perfect through suffering. (Heb. 2:10)

He who conquers shall have this heritage, and I will be his God and he shall be my son. (Rev. 21:7)

In contrast with dozens of New Testament passages that speak of "sons" or "children" in the foregoing manner, there is only one text in the New Testament that speaks of God's "sons and daughters" (2 Cor. 6:18).[127] Here, St. Paul seems to be paraphrasing a passage from Isaiah that uses metaphorical speech pertaining to the order of creation (cf. Isa. 43:6–7; Jer. 31:9). Typically, however, the Old Testament places a *singular* emphasis on sonship, preparing the way for Christ by speaking of Israel as God's firstborn son (cf. Exod. 4:22) and of the Davidic king and Messiah as God's son (e.g., Ps. 2:7, "I will tell of the decree of the Lord: He said to me, 'You are my son, today have I begotten you'"). All of this reaches a climax in the two "filial epiphanies" of the Gospels, at the baptism of Jesus and at His Transfiguration:

---

[127] It should be noted that "brothers and sisters" is a normal way of speaking about Christians within the community of the Church, because in *that* context we are considering God simply as Father and the Church as Mother; it is not a Trinitarian way of speaking but a father-mother-child triad. Thus, too, we call nuns "sisters," and the famous Easter hymn begins: "O Filii et Filiae ... "

And when Jesus was baptized, he went up immediately from the water, and behold, the heavens were opened and he saw the Spirit of God descending like a dove, and alighting on him; and lo, a voice from heaven, saying, *"This is my beloved Son, in whom I am well pleased."* (Matt. 3:16–17, emphasis mine; cf. Mark 1:11; Luke 3:22)

He was still speaking, when lo, a bright cloud overshadowed them, and a voice from the cloud said, *"This is my beloved Son, with whom I am well pleased; listen to him."* (Matt. 17:5, emphasis mine; cf. Mark 9:7; 2 Pet. 1:17)

The baptism of Jesus in the Jordan is, to use the language of St. Thomas Aquinas, the exemplar cause of our own baptism: we become beloved "sons in the Son" after the model of His sonship.[128] By the power of the Holy Spirit, we are made to participate in Christ's *natural* sonship, being made like unto Him as He is like unto the Father. This is what our adoption consists in, as St. Paul so carefully and frequently teaches. The Transfiguration, too, shows us what we, the members, are to become in our resurrection, provided we are united to Christ in a death like His.

For their part, the Fathers and Doctors of the Church unanimously follow Scripture's preferred way of speaking of "sons in the

[128] Christ's baptism is the exemplar cause of our baptism (*ST* III, Q. 39). While Christ's Passion is the efficient cause of man's salvation, all of His actions and sufferings are instrumental causes of our salvation (III, Q. 48, art. 6). Our baptism applies to us the grace that Christ merited for us by all the mysteries of His life, culminating in His Passion: "The sacraments of the Church derive their power specially from Christ's Passion, the virtue of which is in a manner united to us by our receiving the sacraments" (III, Q. 62, art. 5).

Son," a rule we see observed with utter consistency throughout the ages, in the great monastic and Scholastic authors, and in all the great modern theologians and spiritual authors, such as Newman, Mersch, Marmion, Scheeben, Journet, and Ratzinger.[129]

But why is this consistency and clarity of sonship language so important?

Our fundamental filial relationship with God is not in any way conditioned by our sex. We are Christians not inasmuch as we are men or women but inasmuch as we are human persons made unto the image and likeness of God, and therefore redeemable and savable. We participate in the *sonship* of the natural Son of God—the God in whom there is no natural daughter—even as we participate in the *bridal* nature of the Church, who is a she, not a he.

In comparison with Christ, we are all brides; in comparison with the Father, we are all sons. Yes, the images clash and refuse to meld—in the order of nature, one cannot be simultaneously a son and a bride—because we are dealing not with natural realities but with a supernatural mystery of divinization so profound that no single way of speaking can fully express it. And yet, the precise images we use, and the language by which we convey them, *do* matter. They cannot be arbitrarily switched around, for we are dealing with definite truths, not with vague mythic metaphors.

To go one step further: in our participatory divine sonship, there is not a natural filiation like the one we have to both of our

---

[129] For two especially good overviews, see Emile Mersch, S.J., "*Filii in Filio*: The Life Imparted by the Trinity," in *The Theology of the Mystical Body*, trans. Cyril Vollert, S.J. (St. Louis: B. Herder, 1951), 325–74, and John Saward, *Cradle of Redeeming Love: The Theology of the Christmas Mystery* (San Francisco: Ignatius Press, 2002), 234–81, esp. 267–81.

parents. In the natural order, we proceed *as* male or female *from* a man-woman couple. Supernaturally, however, we proceed *as* the Son from the Father; God is Father, not Mother, nor is the Son a Daughter. Hence, when speaking of our relationship to God in Christ, we must *not* bring in sex or gender ("God's sons and daughters"), for such language necessarily implies a relationship of natural or physical generation, which is the basis and origin of sexual differentiation. In other words, whether we are male or female is not relevant to divinization. *That*—and not some proto-feminist leveling—is the meaning of St. Paul's famous phrase: "There is neither Jew nor Greek, there is neither bond nor free, there is neither male nor female. For you are all one in Christ Jesus" (Gal. 3:28). We are one *in Him*; He Himself is our unity, our identity, our salvation. God does not offer salvation more to men than to women, or to women more than to men; He offers it to *man*, the rational animal, as Scripture emphasizes: "And God created man to his own image: to the image of God he created him: male and female he created them" (Gen. 1:27). In the world, in human society, in our mutual dealings with one another, and in the sacramental economy, in which natural realities are "borrowed," so to speak, by supernatural ones that speak through them, sex and gender matter a great deal: *either* men *or* women must fulfill certain functions, and therefore the maleness of Christ is absolutely relevant to the question of who may be and serve as a priest or minister *in persona eius*. But human sexual dimorphism does not apply to the divine nature in itself, and it is a mistake to assert it by the language of "sons and daughters."

When we use the expression "God's sons and daughters," we are speaking metaphorically of creatures in their relation to the Creator. In *that* way, all human beings, regardless of religion, faith, baptism, are "God's sons and daughters" — creatures that are like Him in having intellect and free will. But this says nothing about our incorporation into Christ as our Head, our insertion into the mystery of the Blessed Trinity, our taking on the specific likeness of the Son of God so that when the Father looks upon us, He sees His beloved Jesus. Through sanctifying grace, we are made like the Son in His constitutive Sonship. In this analogical (*not* metaphorical) way of speaking, no one is ever a "daughter" of the Father, because there is no Daughter in God to whom we may be specifically likened. As said above, there is no Daughter in the Trinity, only Father, Son, and Holy Spirit. Hence, if we want to talk about this magnificent gift of divinization and filiation, if we want to refer to that which makes us actually Christian, we cannot and must not speak of being "God's sons and daughters." We may *only* speak of being "God's sons," or "sons in the Son." The moment the word "daughter" enters in, what is specifically Christian is evacuated, and something generically monotheistic replaces it.

When I first published these thoughts, a reader attempted to refute me thus: "Men are sons. Women are daughters. Case closed. As for the use of the image of bride and groom, perhaps that is overstated and overused these days. There are other metaphors that may be more helpful in most circumstances. And even in relationship to Christ, we are not really a bride, in the sense of an equal partner in marriage. Metaphorical language is great. But its use must ring true. Otherwise, it will just be perceived as silliness.... There is no earthly way we can speak with precision on matters regarding the essence of God. It is precisely because they are so far beyond human comprehension that we need to use artistic language to communicate a better sense of it all. And such language will not always fit."

What is astonishing about this line of argument is that it completely shreds dogmatic theology about the Trinity, the Incarnation, and the elevation of mankind to divine sonship—what church councils and spiritual writers have taught confidently for centuries evaporates into thin air. How many times does one need to repeat that the language of sonship is *not* metaphorical but analogical in the strict theological sense? The issue is not about mere poetic comparisons but about a metaphysical assimilation of human beings to Him who is the Son of God in truth. There is a likeness between Father and Son that there is not between a father and a daughter. Adoptive likeness to God is a participation in the divine nature itself, and God has revealed himself as Father and Son, not as Father and Daughter. For the inclusive language to ring true, God would have to be Father and Mother in Himself/Herself so that the likeness could be carried through consistently. With the traditional language, on the contrary, we are saying that women have the *very same participation* in Christ Jesus that men have—not a different (and more metaphorical) relationship.[130]

---

[130] On this point, Barry Pearlman writes: "It must be borne in mind that, while concepts such as substantial union (*homoousios*) were foreign to the Jewish mindset, yet on the other hand names given to individuals did serve to express the substantial identity of a person. To be someone's son was to belong to his heritage, community, authority, and lineage: entitled to be the recipient of everything that belonged to the *name* of the father. These ideas are obscured when the Bible is translated by inclusive language" (*A Certain Faith: The Catholic Alternative* [Brooklyn, NY: Angelico Press, 2021], 114). And, one might add, when liturgical texts are translated by inclusive language. Pearlman again: "Jesus possesses his inheritance as his filial right precisely because he is the Son sent by the Father" (ibid., 116).

By trying to be inclusive, the language of "sons and daughters" actually ends up being *exclusive*. For all of us are sons, and all of us are brides. The modern linguistic convention distributes these identities, under the influence of an excessively sexualized conception of the human person. It's as if women cannot have a certain relation to God that men can have (namely, that of sons, like the natural Son Jesus Christ), and as if men cannot have a receptive stance vis-à-vis God the way women can (namely, that of brides, like the Church in whom they exist). In reality, every Christian enjoys all of these privileges, some of which are best described by strictly masculine language and some by strictly feminine language. The greatest honor of a man or woman is that he or she is re-created in the image of the Son, *as a son* — and, in an astonishing perfection of our creatureliness, the same man or woman stands to Christ as a chaste virgin to her Lord. As St. Paul writes to the Christians of Corinth, "I feel a divine jealousy for you, for I betrothed you to Christ to present you as a pure bride to her one husband" (2 Cor. 11:2). It would be just as ridiculous to talk of men and women as "brides and bridegrooms of Christ" as to talk about men and women as "sons and daughters of the Father."

Given the massive witness of Scripture and Tradition concerning a central dogma of the Faith — our adoptive sonship in Christ through water and the Holy Spirit — it is a matter of no small concern that the revised English translation of the modern *Roman Missal* issued by Paul VI adopts the very language that is theologically problematic, in spite of the fact that the Latin original certainly need not be translated thus. While it's true that the Latin plural *filii* can be translated "sons," "children," or "sons and daughters," only the first option remains rooted in the Christology we've been looking at. The other possibilities distract us from our status as adopted sons of God who are re-created in the image of the beloved Son. The modern *Roman Missal*, in an attempt to translate the original Latin more inclusively, overshot the mark and sacrificed the true meaning. Here are three of many instances:

> Almighty ever-living God, whom, taught by the Holy Spirit, we dare to call our Father, bring, we pray, to perfection in our hearts the spirit of adoption as your sons and daughters [*adoptionis filiorum*], that we may merit to enter into the inheritance which you have promised. (Collect, Nineteenth Sunday in Ordinary Time)

> O God, by whom we are redeemed and receive adoption, look graciously upon your beloved sons and daughters [*filios dilectionis tuae*], that those who believe in Christ may receive true freedom and an everlasting inheritance. (Collect, Twenty-Third Sunday in Ordinary Time)

> Look, we pray, upon your people's offerings and pour out on them the power of your Spirit, that they may become the Body and Blood of your beloved Son, Jesus Christ, in whom we, too, are your sons and daughters [*filii tui*]. (Eucharistic Prayer for Reconciliation I)

Even if the redactors of the translation could plead that they intended no theological assertion but merely wished to avoid giving the impression of excluding women — an inclusive language move, they would say, rather than a doctrinal assertion — nevertheless the venerable axiom *lex orandi, lex credendi* reminds us that there is a mutual, reciprocal influence between how one prays and what one believes. The liturgy cannot avoid forming us with its formulas and will teach well or badly depending on the soundness of its formulations. The language of the liturgy shapes our minds, our hearts. It is, without a doubt, the primary source of doctrinal formation for practicing Catholics, especially in an age bereft of substantive catechesis.

As servants of the unchanging truth of Divine Revelation, we have a solemn responsibility to use theological language precisely, whether we are reading a liturgical text or speaking in our own words. If we want to avoid transmitting over time a distorted doctrine of the Trinity, of our adoptive filial relationship to the Father in and through His only-begotten Son, and of the nature of the Church as "spiritually feminine," the Bride of Christ and the Mother of the faithful, we would do well to avoid referring to "God's sons and daughters." Let us speak of God's "children" (as other passages do, such as Heb. 2:13 and 1 John 3:1–2), and even, when appropriate for the context, of God's "offspring" (cf. Acts 17:28–29), and of "brethren [brothers and sisters] in Christ." But let us also take special delight in proclaiming the wondrous truth that all of us who were baptized into Christ have put on Christ (cf. Gal. 3:27) and thus are "sons in the Son," to *each* of whom our heavenly Father can truly say: "This is my beloved Son, in whom I am well pleased."[131]

In his *Commentary on the Rule of St. Benedict*, Dom Paul Delatte beautifully writes:

---

[131] As for the modern translation with its implicit theological error, it is the duty of the Church's hierarchy to correct it as soon as may be. Meanwhile, in keeping with Canon 928 of the 1983 *Code*, a priest is always free to celebrate the Novus Ordo *in Latin*: "The Eucharistic celebration is to be carried out in the Latin language or in another language provided that the liturgical texts have been legitimately approved."

With baptism and faith in Our Lord Jesus Christ, all these distinctions vanish; and in spite of the diversity of our individual circumstances, in spite of the plurality of our natures, we are all one in Our Lord Jesus Christ. The same divine sonship is enjoyed by all, the same blood circulates in all veins, all have the same name, the same spirit, the same nourishment, the same life. This levelling is accomplished, not by the degradation of any, but by the elevation of all to the stature of Our Lord: "unto the measure of the age of the fulness of Christ" (Eph. 4:13).[132]

A sublime expression of this mystery is given to us in the prayer written by St. Elizabeth of the Trinity:

O Consuming Fire, Spirit of Love, descend into my soul and make all in me as an incarnation of the Word, that I may be to Him a super-added humanity wherein He renews His mystery; and You, O Father, bestow Yourself and bend down to Your little creature, seeing in her only Your beloved Son, in whom You are well pleased.[133]

---

[132] *The Rule of Saint Benedict: A Commentary by the Right Rev. Dom Paul Delatte*, trans. Dom Justin McCann, O.S.B. (Eugene, OR: Wipf and Stock, 2000), 44. Another disciple of the *Rule*, Dom Gabriel Sortais, O.C.S.O. (1902–1963), wrote as follows *to a nun* on January 29, 1956: "You are a son of God. Nothing can change that." Such language was normal and accepted, before the postconciliar theological meltdown. See Guy Oury, O.S.B., *Dom Gabriel Sortais: An Amazing Abbot in Turbulent Times*, trans. Brian Kerns, O.S.C.O. (Kalamazoo, MI: Cistercian Publications, 2006), 86.

[133] From the prayer "Ô mon Dieu, Trinité que j'adore" (O my God, Trinity whom I adore) of November 21, 1904. There are several translations of this prayer. For the full text with notes,

Why did St. Elizabeth pray that the Father look upon her and see "only His beloved Son"? There are two possible answers. The first is that she was speaking truthfully and correctly, according to divine revelation. The other is that she was the product and victim of a patriarchal culture that exalted men and devalued women, having "internalized the misogyny" of her age. We may confidently choose the former, which is supported by Scripture, Tradition, and the Magisterium, whose triple witness cannot be in error. Human language does not exhaust divine realities, but there are still right and wrong ways of speaking, as the entire history of doctrine indicates, beginning with the credal formulas and anathemas of the ecumenical councils. Being a son and being a daughter are obviously biologically different, but one must not transfer human biology into the transcendent (and immaterial) Father-Son relationship.

Living in an age characterized by enormous and ever-increasing confusion about nature, personhood, and sexual identity, we need to be more attentive to revealed truth and adhere firmly to traditional theological language when we write or speak or pray.

Dear bishops, priests, and deacons: We love you, we pray for you, and we appreciate the sacrifice of time, prayer, and study you put into your homilies by which you transmit the Gospel to us and strengthen our discipleship. But if you are intending to preach the Good News of our divine sonship in Christ rather than a generic pre-Christian monotheism, *please* stop saying "God's sons and daughters."

---

see Elizabeth of the Trinity, *The Complete Works,* vol. 1, trans. Aletheia Kane, O.C.D. (Washington, DC: ICS Publications, 1984), 183–91.

9

How *Not* to Understand Active Participation

Historian Yves Chiron, in his superlative biography of Annibale Bugnini, notes the rising popularity of a phrase — today more likely to elicit the rolling of eyes — that was bandied about in the 1950s and 1960s:

> The "active participation of the faithful" in the liturgy was one of this period's recurring themes well before it became the watchword of the reform that Vatican II envisaged. In September 1953, Cardinal Lercaro, Archbishop of Bologna, made it the theme of his keynote address at the International Meeting for Liturgical Studies at Lugano, Italy: "Active participation, the fundamental principle of Pius X's pastoral and liturgical reform." Two years later, he published a diocesan liturgical directory for Bologna with this meaningful title: *A messa, figlioli! Direttorio liturgico per la partecipazione attiva dei fedeli alla santa messa letta* ("To Mass, My Children! Liturgical Directory for the Active Participation of the Faithful at Low Mass"). This directory circulated widely.[134]

---

[134] Yves Chiron, *Annibale Bugnini: Reformer of the Liturgy*, trans. John Pepino (Brooklyn, NY: Angelico Press, 2018), 54.

As an author myself, I am often struck by the discrepancies between positions attributed to authors and the actual positions held by the same authors upon a closer look. Pope St. Pius X was held aloft as the author of this mantra "active participation," but was Cardinal Lercaro — or any of the lesser lights who said the same kind of thing across the decades — actually being faithful to the thought of this Roman pontiff?

In the motu proprio *Tra le Sollecitudini* of 1903, Pope Pius X called for a reform to sacred music, not in order to bring it up to date (*aggiornamento*) but precisely to move it away from the fashions of the day — Italian operatic-style church music, which was very *au courant* — and back to a healthy condition characterized by music truly suited for the liturgy, which he identified as Gregorian chant and music inspired by and compatible with it, such as Renaissance polyphony. Before he lays down specific rules for sacred music, however, Pius X first enunciates the general rule that motivates and justifies his actions:

> It being our ardent desire to see the true Christian spirit restored in every respect and preserved by all the faithful, we deem it necessary to provide before everything else for the sanctity and dignity of the temple, in which the faithful assemble for the object of acquiring this spirit from its indispensable fount, which is the active participation in the holy mysteries and in the public and solemn prayer of the Church.

As usual with older papal documents, the wording here is exquisitely crafted so that each idea fits into the whole in its proper order. The purpose or final cause for Pius X's reform is "to see the true Christian spirit restored and preserved"; this he says against the backdrop of a Europe ravaged by anticlericalism and encroaching secularism. He then identifies the means by which this purpose will be achieved. First and foremost, "the sanctity and dignity of the temple" must be provided for. All that conduces to the holiness and nobility of Catholic worship has to be put in place first so that the second step may occur: the faithful assembling there to acquire the Christian spirit from its "indispensable fount." The "active participation" of the people—a phrase used here for the first time[135]—is not portrayed as the goal or end, nor has it priority over the soundness and fittingness of the worship.

Put more simply: the end is the true Christian spirit. The means are twofold. On the one hand is the public and solemn prayer of the Church itself, which ought to be excellently done, with sanctity and dignity. On the other is the active participation of the faithful in that prayer so that its spirit may become theirs. Note here that Pius X is assuming that the faithful will be assimilated to the spirit of the liturgy itself. What it is, they also will be; what it is not, they can never become.[136]

---

[135] In the Italian version of the motu proprio, the phrase is *partecipazione attiva*. The Latin version, interestingly, does not have the word "active" but only the word "participation." For further commentary (with which I do not necessarily agree), see Carol Byrne, *Born of Revolution: A Misconceived Liturgical Movement* (n.p.: Holyrood Press, 2020), 13–24. In Vatican II's *Sacrosanctum Concilium* §14, the phrase would be *participatio actuosa*. For an extended discussion of the meaning of this phrase, see Kwasniewski, *Noble Beauty*, 191–213.

[136] Ferdinando Antonelli, who was closely involved in the liturgical reforms of the twentieth century, had this to say about the 1958 Instruction on Sacred Music, which, though controversial in some points, reiterated many traditional elements of the liturgy: "The Instruction, be it said at once, is not meant as a floodgate for the liturgical movement. Rather, it is meant as a dike to protect it, in order that the movement, remaining within

Now, compare the above text to another one, this time from the Second Vatican Council's *Sacrosanctum Concilium* of 1963, sixty years later.

> In the restoration and promotion of the sacred liturgy, this full and active participation by all the people is the aim to be considered before all else; for it is the primary and indispensable source from which the faithful are to derive the true Christian spirit; and therefore pastors of souls must zealously strive to achieve it, by means of the necessary instruction, in all their pastoral work.

It cannot escape our notice that this text turns things on their head. Where Pius X had said that what should be "provided for before everything else" is the "sanctity and dignity of the temple," Vatican II says that "the aim to be considered before all else" is "full and active participation by all the people." In doing so, it inverts the hierarchy of goods. Now the worship of God and its right condition becomes secondary to the people's involvement. The activity of the faithful is to take priority in liturgical reform and conduct.

We know what this led to in practice: the holiness and nobility of worship done for God's glory suffered grave damage because all attention was focused on getting people "involved" in ways both legitimate and illegitimate. Instead of placing the

---

the riverbed of the great principles repeatedly inculcated by the Holy See, may truly carry the living waters of the Savior to all the faithful through an ever more active and conscious participation in the liturgical life of the Church" ("L'istruzione," *L'Osservatore Romano*, October 2, 1958; English translation in *Worship* 32 [1958], 628). Note that he speaks in the same manner as Pius X.

objective good of authentic liturgy first and the subjective good of participation second, which is the correct order, Vatican II implies that the subjective good takes precedence and should even determine the content of the objective good. So while superficially it may seem that the two documents are saying the same thing, a closer look shows that they diverge on a point of no small importance. Cardinal Lercaro blundered, therefore, in asserting that "active participation [is] the fundamental principle of Pius X's pastoral and liturgical reform."

Nor should we be surprised that Pius X's views are much more akin to those of his immediate predecessor, Leo XIII. In his splendid letter *Testem Benevolentiae* of 1899, Leo teaches that the primary work or activity of the laity is to live as faithful Christians in the world and to raise up prayer to God, while the primary work of the clergy is to preach sound doctrine and to celebrate glorious liturgies in honor of God, the Greatest and Best:

> The Scriptures teach us that it is the duty of all to be solicitous for the salvation of one's neighbor, according to the power and position of each. The faithful do this by religiously discharging the duties of their state of life, by the uprightness of their conduct, by their works of Christian charity and by earnest and continuous prayer to God. On the other hand, those who belong to the clergy should do this by an enlightened fulfillment of their preaching ministry, by the pomp and splendor of ceremonies, and especially by setting forth that sound form of doctrine which Saint Paul inculcated upon Titus and Timothy.

The Church will be better off when we have a lot more of "that sound form of doctrine" and "pomp and splendor of ceremonies" so that before everything else, the sanctity and dignity of the temple may be duly provided for — and in *this* way, the faithful may come to participate most fruitfully in the holy mysteries.

A division of roles in the one Body of Christ

A prelate in the Church who understands the mind of Pius X and the broader tradition to which he gives voice is Archbishop Alexander Sample. The pastoral letter on sacred music that he issued to the diocese of Marquette in 2013, *Rejoice in the Lord Always*, is impressive for its thoroughness, clarity, and fervor. He tackles the most contentious issues in church music today with a serene confidence in the wisdom of the Church's Magisterium and with a pastor's patient willingness to spell out first principles and draw forth the right conclusions.

Looking back on all the years I have been studying and discussing the sacred liturgy — its theology, history, ceremonies, rubrics, canon law, music, and so forth — I would say that the single most misunderstood concept of the twentieth century has been "active participation." The phrase itself, coined as we have seen by Pope St. Pius X and disseminated in his 1903 motu proprio *Tra le Sollecitudini*, has often been interpreted in a manner diametrically opposed to St. Pius X's own teaching and that of his successors.

Participatio actuosa could be rendered "a thoroughly actualized sharing": a sharing in the mysteries of Christ that is not merely potential or possible or distant or sleepy, but deeply involved, closely bound up with the unfolding action, attentive in mind and receptive in heart, and ready to do whatever it is appropriate to be doing at any given moment in the ebb and flow of the liturgy.[137]

---

[137] Obviously this will not be the same for everyone in the church — or even for one and the same person on different days, since

Clearly, this does not and cannot mean doing everything that is to be done: for example, the layman can never recite the Eucharistic Prayer, the deacon or priest reading the Gospel does not say "*Laus tibi, Christe*" ("Praise to you, Lord Jesus Christ"), and the celebrant does not say "*Et cum spiritu tuo*" ("And with your spirit").[138]

There are a variety of different roles, and, as the Second Vatican Council correctly stated, each person should do *all* of that which belongs to his role — and *only* that.[139] The liturgy in this way is a reflection of the hierarchical structure of the Church, which reflects the structure of the entire cosmos, from angels to atoms, itself reflected in the microcosm of the human soul with its powers of intellect, will, sensitive appetite, and so forth. Everything in God's good creation is hierarchically ordered, and the virtue of each part is to belong to the whole in the right way, doing all that belongs to the part and only that which belongs

---

"whatever is appropriate" often includes several possibilities. For example, vocalization of prayers can be and often is appropriate for public worship, but it is not always obligatory, and sometimes it is less helpful spiritually for assimilating the riches of the liturgy.

[138] There are rare occasions when a priest saying Mass on his own may make certain responses, but this is only on account of the lack of the server who ought, by tradition and by law, to be present. The 1917 *Code of Canon Law* (canon 813) mandated the presence of at least one server; the 1983 *Code of Canon Law* repeats the rule but allows an exception "for good and reasonable cause" (canon 906).

[139] *Sacrosanctum Concilium* §28: "In liturgical celebrations each person, minister or layman, who has an office to perform, should do all of, but only, those parts which pertain to his office by the nature of the rite and the principles of liturgy."

to the part. To act otherwise is to introduce disorder, disruption, confusion, rivalry, anarchy — the vices characteristic of the fallen angels and of human beings inasmuch as they are unrepentant sinners.

This is the normal Catholic worldview, and Archbishop Sample brings it to bear on the particular question of music and musicians for the Mass.[140] The principle of *participatio actuosa* is not at all violated by a division of labor or distribution of functions:

> Those responsible for sacred music in the Mass must foster and enable the *participatio actuosa* (active participation) of all the faithful; all should have the opportunity to participate fully and consciously in the sacred action of the Mass. This does not mean that everyone present has to sing everything all the time; the sacred music of the Mass pertains to different participants in different ways depending on its structure and its position in the rite. The congregation should be encouraged and enabled to sing whenever appropriate, and when the singing is properly rendered by the cantor or choir alone, participate interiorly through engaged and prayerful silent reflection. Likewise, the musicians should be attentive and prayerfully engaged in the parts of the Mass which do not necessarily involve music, both for their own spiritual good and so as not to become a distraction to others. They should participate in the Mass, observing all of the appropriate

[140] It is true that this pastoral letter addresses the Novus Ordo, but the principles enunciated are the same as Pius X's and would apply, *mutatis mutandis*, to the traditional Roman rite as well.

postures and gestures of the congregation to the fullest
degree possible.[141]

In this brief and clear summary, the episcopal author follows in
the footsteps of Pope John Paul II, who addressed the contentious
issue directly in one of the most important liturgical catecheses
of his pontificate:

> Only by being radically faithful to this doctrinal foun-
> dation [concerning the essential distinction between
> ministerial priesthood and the common priesthood of
> the faithful] can we avoid one-dimensional and unilateral
> interpretations of the Council's teaching. The sharing of
> all the baptized in the one priesthood of Jesus Christ is
> the key to understanding the Council's call for "full, con-
> scious, and active participation" in the liturgy (SC §14).
> Full participation certainly means that every member of
> the community has a part to play in the liturgy.... But
> full participation does not mean that everyone does every-
> thing, since this would lead to a clericalizing of the laity
> and a laicizing of the priesthood; and this was not what
> the Council had in mind. The liturgy, like the Church,
> is intended to be hierarchical and polyphonic, respecting
> the different roles assigned by Christ and allowing all the
> different voices to blend in one great hymn of praise.
>
> Active participation certainly means that, in gesture,
> word, song and service, all the members of the community
> take part in an act of worship, which is anything but inert

---

[141] *Rejoice in the Lord Always*, 10. The document is available at
www.dioceseofmarquette.org/images/files/PastoralLetter-Rejoice
InTheLordAlways.pdf.

or passive. Yet active participation does not preclude the active passivity of silence, stillness, and listening: indeed, it demands it. Worshippers are not passive, for instance, when listening to the readings or the homily, or following the prayers of the celebrant, and the chants and music of the liturgy. These are experiences of silence and stillness, but they are in their own way profoundly active. In a culture which neither favors nor fosters meditative quiet, the art of interior listening is learned only with difficulty. Here we see how the liturgy, though it must always be properly inculturated, must also be countercultural.[142]

If this light-filled teaching of John Paul II, reflected in the mirror of Alexander Sample's pastoral letter, could shine brightly in the Catholic world, an era of misguided attempts at inculturation and *aggiornamento* would give way to a joyful embrace of the treasury of sacred music and sacred art so highly praised by Pius X and his successors, who saw how well it suits "the sanctity and dignity of the temple." For the visible temple is itself a symbol of Christ (cf. John 2:19–21), our eternal High Priest and Victim, our Savior and our God, the Head of the Mystical Body of which we are privileged, through no merits of our own, to be the members. To the extent that this shift to a supernatural perspective happens, parishes and religious communities will begin to find their way out of the parched desert of worldliness and into the enclosed garden of the Church's traditions, lush and life-giving.

---

[142] *Ad limina* Address to the Bishops of the Northwestern United States, October 9, 1998. Over the years I have cited this text perhaps more than any other by John Paul II, and have gone so far as to suggest that it should be inscribed on a bronze plaque mounted in the vestibule of every parish church.

10

When Piety Is Mistaken for Passivity,
and Passivity for Piety

This chapter will have two contrasting parts. In the first part, I will defend being a "silent spectator" at Mass, one who looks and listens or, perhaps, prays the Rosary. In the second part, I will suggest that there may be, among traditionalists today, a danger of bending the stick so far in this direction that one risks cultivating a habit of liturgical passivity and self-alienation rather than a habit of true devotion.

Pope Pius XII subtly corrects Pope Pius XI

Almost a century ago, Pope Pius XI issued an Apostolic Constitution on Sacred Music *Divini Cultus*, promulgated on December 20, 1928. This document has many fine passages. Nevertheless, there is one phrase in section 9 that might give us pause:

> In order that the faithful may more actively participate in divine worship, let them be made once more to sing the Gregorian chant, so far as it belongs to them to take part in it. It is most important that when the faithful assist at the sacred ceremonies, or when pious sodalities take part with the clergy in a procession, they should not be merely

detached and silent spectators [*non tamquam extranei vel muti spectatores*] but, filled with a deep sense of the beauty of the Liturgy, they should sing alternately with the clergy or the choir, as it is prescribed.

The notion that laity who sit or kneel quietly at Mass and do not vocally participate are "detached and silent spectators" is something of a caricature, and the mantra-like use made of this phrase in subsequent decades of an increasingly audacious Liturgical Movement culminated in a heavy-handed enforcement of "active participation" by authorities (real and self-appointed), which has numbered among its casualties the interior participation that often thrives on silence and sacred music. The majority of the faithful, even those who may practice paraliturgical devotions during Mass, are still participating in the mystery of the Holy Sacrifice. Following a missal word-for-word, which seemed to be the ideal of the Liturgical Movement, is not only *not* required but can even be an impediment to offering up the holy oblation in peace.[143]

Pope Pius XII's encyclical *Mediator Dei* contains the best treatment of participation—and of the related topics of the priesthood

---

[143] In Chiron's *Bugnini*, we learn about the younger Bugnini's radical liturgical experiments in the 1940s, where he began manipulating the liturgy for the sake of "participation." In Bugnini's own words: "I suddenly wondered: how could I have this people, with their elementary religious instruction, participate in the Mass? Above all, how could I make the children participate? I started out by painting big signboards with the easier responses for the people to say in Latin.... Then I did the same with signposts in Italian.... I knew that I had found the formula: the people willingly followed the Mass. The 'inert and mute' assembly had been transformed into a living and prayerful assembly" (p. 25). Note how Bugnini himself reverts to the formula of Pius XI.

of the faithful and how they offer the sacrifice of the Mass in union with the priest—to be found in any magisterial document.[144] In paragraph 80 he writes:

> It is therefore desirable, Venerable Brethren, that all the faithful should be aware that to participate in the Eucharistic Sacrifice is their chief duty and supreme dignity, and that not in an inert and negligent fashion, giving way to distractions and day-dreaming, but with such earnestness and concentration that they may be united as closely as possible with the High Priest, according to the Apostle, "Let this mind be in you which was also in Christ Jesus" (Phil. 2:5). And together with Him and through Him let them make their oblation, and in union with Him let them offer up themselves.

Pius XII explains in paragraph 106 the purpose of any actions by which the faithful join in more directly with the liturgy taking place, such as following a daily missal or chanting the responses and the Ordinary—"their chief aim is to foster and promote the people's piety and intimate union with Christ and His visible minister and to arouse those internal sentiments and dispositions which should make our hearts become like to that of the High Priest of the New Testament"—but then cautions against

---

[144] See §76 to §111. There is no question that the traditional liturgy accentuates the one who is sacramentally configured to Christ in Holy Orders and who represents the Head of the Church within the assembly, the *ekklesia*. However, this would seem to cancel out the common priesthood of the faithful *only* if one had an activistic notion of what it means to exercise this universal baptismal priesthood, which, in reality, is one of consent and self-offering.

those who, "led away by false opinions, make so much of these accidentals as to presume to assert that without them the Mass cannot fulfill its appointed end":

> Many of the faithful are unable to use the *Roman Missal* even when it is written in the vernacular; nor are all capable of understanding correctly the liturgical rites and formulas. So varied and diverse are men's talents and characters that it is impossible for all to be moved and attracted to the same extent by community prayers, hymns, and liturgical services. Moreover, the needs and inclinations of all are not the same, nor are they always constant in the same individual. Who, then, would say, on account of such a prejudice, that all these Christians cannot participate in the Mass nor share its fruits? On the contrary, they can adopt some other method which proves easier for certain people; for instance, they can lovingly meditate on the mysteries of Jesus Christ or perform other exercises of piety or recite prayers which, though they differ from the sacred rites, are still essentially in harmony with them.

This was Pius XII's typically nuanced response to a complex situation. On the one hand, he applauded efforts made to inform the laity about the actual liturgical rites so that worshipers might harness their riches, as Dom Prosper Guéranger had done with his *The Liturgical Year* and *Explanation of the Prayers and Ceremonies of Holy Mass*.[145] On the other hand, he rebuked the haughty proponents of "objective piety" who considered it wrong

---

[145] For the latter, I recommend the 2017 edition from Angelico Press, which bears the title *The Traditional Latin Mass Explained*.

for Catholics to "tell their beads" during the Mass. It is as if the pope were saying to each Catholic who assists at Mass: Pursue whatever it is that will most unite you in mind and heart to the mysteries of Christ and especially to His Sacrifice. For different people, this will take different forms, and even for the same person, it will take different forms at different times.

When my son interviewed Bishop Athanasius Schneider in June 2018 at the Sacred Liturgy Conference in Oregon, he asked him how the Rosary and the Mass complement one another, how they might "work together." I was delighted to read the good bishop's profound answer:

> The Rosary is a beautiful synthesis of the entire mystery of the Incarnation, redemption, and work of salvation. And the Holy Mass is the recapitulation of the work of salvation. Christ became incarnate for what reason? To offer Himself as the Lamb of God and to offer Himself on the Cross for the salvation of humankind, and to glorify the Father. This is what it means. When we pray the Rosary, which we can pray even during Mass, we do participate very actively in the Joyful Mysteries, centered around the Incarnation—and the Holy Mass is a continuation of the coming of Christ in the Incarnation, under the veils of the sacred species of bread and wine. And then the Sorrowful Mysteries, of course, they are the specific meditation of the Holy Mass: they help us to contemplate the real presence of Golgotha under the sacramental veil. And then the Glorious: Christ present in the holy Host is the Risen One, the Glorified One, with His luminous wounds.
>
> So we have in the prayer of the Rosary a really beautiful synthesis of the entire Mass. And therefore in olden

times, those who could not read, I mean the peasants and farmers, *did* participate in the Mass with the Rosary. Often times after the Council, priests ridiculed these people, and humiliated them for praying the Rosary. But this is bad; it is unjust. They participated more deeply by praying the Rosary, because they are meditating on what is now going on at the altar with the Rosary, the prayer of the Gospel, because the words of this prayer are of the holy Gospel.

And so, of course, I do not want to say that we should *only* pray the Rosary during holy Mass, but it is a *possible* way of participating—not the only one, maybe not the main one, but it is legitimate. This I would say for people who have a special affinity for this.[146]

As Pius XII said, and as Bishop Schneider beautifully explained, we should have no objection to people praying the Rosary during the traditional Latin Mass. I remember when I used to parrot the fashionable objections against such "private devotions" and "subjective piety." But sooner or later, I learned a different lesson, thanks to my encounters with priests who took their time in celebrating the Tridentine Mass. This was a new phenomenon: I had so much time on my hands that I could read the propers of the Mass five times and still be left wondering what to do with myself. So I tried praying the Rosary and was surprised at how well it worked. (These "peasants and farmers" knew a thing or two—a tough lesson for a kid who grew up in suburban New Jersey!) Or I prayed the preparatory Psalms from my *Saint Andrew's Daily Missal* of 1945—Psalms 83, 84, 85, 115,

---

[146] For the full transcript, see "Bishop Schneider on Chastity vs. a Society 'Becoming Ever More Cruel,'" *OnePeterFive*, September 21, 2018.

and 129 — or a Litany during the Offertory and the Canon, and often the prayer of St. Ambrose or St. Thomas while the priest recited his prayers immediately before Communion. So far from detaching me as a silent spectator, all of these practices enriched my offering of the prayer of the Mass, the prayer of Christ.

Liturgical quietism and the deactivation of the laity

All this being said, however, I have noticed in some pockets of the Catholic traditionalist world the pendulum swinging to the opposite extreme, the contrary of outward participation and intelligent assimilation of the liturgy. I will call it a *refusal* to engage the liturgy at a bodily level, be this in gestures, reading along, or singing; almost a *taking pride in* saying or singing nothing and making as few motions as possible.[147] There are many examples of the phenomenon; I will offer a few for consideration.

If you are literate and can follow the orations (collect, secret, postcommunion), or ponder the Epistle and Gospel, why would you not do it — at least sometimes? Why sit there and let the foreign words float over your head while you think about something other than what the liturgy is presenting to God on your behalf and with you (at least partly) in mind? Yes, it's efficacious *ex opere operato*, but you can also make it your own prayer and your own meditation. It seems a perfect occasion for having the Church's words in your soul, illuminating your mind and warming your heart. Even laity who know enough Latin to understand what the priest is saying or singing without aid of a translation will find a hand missal useful when church architecture, acoustics,

---

[147] For a brilliant parody of this mentality, see Charles Branson, "Subverting Prayer with Bodily Action and Mental Traction," *Creative Minority Report*, May 27, 2020.

idiosyncratic pronunciation, or speed of delivery makes it difficult to follow the Latin of the priest.

If you know the melody of Credo III and can sing it, why would you not sing it? The profession of faith is yours, too, and there's no reason to consider it exclusively the property of the choir or schola. Congregational singing of the Ordinary is something the twentieth-century popes spoke consistently in favor of, and for good reason.

If you know that it's a custom to strike your breast three times with the servers at the Confiteor, or during the Agnus Dei and the "Domine, non sum dignus," why wouldn't you do it? And if the faithful don't know it, why couldn't the priest tell them about it in a sermon? The same could be said of the many times when the priest makes the sign of the cross ("Adjutorium nostrum in nomine Domini ..."; "Indulgentiam, absolutionem, et remissionem peccatorum nostrorum ..."; "in gloria Dei Patri"; "vitam venturi saeculi"; etc.). Admittedly, many of the faithful do cross themselves at these moments, which is a beautiful custom; why should it not be universal? What about the slight bowing of the priest's head at certain points in the Gloria and in the Creed? Such actions, for me at any rate, remind me all the more forcefully of what we are praying and why. When bowing the head at "simul adoratur et conglorificatur," one is aware *in one's very muscles* as well as in one's intellect that the Holy Spirit is God, deserving of adoration (*latria*).

When the priest turns toward us with the Blessed Sacrament, why shouldn't we say together: *Domine, non sum dignus ut intres sub tectum meum, sed tantum dic verbo, et sanabitur anima mea* (O Lord, I am not worthy that Thou shouldst enter under my roof, but only say the word, and my soul shall be healed)?

Now, I am not suggesting (*quod absit!*) that rubrics be imposed on the faithful, for we have seen how harmful such regimentation has been in the sphere of the Novus Ordo.[148] I am merely point-ing out a kind of *passivity* among the faithful that inhibits a fuller response to the texts and motions of the liturgy.[149] For, as Hilary White insightfully put it, liturgy is "theology in motion," and this means *our* motion, to the extent that it pertains to us.[150]

At this point, many readers may be itching to accuse me of being in cahoots with the tumid Liturgical Movement, of trying to sacerdotalize the laity, of importing Novus Ordo expectations into a classical context where they do not belong, of confusing *participatio actuosa* with activism, etc. But all of this I have argued against elsewhere (particularly in my 2020 book *Reclaiming Our Roman Catholic Birthright*), and nothing I am saying need be con-strued as implying or promoting those errors. What I object to is a situation in which there is *nothing* in common between the two parts of the church—the nave and the sanctuary—except that the people in each part happen to be in the same building at the same time with the same generic intention. This strikes me as a low-water mark in the practice of liturgy and a fruitful cause of the evils of liturgical reform. The solution isn't to change the liturgy or to force laity to do something; the solution is that clergy and laity alike should learn how to *know and love* the liturgy as it

---

[148] See my article: "Should the Postures of the Laity at the Tradi-tional Latin Mass Be Regulated, Legislated, or Revised?," *New Liturgical Movement*, April 27, 2020.

[149] For the record: I am not a proponent of the so-called dialogue Mass. The kind of responses I have in mind are those that are sung during a High Mass ("Et cum spiritu tuo," "Gloria tibi, Domine," "Amen," etc.) and the Ordinary of the Mass (from the "Asperges" through the final "Deo gratias").

[150] For many examples of bodily participation in the *usus antiquior*, see "How the *Usus Antiquior* Elicits Superior Participation," in Kwasniewski, *Noble Beauty*, 191–213.

stands and to insert themselves into it with their powers of soul and body. Unlike the "pastoral priests" who are bent on repeating the errors of the past, we must be intelligent supporters and sustainers of the liturgical tradition as it comes down to us.[151]

This *does* require some preaching specifically on the liturgy, and ongoing catechesis. The family of St. Thérèse of Lisieux read aloud Dom Guéranger's *The Liturgical Year*, which formed the souls of the Martins. Lest it be thought that no one today could read such a book within the family, I happen to know of a family that did it—with about a dozen children, ranging from infants at the breast to young adults. More is possible than we tend to think.

I am convinced that it is too trite and simplistic to say, "Well, all that the priest says at the altar belongs to him, it's *his* business; all the stuff the schola sings is *their* business; and the laity should just do their own thing." No. The liturgy belongs to everyone in the church, because it belongs to Christ our Head. It is our common inheritance and activity. We have different offices and roles within it, but the liturgy is not like a pie divided up into different pieces that are served up to different people. It is a common good, like a philosophical truth or a theological mystery that can be equally and fully possessed by everyone at the same time. What the priest is doing and saying is also mine, albeit in a different mode.[152] When the schola sings the propers, they are

---

[151] See my articles "Traditional Clergy: Please Stop Making 'Pastoral Adaptations,'" *New Liturgical Movement*, June 11, 2018, and "The Ill-Placed Charges of Purism, Elitism, and Rubricism," *New Liturgical Movement*, July 9, 2018.

[152] As mentioned above, Pius XII's explication of this point in *Mediator Dei* (§76–§111) remains unsurpassed.

my prayers, too, sung on my behalf—words that the Church places before me and within me.

It is also trite and simplistic to say "participation is interior" and then leave it at that. Yes, it *is* principally interior and spiritual. As we all know, without this inner component, any amount of physical activity is useless or worse. But "principal" implies a comparison with something else that is secondary. The soul of man is primary, and his body is secondary—yet you cannot have a man without both. The liturgy is a physical action, and the man who participates in it is a physical being who engages with it through his bodily senses. Thus the body should be engaged as much as is consistent with the role a given person has in the liturgy. That means not only kneeling, but also beating the breast, making the sign of the cross, bowing the head, and singing the responses and the Ordinary.

Ultimately, the right disposition is not passivity; we must not simply sit or kneel and otherwise keep as still as schoolchildren in the 1950s, afraid to call down on our heads the displeasure of the sister in charge. The right disposition is *receptivity*—and this means receiving not only invisible graces but also the particular goods that the liturgy itself, in all its human richness, offers us as creatures of body and soul.

III

Restoration

11

Healing the Rupture: A Call for
the Restoration of Minor Orders

Bishop Athanasius Schneider

Pope Benedict XVI reiterated the following principle, perennially valid in the life of the Church since apostolic times: "In the history of the liturgy there is growth and progress, but no rupture."[153]

The theory that minor liturgical services (which do not require sacramental ordination) are a particular form of the exercise of the common priesthood—expressed by Pope Paul VI in the Apostolic Letter *Ministeria Quaedam* (August 15, 1972), disseminated in the life and practice of the Church, and now juridically sanctioned by Pope Francis with the motu proprio *Spiritus Domini* (January 10, 2021)—is alien to the two-thousand-year tradition of the universal Church, both in the East and in the West, and represents a novelty that comes close to the liturgical views of certain Protestant communities. Further,

[153] Letter to the bishops *Con Grande Fiducia* on the occasion of the publication of the Apostolic Letter *Summorum Pontificum*, July 7, 2007.

it also manifests a yielding to the demands of the feminist move-ment in the life of the Church, since it positions women within the presbytery by dressing them in clerical robes such as the alb, the common vestment of clerics of different degrees (bishop, presbyter, deacon).

If minor liturgical services were a peculiar form of exercising the baptismal priesthood, the apostles and the subsequent con-stant and universal tradition of the Church would have admitted women to liturgical services in the presbytery or at the altar. The tradition, however, of not admitting women to the altar dates back to apostolic times (cf. 1 Cor. 14:34) and has always been maintained in the tradition of the Church both in the East and in the West.[154]

At the end of the fifth century, Pope St. Gelasius I reiterated the apostolic tradition of not admitting women to the liturgical service at the altar: "With impatience, we have heard that divine things have undergone such contempt that women are encour-aged to serve at the sacred altars, and that all tasks entrusted to the service of men are performed by a sex for which these [tasks] are not appropriate" (Mansi VIII, 44). In the *Capitula Martini*, a sixth-century Gallic collection of canons which originates from both Greek and Western sources, the same apostolic tradition is again recalled in these terms: "Women are not permitted to enter the sanctuary" (canon 42).

The specific norms of the *Corpus Iuris Canonici* and that of the *Code of Canon Law* of 1917 (canon 813) are a further testimony of the constant and universal tradition of the Church received from apostolic times of not admitting women to the liturgical ministries at the altar. The decree of Pope Gregory IX in the

[154] See the fourth-century Synod of Laodicea, canon 44.

Corpus Iuris Canonici says: "Care must be taken that no woman presumes to walk to the altar or to minister to the priest or to stand or to sit within the chancel" (c. 1, X). Pope Benedict XIV is another witness to this constant tradition of the Church, as we read in his encyclical *Allatae Sunt* of July 26, 1755:

> Pope Gelasius in his ninth letter (chap. 26) to the bishops of Lucania condemned the evil practice which had been introduced of women serving the priest at the celebration of Mass. Since this abuse had spread to the Greeks, Innocent IV strictly forbade it in his letter to the bishop of Tusculum: "Women should not dare to serve at the altar; they should be altogether refused this ministry." We too have forbidden this practice in the same words in our often repeated constitution *Etsi Pastoralis*, sect. 6, no. 21.

In a recent manifesto by a group of French women in reference to the motu proprio *Spiritus Domini*, we can read the following wise words: "We believe that our specific vocation is not a mirror of the man's, and that it does not need to be ennobled by service at the altar."[155]

The opinion that argues that the dignity of the common priesthood must be ennobled by first placing the laity — both men and women — in the presbytery and at the altar, and then giving them the task of performing minor ministries in the liturgy ultimately means a form of clericalization of the laity and, above all, of women. Furthermore, this shift indicates not a promotion

---

[155] See "Appel à approfondir la vocation de la femme," accessed at https://lavocationdufeminin.fr/appel-a-approfondir-la-vocation-de-la-femme/, March 15, 2021.

of the laity but, on the contrary, a subtle discrimination against the laity and women, as it reserves to them only the lesser duties in the sanctuary while it reserves to the clergy the most important or major duties. Furthermore, the application of the word "ministry" to the exercise of the common priesthood in the liturgy contains the Protestantizing danger of a confusion between the ministerial and common priesthoods.[156]

The Church has always understood the liturgical expression of the common priesthood as that of the laity participating in the sacred liturgy by being gathered for prayer in the nave of the Church and not in the presbytery, i.e., the part of a church that is separated from the nave and given over to the execution of the ceremonies by the ministers. The laity thus participate in the liturgy by being in their place outside of the presbytery (as already indicated by Pope St. Clement I in the first century). Consequently, as Professor Kwasniewski explained in the previous chapter, the lay faithful liturgically express their common priesthood with responses, songs, bodily gestures, genuflections, bows—even with silence.[157] The greatest and most worthy liturgical realization of the common priesthood consists in the worthy and fruitful sacramental reception of Holy Communion.

The principal expression of the common priesthood outside the strictly liturgical sphere consists in the service of the laity in the family: in the domestic church, in the domestic "liturgy" at home. Mainly, however, the expression of the common priesthood

---

[156] In other words, if the laity's greatness is correctly understood to be of a different character from that of the clergy, then there is no discrimination in not having them perform *any* of these clerical duties, lesser or greater.

[157] See the Second Vatican Council's Constitution on the Sacred Liturgy, *Sacrosanctum Concilium*, §30.

consists in the sanctification of the secular field—as Professor Kwasniewski already indicated, quoting this powerful passage by Pope Paul VI's Apostolic Exhortation *Evangelii Nuntiandi*:

> [The laity's] primary and immediate task is not to establish and develop the ecclesial community—this is the specific role of the pastors—but to put to use every Christian and evangelical possibility latent but already present and active in the affairs of the world. Their own field of evangelizing activity is the vast and complicated world of politics, society and economics, but also the world of culture, of the sciences and the arts, of international life, of the mass media. It also includes other realities which are open to evangelization, such as human love, the family, the education of children and adolescents, professional work, suffering. The more Gospel-inspired lay people there are engaged in these realities, clearly involved in them, competent to promote them and conscious that they must exercise to the full their Christian powers which are often buried and suffocated, the more these realities will be at the service of the kingdom of God and therefore of salvation in Jesus Christ, without in any way losing or sacrificing their human content but rather pointing to a transcendent dimension which is often disregarded. (n. 70)

However, through Paul VI and now Pope Francis, a drastic break with an almost bimillennial tradition of the universal Church (East and West) has been carried out through the abolition of the subdiaconate and minor orders (Paul VI) and through the change of the significance of these lesser liturgical ministries (Paul VI and Francis). According to the *lex orandi* of the Church, the proper significance of the subdiaconate and of all the minor ministries at the altar derives not from the common priesthood but from the diaconate. The subdiaconate and minor orders are therefore an expression, through non-sacramental ordinations, of the humble service of the ministerial priesthood (episcopate and presbyterate) and of the sacramental diaconate. In a broader sense, the same also applies to altar boys, who must therefore be of the male sex to maintain the link with the ministerial priesthood and the sacramental diaconate at the symbolic level.

In keeping with Pope St. Stephen I's principle "let them innovate nothing, but keep the traditions," the practice and doctrine of the Church of Rome should correspond to what has been taught and done by the preceding tradition, which dates back to apostolic times. There should be no drastic innovations. Of course, all the minor orders and the subdiaconate existed in Stephen's time, and the Council of Trent later taught that the minor orders have been "received into the Church since apostolic times."[158]

With humility, respect, and candor—the *parrhesia* so often encouraged by Pope Francis—we should ask the Roman Church to return to the *sensus perennis universalis ecclesiae* by re-establishing the minor orders with the same theological significance that the Church has always expressed in her *lex orandi*. At the same time, the laity—especially women—should be taught the true meaning of their common priesthood in the liturgy and the highest source of their dignity. Our model is the common priesthood of the Most Blessed Virgin Mary, who was precisely not a "deaconess" nor a "liturgical agent at the altar" but simply the handmaid of the Lord who listened to the word of God with a good and

---

[158] Session XXIII, *Decree of Reform*, canon 17.

perfect heart, kept it, and made it fruitful in the world (cf. Luke 2:51; 8:15).

May the Blessed Virgin Mary, the Mother of the Church, with St. Joseph, her chaste Spouse and Patron of the Universal Church, impetrate for us the grace that those who bear responsibility in and for the Church in our day may endeavor to heal the rupture caused by the documents *Ministeria Quaedam* and *Spiritus Domini* and may promote the restoration and organic growth of a tradition constant and universal since apostolic times.

12

On the Status of Minor Orders
and the Subdiaconate

Arising more and more often nowadays is the question: What exactly is the status of the minor orders (porter, lector, exorcist, acolyte) in the Roman rite? We can add to this list the major order of subdeacon. In spite of their immense antiquity, which ought to have gained them the principled support of the liturgical reform—they are, for example, more ancient than the season of Advent—the minor orders were abolished in the form in which they had existed previously (or at least, it seemed to observers that they were abolished) by Paul VI in his Apostolic Letter *Ministeria Quaedam* of 1972. Yet from 1972 onward, minor orders and the subdiaconate have never ceased to be conferred in this or that corner of the Catholic world. On the contrary: with increasing frequency, thanks to the good fruits of John Paul II's *Ecclesia Dei* and Benedict XVI's *Summorum Pontificum*, these orders are routinely imparted to the many young candidates who flock to traditional priestly and religious communities that retain the classical Roman rite, like the Priestly Fraternity of St. Peter and the Institute of Christ the King Sovereign Priest. It certainly seems like an odd situation, when something that is not supposed to exist anymore not only continues to exist but has become stronger.

As far as I can tell, there are only two explanations that have been or can be given.

The view we might dub "conservative" would say that the minor orders and subdiaconate were in fact abrogated and their functions reassigned—but that even as the old liturgical tradition continued alongside the new and was eventually regularized by the Vatican, so, too, the use of the ceremonies for conferring the suppressed orders were regularized *in that specific context* and are efficacious *in that context*. It's "praetercanonical," something outside the normal framework envisaged and provided for by church law.

The weakness of this position is that it leans too much on canon law. Canon law is not some kind of inerrant or infallible thing. It's simply a compilation of ecclesiastical jurisprudence. It can be badly done; it may contain omissions and require correction or supplementation. The current *Code of Canon Law*'s silence on the minor orders and the subdiaconate does not logically preclude the possibility of their continuing existence. Not all things in Heaven and on earth are contained in the 1983 *Code*.

With this, we segue into the "traditionalist" position, which maintains that no pope has the authority to abolish a bimillennial tradition like the minor orders and the subdiaconate, just as no pope—strain he ever so many a pontifical muscle—could abolish the immemorial Roman Mass codified (but not created!) by St. Pius V in 1570. On this view, Paul VI's attempt to do both of these things wasn't worth the paper it was written on. This has already, in a sense, been recognized regarding the Mass by Benedict XVI when he said in *Summorum Pontificum* and in *Con Grande Fiducia* that the old missal was never abrogated—even though nearly everyone, except a tiny number of traditionalists, acted as if it had been.[159] Due to craven ultramontanism, however, people went along with the pretense and still act as if the minor orders and the subdiaconate were or are suppressed. Traditional religious and clerical communities, on the other hand, know better and continue to follow the settled and venerable Roman tradition. The episcopal use of the old *Pontificale Romanum* has increased in keeping with the growth in membership of such communities. These developments allow us to see, in light of the perennial doctrinal principles declared in the motu proprio *Summorum Pontificum* and its accompanying letter, that the subdiaconate and minor orders have no more been abolished than has the ancient usage of the Roman Rite itself, nor could they be.

At very least, something like the conservative view has to be true. Otherwise, in conferring minor orders today (and most of all, the subdiaconate), one would be guilty of simulating a conferral that cannot happen—a sort of contraceptive liturgy. It is impossible that the Church should continue to use such rites without their being efficacious in accomplishing what they intend to accomplish. A sacramental theologian of Scotistic subtlety might rejoin that a third possibility exists: that these rites are not efficacious *in se*—they actually do nothing to the

---

[159] The pertinent language in *Summorum Pontificum* read as follows: "It is, therefore, permissible to celebrate the Sacrifice of the Mass following the typical edition of the Roman Missal promulgated by Bl. John XXIII in 1962 and never abrogated"; and in the Letter to Bishops *Con Grande Fiducia*: "this Missal was never juridically abrogated and, consequently, in principle, was always permitted." The motu proprio of Pope Francis, *Traditionis Custodes*, while it intends to abrogate *Summorum Pontificum*, does not abrogate the classical Roman Rite, which is not, in fact, something a pope could do, since it would entail canceling out the immemorial tradition of the Church of Rome.

recipients—but their content, being piously edifying, offers an occasion of grace for the devout in their progress toward the diaconate and priesthood. It would be essentially fancy playacting in the sight of God, publicly marking stages of formation.

All of these positions seem ecclesiologically unsatisfactory in one way or another. The least problematic is to maintain that the old rites, when used today, confer the orders they intend to confer, while admitting that *how* the order is regulated in the Church is governed by the 1983 *Code of Canon Law*. With the 1983 *Code*, *Ministeria Quaedam* became a moot point—of historical interest, no doubt, but superseded. Hence, by the only code currently in force, reception of tonsure does *not* make one a cleric; a man becomes a cleric with the diaconate. He can freely take upon himself the obligation to recite the Divine Office that once came with the subdiaconate, but he is not bound *by law* until he is ordained a deacon.[160] That is not to say that this canonical

---

[160] To make sense of the efficacy of the ceremony of tonsure when conferred post-1983, some have proposed a distinction between "liturgical cleric" and "canonical cleric," similar to the distinction between "liturgical Sunday," which begins with First Vespers, and "canonical Sunday," which begins at midnight. The tonsure ceremony itself says that those who receive it receive clerical privileges: "Filii carissimi, animadvertere debetis, quod hodie de foro Ecclesiae facti estis, et privilegia clericalia sortiti estis" (Dearly beloved children, you ought to ponder well that you are placed today under the jurisdiction of the Church and are put in possession of clerical privileges). If we accept that these ceremonies are not empty, then they must confer something. Understood as liturgical clerics, the tonsured at least receive certain rights whose visible exercise is highly significant within the body of the Church: the right to wear the cassock, Roman collar, fascia/cincture, surplice, and biretta; the right to sit in Choir; the right to receive Communion, blessings, etc., at

formulation from 1983 is a good one and should not be changed in the future. Nor is it to say that the personal commitment of a seminarian is not serious prior to the reception of the diaconate. There is a whole culture that goes with the minor orders: they set their recipient apart for liturgical offices and activities and prepare a man step by step, through lower forms of ministry, to receive the higher forms of the major orders, by which he is decisively inserted into the exercise of the priesthood of Jesus Christ in the Church.

Catholics have long been told that they should engage in ecumenism, but the one ecumenism that was oddly forbidden was respecting the traditions we hold in common with the Eastern Churches. The lectorate and the subdiaconate still abide in the East. Rather than thinking they have somehow vanished into thin air, it is far more plausible to assume that they abide — and must abide — in the Roman Church as well, albeit in a condition of widespread underappreciation and underuse that carries the disgrace of ingratitude to Divine Providence and has, with the passage of decades, compounded occasions of ingratitude, unfittingness, and irregularity.

The conferral of the minor orders is more than a mere delegation but less than a sacramental ordination in the full sense, which inscribes an indelible mark or character on the soul. If (as in the most common theological opinion) the minor orders do not confer a character and are not part of the sacrament of order but are instituted by the Church, they should be classified

---

the altar; and the right to handle the sacred vessels with bare hands. Since the ceremonies of the Church are not empty, this must mean something at least liturgically, if not canonically.

as sacramentals.[161] This seems in keeping with the definition of sacramentals given in the 1917 *Code*: "things or actions which the Church uses in a certain imitation of the sacraments, in order, in virtue of her prayers, to achieve effects, above all of a spiritual nature."[162] Specifically, the ceremonies are constitutive blessings that permanently depute persons or things to divine service by imparting to them some sacred identity, by which they assume a new and distinct spiritual relationship. When persons are their objects, these blessings entitle them to the receipt of actual graces for the performance of their ministries, much like the sacramental graces associated with the reception of the sacraments, and similar to the blessing of an abbot.[163] This then makes the men in minor orders to be *sacramentalia permanentia*—blessed and consecrated objects of a sort. For instance, the blessing of a rosary is a sacramental; the blessed rosary itself is a sacramental; the use of the blessed rosary is a sacramental. Likewise, we can say that the ceremonies conferring the minor orders are sacramentals, those in minor orders are sacramentals, and the exercises of their offices are sacramentals.

So the ceremonies of the minor orders and of the subdiaconate confer both the right to perform the ministries and also the

---

[161] See Ott, *Fundamentals*, Bk. 4, pt. 3, §2.VI, no. 1, p. 477.

[162] CIC (1917), canon 1144.

[163] Theologians argue that marriage confers a quasi-character, because it instills in the spouses an enduring disposition and right to receive sacramental grace, as long as the spouses are alive. If the minor orders are held to be sacramentals, they can be seen as asking God to instill a lifelong disposition and right in the souls of the men who receive them so that they would perform their duties worthily with divine assistance.

promise of actual graces in carrying them out.[164] If we humbly allow ourselves to be guided by the traditional rites of the *Pontifical*, we can see that there is a solemn imparting of new responsibilities and the assurance of graces to fulfill them worthily. The Church has always endeavored to follow the exhortation of St. Paul: "Let all things [in public worship] be done to edification.... Let all things be done decently, and according to order."[165] Following apostolic and ancient discipline in regard to the *ordines* or ranked ministers of the Church ought to matter to us. To hold it as a thing of no worth would be an imperfection, even a vice, for we must never treat longstanding ecclesiastical tradition as deserving of contempt or rejection. As St. Thomas Aquinas writes: "The various customs of the Church in the divine worship are in no way contrary to the truth: wherefore we must observe them, and to disregard them is unlawful."[166]

---

[164] These two, the right and the promise, are separable from each other: historically, one who was removed from the clerical state would lose the right to perform the ministry, but the promise of divine assistance, if one were to perform the ministry, remains, since one would not be re-ordained to the minor orders if one were to re-enter the clerical state. Since they are separable, this indicates that the conferral of a minor order is in fact more than just a conferral of a duty. It is a more speculative question to ask whether someone who was ordained an acolyte but was later removed from the clerical state would still receive the graces to which his office entitled him were he to perform at Mass the ministry of an acolyte without having been reinstated.

[165] 1 Cor. 14:26, 40. For commentary on the first Epistle to the Corinthians, see "St. Paul Tells Us How to Fix Our Liturgical Problems," in Kwasniewski, *Holy Bread of Eternal Life*, 35–42.

[166] *ST* II-II, Q. 93, art. 1, ad 3. Note that this argument cannot be flipped around and made a justification for novel practices, because the condition for the legitimacy of replacing traditional

Ministers of Christ

In a magnificent passage from the *Summa theologiae*, the Angelic Doctor holds forth on the appropriateness of the Church's manifesting an orderly diversity of offices and ways of life, as she did throughout her history and well into modern times, and as she will continue to do, wherever sound theology prevails. The vision presented here is at the furthest possible remove from the democratic egalitarianism, traffic of interchangeable functionaries, and lack of architectural and ministerial boundaries characteristic of the postconciliar era. Thomas writes:

> The difference of states and duties in the Church regards three things.
>
> In the first place, it regards the perfection of the Church. For even as in the order of natural things, perfection, which in God is simple and uniform, is not to be found in the created universe except in a multiform and manifold manner, so too, the fullness of grace, which is centered in Christ as head, flows forth to His members in various ways, for the perfecting of the body of the Church. This is the meaning of the Apostle's words (Eph. 4:11–12): "He gave some apostles, and some prophets, and other some evangelists, and other some pastors and doctors for the perfecting of the saints."
>
> Secondly, it regards the need of those actions which are necessary in the Church. For a diversity of actions requires a diversity of men appointed to them, in order that all

---

practices with novel ones is that the former have been discovered to be contrary to some truth and in need of change or suppression. But Aquinas would not grant this possibility—nor should we.

things may be accomplished without delay or confusion; and this is indicated by the Apostle (Rom. 12:4–5), "As in one body we have many members, but all the members have not the same office, so we being many are one body in Christ."

Thirdly, this belongs to the dignity and beauty of the Church, which consist in a certain order; wherefore it is written (1 Kings 10:4–5) that "when the queen of Saba saw all the wisdom of Solomon … and the apartments of his servants, and the order of his ministers … she had no longer any spirit in her." Hence the Apostle says (2 Tim. 2:20) that "in a great house there are not only vessels of gold and silver, but also of wood and of earth."[167]

In an objection that might have been penned in 1970, St. Thomas initially argues against his position by saying that "the faithful of Christ are called to unity," and, since distinction is opposed to unity, therefore no distinction of states and duties should be found in the Church. In his reply, St. Thomas notes that, on the contrary, it is precisely a diversification of ranks and roles that allows for the entire body of the Church to achieve its optimal condition, as each part contributes something different and necessary to the whole:

> The distinction of states and duties is not an obstacle to the unity of the Church, for this results from the unity of faith, charity, and mutual service, according to the saying of the Apostle (Eph. 4:16): "From whom the whole body being compacted," namely by faith, "and fitly joined

---

[167] *ST* II-II, Q. 183, art. 2.

together," namely by charity, "by what every joint sup-
plieth," namely by one man serving another.[168]

This age-old wisdom, already anticipated in the hierarchy of
ancient Israel, is represented still more vividly and put into daily
practice by the four minor orders of porter, lector, exorcist, and
acolyte, the three major orders of subdeacon, deacon, and priest,
and the episcopacy in its unbroken succession from the apostles.
It finds rich expression in a multitude of religious orders and communities for consecrated men and women and in a proliferation
of third orders, confraternities, oblateships, and lay movements.
It renews itself in the faithful and fruitful callings of husbands and
wives, fathers and mothers, from whom all the children of God
arise. How blessed and privileged we are to occupy the places we
do in the great house of the Lord—be it in the sanctuary or in
the nave, in the workshop or at the hearth. We serve Him best
by serving Him in our station, according to our rights and duties.
It is time, it is well past time, that we stop being embarrassed
about the good of hierarchy and start rejoicing in it, as did Our
Lord, His most holy Mother, His foster father, His apostles and
disciples, and all the saints who have followed Him in unity of
faith, charity, and mutual service.

[168] *ST* II-II, Q. 183, art. 2, ad 1.

13

The Latin Mass as the Antithesis
of Gender-Bending Ideology

To the extent possible, I attend daily Mass at a chapel run by
the Priestly Fraternity of St. Peter. Although I seldom take up
my missal for the Ordinary of the Mass, I always consult it for
the Propers, and I try to pray them deeply and to draw wisdom
from them. In fact, it would be no exaggeration to say that I keep
learning my faith anew, and learning it better, from the Mass.
It is a school in which I am always enrolled, one in which the
teaching is quiet, respectful, consistent, earnest, and efficacious.
The learning is delightful, because it happens without deliberate
didacticism, tedious verbosity, or embarrassing gimmicks. It happens more the way a swimmer gets wet if he dives in.

Last year, in a certain week of saints' feasts (November 16
through November 20), I couldn't help noticing how resolutely
the traditional Mass presents the feminine and masculine sides
of human nature and of the Christian life. One thing is certain:
it is absolutely *not* androgynous.

November 16, for example, is St. Gertrude the Great, for
whom the Epistle is taken from the Common of Virgins and
includes the verse: "I am jealous of you with the jealousy of

Ministers of Christ

God. For I have espoused you to one husband, that I may present you as a chaste virgin to Christ" (2 Cor. 11:2). This verse is being applied to Gertrude, of course, but it also describes the entire Church as the chaste Bride of Christ. The Gospel is about the ten virgins who go out to meet the bridegroom and the bride (Matt. 25:1–13), while the Offertory is about the virgin handmaids of the princess being presented before her husband, the king (cf. Ps. 44:15–16). In the spiritual order, we are *all* receptive and made fruitful by Christ the King. That is our basic baptismal vocation.

November 17, in contrast, is St. Gregory the Wonderworker, a mighty man of valor. The Introit nobly announces: "The Lord ... made him a prince, that the dignity of priesthood should be to him for ever." The Lesson from Sirach strikes the same note: "He glorified him in the sight of kings, and gave him a crown of glory ... gave him a great priesthood" (cf. 45:3–20). The Gospel (Mark 11:22–24) speaks of the immense power of prayer made with faith — a faith that can move mountains, as Gregory actually did on one occasion to clear space for the building of a church. The Offertory antiphon: "I have found David My servant.... My hand shall help him, and my arm shall strengthen him" (cf. Ps. 88:21–22). The Communion antiphon: "This is the faithful and wise steward, whom his lord setteth over his family" (cf. Luke 12:42). It's all very active and virile. We are now looking at the ordained priesthood, a special participation in Christ the Bridegroom, at once the Head of His spouse and the one who lays down His life for her.

November 18 is the dedication of the basilicas of SS. Peter & Paul. And what is the Lesson? "In those days I saw the holy city, the new Jerusalem, coming down out of heaven from God, prepared as a bride adorned for her husband" (Rev. 21:2–5).

The theme of the bridal church is once more emphasized. This theme is brought into even greater prominence when the priest uses the Gallican preface for the occasion, as all priests are now permitted to do, and as our local chaplain did:

> It is truly meet and just, right and for our salvation, that we should at all times and in all places give thanks unto Thee, O holy Lord, almighty Father, eternal God: Who, being the Giver of all good things, dost dwell in this house of prayer which we have built and dost sanctify through unceasing operation Thy Church, which Thou Thyself hast founded. For this indeed is a house of prayer, expressed in the semblance of visible buildings, a temple for the indwelling of Thy glory, the unchangeable seat of truth, the sanctuary of eternal charity. This is the ark that leads us, snatched from the deluge of the world, into the port of salvation. This is the beloved and only Spouse, whom Christ bought by His own Blood, whom He quickeneth with His Spirit: in whose bosom we are reborn through Thy grace, nursed with the milk of Thy Word, strengthened with the Bread of Life, and warmed by the aid of Thy mercy. She fighteth faithfully on earth, assisted by her Spouse, and, crowned by Him, doth gain everlasting victory in heaven. And therefore with the Angels and Archangels, with the Thrones and Dominions and with all the hosts of the heavenly army, we sing a hymn to Thy glory, evermore saying: *Sanctus, sanctus, sanctus* ...

November 19 is the feast of St. Elizabeth of Hungary. The Lesson is from Proverbs 31:10–31, which paints a memorable portrait, worth quoting in full:

Who shall find a valiant woman? Far and from the uttermost coasts is the price of her. The heart of her husband trusteth in her, and he shall have no need of spoils. She will render him good, and not evil, all the days of her life. She hath sought wool and flax, and hath wrought by the counsel of her hands. She is like the merchant's ship, she bringeth her bread from afar. And she hath risen in the night, and given prey to her household, and victuals to her maidens. She hath considered a field, and bought it: with the fruit of her hand she hath planted a vineyard. She hath girded her loins with strength, and hath strengthened her arm. She hath tasted and seen that her traffic is good: her lamp shall not be put out in the night. She hath put out her hand to strong things, and her fingers have taken hold of the spindle. She hath opened her hand to the needy, and stretched out her hands to the poor. She shall not fear for her house in the cold of snow: for all her domestics are clothed with double garments. She hath made for herself clothing of tapestry: fine linen and purple is her covering. Her husband is honourable in the gates, when he sitteth among the senators of the land. She made fine linen and sold it, and delivered a girdle to the Chanaanite. Strength and beauty are her clothing, and she shall laugh in the latter day. She hath opened her mouth to wisdom, and the law of clemency is on her tongue. She hath looked well to the paths of her house, and hath not eaten her bread idle. Her children rose up, and called her blessed: her husband, and he praised her. Many daughters have gathered together riches: thou hast surpassed them all. Favour is deceitful, and beauty is vain: the woman that feareth the Lord, she shall be praised.

Give her of the fruit of her hands: and let her works praise
her in the gates.

Although the Church applies it to the holy women saints, this
reading deserves to be read above all as a parable about Holy
Mother Church herself—a parable that takes flesh, with spotless
perfection, in the Blessed Virgin Mary.

November 20 is the feast of St. Felix of Valois, who belonged
to the royal family, renounced his goods, retired to a desert, and
eventually founded an institute for redeeming captives from
the Muslims. The Common Mass assigned for him—*Justus ut
palma*—is, once again, thoroughly manly, as is the proper Collect of the day.

What we see, in other words, is something like a liturgical
dialogue between bride and bridegroom, like a shuttle weaving
back and forth, producing a tapestry all the more beautiful for
the contrasting functions of warp and woof. And, since the feasts
are not optional and the readings are in harmony with the sanc-
toral cycle, all of this is *always* presented, year after year, to the
faithful who assist at daily Mass. Over time, these faithful cannot
help but be formed in traditional (that is, God-given) intuitions
about the roles of men and women, about what is appropriate to
masculinity and femininity, and about the ideals we should set
before us and the models we should strive to imitate.

Although family culture and catechesis surely play the largest role in developing a healthy understanding of the sexual
duality of human nature and the various ways, in practice, that
complementarity can be lived out—surely it is not "one size
fits all," for there are single women who have not yet chosen a
path, consecrated virgins, wives, mothers, and widows, just as
there are bachelors, religious brothers, priests, husbands, fathers,

widowers—nevertheless, there can be no doubt that the traditional prayer of the Church plays a formative role by giving us shining and unambiguous exemplars from which we receive principles of thought and action. We see these exemplars both in the conducting of the liturgy itself, with its masculine ministries and the veil-wearing of the women, and in the *cultus* of the saints presented to us with such appropriate Mass formularies.

One thing I particularly love about the traditional liturgy is the way it depicts women with images of royalty, dignity, and power—not priestly and kingly power, since that would not be fitting or even possible, but rather the power of the daughters of kings and the power of queens who serve in order to reign. In other words, the distinction is not "men are in charge and women are indentured servants," but men and women alike rule in their proper domains. They are perfected by what they have in common as the baptized, as well as by what differentiates them in their specific vocations. All Christians are together the Bride of Christ, the Church. Consecrated virgins, led by the Blessed Virgin, are Christ's bride in the fullest way possible. Mothers of Christian families emulate the maternity of the Church and of the Mother of God. All priests, as such, stand in the place of Christ the divine Bridegroom and exercise divine paternity; all fathers of families exercise a likeness of that same divine fatherhood. The Tridentine Mass has the power to accentuate and develop what is masculine in men, what is feminine in women, what is human in all of us, and what is divine in us by God's gift.

At a time when traditional sexual roles are scorned by secular society, when the very worth of mankind is called into question, the restoration of our traditional worship is all the more important in avoiding gender dysphoria, misanthropy, abortionism, and other such psychological diseases that rarely, if ever, occurred in healthy societies but that are now proliferating in a decadent Western world unmoored from nature and grace. These diseases can be prevented by the proper care of the soul. It is the great liturgical rites of Catholic tradition that serve as nutriments, preventatives, vitamins, and cures. Even if these rites are not enough by themselves to ensure health in the world, we will never have health in the Church without them.

14

The Theology Behind Women
Wearing Veils in Church

The noble Latin language that nourished piety for centuries. The serenity of Gregorian plainsong. The splendor of priestly attire. The visible emphasis on the sacrificial nature of the Mass, wherein the Lord of glory makes His offering upon the Cross present anew for the benefit of the living and the dead.

To one degree or another, all of these things and more quickly disappeared after the Second Vatican Council under the specious pretext that "modern man" needed something other — something more approachable and up-to-date — than solemnity, silence, and sacredness. This was a huge mistake, as observant members of the laity, clergy, and episcopacy have acknowledged with increasing frankness as time goes on. The work of recovery has largely occurred at the grassroots level.

In discussions of postconciliar reforms, Catholics often dwell on things like the banishment of Latin, chant, *ad orientem*, and kneeling for Communion. This is not surprising, as these changes are the most noticeable, and their cumulative effect on the character of Catholic worship has been the most profound. But there have been other subtle changes that also, in the long run, affect our understanding of the Faith. One example would be the lack of genuflecting at the passage in the Creed: "*Et incarnatus est de Spiritu Sancto, ex Maria Virgine, et homo factus est.*" Similarly, most people no longer bow their heads out of reverence when the Holy Name of Jesus is spoken.

One such change was the more or less total extinction of the custom of women wearing veils when praying in church. Entering a parish church for Mass prior to the Council, one would have seen all the women with their heads covered, whether by berets, bonnets, veils, or doilies. Although today one occasionally sees women at a Novus Ordo Mass wearing a hat or veil, by and large the custom has vanished outside of places where the traditional Latin Mass has survived or returned. And even in the latter places, the custom is by no means universally practiced. Women who feel defensive might say that canon law doesn't require it, the bishop doesn't ask it, and the parish priest doesn't even mention it. Indeed, those who look upon it as a token of an era in which (they suppose) women were regarded as second-class citizens in the Church rejoice that the chapel veil has gone by the wayside.

Yet before we write off the change as an instance of something old-fashioned that was dropped because it was no longer relevant, we should consider what the custom itself meant and whether it symbolizes an important truth that remains as true for us as for our predecessors. Customs of popular piety often have deeper religious and human roots than we initially think. In this fast-paced world, good things of the past are often left behind not because something better has been found to replace them but because people have forgotten a basic truth that needs, more than ever, to be heard and followed.

The teaching of the Apostle

The tradition of women wearing veils in church is based on the words of St. Paul: "For a man ought not to cover his head, since he is the image and glory of God; but woman is the glory of man. (For man was not made from woman, but woman from man. Neither was man created for woman, but woman for man.) That is why a woman ought to wear a veil on her head, because of the angels" (1 Cor. 11:7–10). The word usually translated "veil" is *exousia*, meaning "power" or "authority."[169] A very literal translation of the passage would read: "the woman should have a power [or authority] over her head." One occasionally sees the text expanded into a paraphrase: "a power over her head, symbolized by a veil." This is clearer, but still, why a *veil*? We must turn to the tradition of the Church for an answer.

According to certain Fathers and Doctors of the Church, this passage refers to the angels who veil their faces before the presence of God, worshiping before His throne:[170]

> I saw the Lord sitting upon a throne, high and lifted up; and his train filled the temple. Above him stood the seraphim; each had six wings: with two he covered his

---

[169] According to Ronald Knox, some commentators maintain that Paul is attempting, by means of this Greek word, to render a Hebrew word that signifies the veil traditionally worn by a married Jewish woman. See *The Holy Bible Translated from the Latin Vulgate by Msgr. Ronald Knox* (London: Baronius Press, 2012), 216, note 4, at 1 Cor. 11:10.

[170] These angels, usually identified as cherubim, are described in this manner in Isaiah, Ezekiel, the Revelation of John, and consistently throughout the Jewish rabbinical tradition. See, for scriptural references, Cornelius a Lapide, *Commentaria in Scripturam Sacram* (Paris: Vives, 1868), 18:355–56.

face, and with two he covered his feet, and with two he flew. And one called to another and said: "Holy, holy, holy is the Lord of hosts; the whole earth is full of his glory." (Isa. 6:2)

The angels cover or veil their faces as a sign of reverence before God's glorious power and majesty. They are under His authority. St. Paul is saying, then, that just as the angels cover their faces before the throne of God, so women ought to cover their heads at worship.

But why only the women? Are not men also standing in the presence of God? The explanation can be found in a series of analogies that St. Paul establishes earlier in the same chapter. "The head of every man is Christ, the head of a woman is her husband, and the head of Christ is God" (1 Cor. 11:3). That is, Christ stands to His Father as the husband stands to Christ, and the husband stands to Christ as the wife stands to her husband — in a sequence of descending authority. Notice how remarkable the last part of this analogy is: the Christian wife, in her relationship to her husband, is being compared to the Second Person of the Trinity in His relation to the Father.[171] Hence, the ultimate meaning of a woman's vocation as a wife and mother is to participate, imitate, and manifest the mystery of Christ's mission. Her self-giving is to mirror the self-giving of Christ.

A specific imitation of Christ and of the Church

To unfold the meaning of this passage further, we should consider what St. Paul says in Ephesians, in which he adds another

---

[171] To put it schematically, wife : husband :: husband : Christ :: Christ : Father. Therefore it would follow that wife : husband :: Christ : Father.

dimension to the symbolism. "Wives, be subject to your husbands, as to the Lord. For the husband is the head of the wife as Christ is the head of the church, his body, and is himself its Savior. As the church is subject to Christ, so let wives also be subject in everything to their husbands" (Eph. 5:22–24). The husband stands to the wife as Christ stands to the Church. From this, we see that by the same token, a wife is called to imitate and participate in the work of the Church, which follows Christ as Christ follows the Father. A great supernatural mystery is foreshadowed in earthly things: the obedience of wives is rooted in and flows from Christ's obedience to the Father and in the Church's submission to her Lord.

The obedience to which a woman binds herself in marriage is a *choice*, a response from the heart to a gift from the Lord, even as a nun vows obedience to her superior as part of her vocation to serve the one Lord. The obedience of the wife is given within the context of a sacrament; it is not a matter of natural dependence or inferiority. A wife submits herself to her husband primarily for the love of God and in obedience to His call. Nor does this sacrifice of self, sustained by the grace of God, endanger the status of the wife as equal to her husband. The opinion that women are not equal to men in both natural and supernatural dignity is heretical, analogous to the heresy of subordinationism which denies the essential equality of the Son with the Father. This is clear from *Casti Connubii* of Pius XI, which teaches that men and women enjoy "equality in difference" and "equality in headship and subordination." As novelist Charles Williams explains:

> The Son is co-equal with the Father (as Origen held, and as was afterwards defined), yet the Son is obedient to the Father. A thing so sweetly known in many relations

of human love is, beyond imagination, present in the midmost secrets of heaven. For the Son in His eternal Now desires subordination, and it is His. He wills to be so; He co-inheres obediently and filially in the Father, as the Father authoritatively and paternally co-inheres in Him. And the whole Three Persons are co-eternal together—and co-equal.[172]

Within the Blessed Trinity, the distinction of Persons does not endanger the unity of the Godhead, essentially and equally shared by Father, Son, and Holy Spirit. This hierarchy-within-equality in the Trinity is reflected in the order of salvation brought about through the Father's sending of Christ, in the bridal relationship of Christ and the Church, and in the order of Christian marriage.

The wound of sinful rebellion was healed by the death of Christ, and the salvation of man was obtained precisely through obedience to the will of God, which began with the Virgin's *fiat*, "Let it be done to me according to Thy word" (Luke 1:38). Similarly, seen as a participation in the mystery of Christ and of His Church, a woman's relationship to her husband is salvific, precisely as a sacrifice freely consecrated to and placed within the one sacrifice of Christ. *All* Christians are called to imitate the Virgin, and all are called to be united to Christ and to one another in Him, but this vocation has a different manifestation in women than it does in men. While Mary is the archetype for all Christians, her life, as a model of true femininity, exhibits certain truths especially applicable to women. The veil and any

---

[172] Charles Williams, quoted in Mary McDermott Shideler, *The Theology of Romantic Love* (Grand Rapids: William B. Eerdmans, 1962), 82–83.

other symbol associated with women must be seen in light of the *fiat* of the Virgin, her abandonment to God's will, the act by which she crushed the serpent's head—just as the submission of Christ to the will of the Father, "even unto death,"[173] was the defeat of Satan. "Behold, I am the handmaiden of the Lord." "Not my will, but Thy will be done."[174] By offering herself, the Virgin became the "helpmate" necessary for the new Adam, the great High Priest, to offer the one Sacrifice for all: His Body and Blood.[175]

The co-responsibility of the husband

In order to have the complete picture, we must remember the pointed teaching St. Paul gives to husbands in Ephesians 5. The Apostle says that husbands are to represent Christ; they are to serve as head of the domestic church. What does this mean? The true authority that comes through the life-giving sacraments has little to do with fallen man's understanding of power, of ruling over others for one's own benefit. "You know that the rulers of the Gentiles lord it over them, and their great men exercise authority over them. It shall not be so among you; but whoever would be great among you must be your servant, and whoever would be first among you must be your slave; even as the Son of man came not to be served but to serve" (Matt. 20:25–28). Husbands are to act as Christ the King—the King enthroned upon the Cross: "Husbands, love your wives, *as Christ loved the Church and gave himself up for her*" (Eph. 5:25). The authority of the husband is truly itself when exercised in imitation of Christ.

---

[173] Matt. 26:38; Phil. 2:8.
[174] Luke 1:38, 22:42.
[175] Cf. Gen. 2:18; 1 Cor. 15:45; Heb. 7:27, 9:12, 9:26, 10:10.

St. Thomas Aquinas captures this point well: "The wife is subject to God by being subject to her husband-under-God" [*subiicitur viro sub Deo*], meaning that she is subject to him inasmuch as he himself is "under God," that is, ruling in accordance with God's commandments.[176]

Thus, in every marriage, husband and wife are called to imitate and manifest, to each other and to the world, the love of Christ and the Church, itself patterned after the mystery of love within the Blessed Trinity. This imitation and manifestation can be accomplished only by the grace of God, the God who is Love. It takes constant prayer and discernment, patience and perseverance. Only through a continual awareness of the greatness of one's vocation to love — to rule and to serve by means of love and for the sake of love — can the balance of hierarchy-in-equality and equality-in-hierarchy be maintained. The proper relationship of wife with husband and the precious gift of childbearing suffered harm from the Fall (cf. Gen. 3:16), as can be seen both in men who abuse their husbandly authority and in men who are too timid or effeminate to embrace its responsibilities. We can see all kinds of problems — in men who dominate for their own selfish gain or lazily refuse to rule for anyone's good, but also in women who refuse to let themselves be ruled at all or else act as doormats and do not challenge abuses of authority. This, I think, is why we find the example of a happily married couple living together in peace and joy so refreshing and encouraging. It shows that it

---

[176] See *Lectura super primam epistolam ad Corinthios*, cap. XI, lec. 3, no. 612; for the Latin text with English translation, see *Commentary on the Letters of Saint Paul to the Corinthians*, trans. F. R. Larcher et al. (Lander, WY: The Aquinas Institute for the Study of Sacred Doctrine, 2012).

can indeed be done—by determined human effort and by God's implored grace.[177]

Thus, in St. Paul's theology, the veil is a symbol of consecration and self-sacrifice. Just as the Church submits herself to Christ and Christ the Son obeys the Father, a wife is "under" the power and protection of her husband. Especially when they are before the Lord in worship, it makes liturgical sense for her to wear an outward sign of this inward truth, a public and visible symbol of her vocation as wife. The veil bears silent witness to her dignity and power *in* her own submission to her husband. It is sacramental in the broad sense: a humble physical thing that signifies a deep spiritual reality. Just as nuns give witness to the world through their habits (including the veil), wives bear witness to the special character of Christian marriage by covering their own heads at Mass.[178] This beautiful symbol gives the wife an opportunity to live her vocation more fully by reminding herself and others, including her daughters, of its Marian character of humility and obedience. One might even go further: this delicate symbol of what is a prime example of the "littleness" of St. Thérèse of Lisieux may be a powerful means of reparation for those who are in rebellion against their identity or who are unfaithful to their callings.

Tradition encoded in symbols

Having examined the theology behind the veil and the role of husband and wife in Christian marriage, it is possible to explain

---

[177] See Leila Marie Lawler, *God Has No Grandchildren: A Guided Reading of Pope Pius XI's Encyclical* Casti Connubii *(On Chaste Marriage)* (Waterloo, ON: Arouca Press, 2021).

[178] See Anon., "The Symbolism of Religious Clothing: Why Nuns Wear What They Do," *OnePeterFive*, October 7, 2020.

another detail in 1 Corinthians 11 that might escape notice. The chapter begins with the Apostle's insistence that the Christians at Corinth uphold the traditions he has passed on to them: "I commend you because you remember me in everything and maintain the traditions even as I have delivered them unto you. But I want you to understand that the head of every man is Christ, the head of a woman is her husband, and the head of Christ is God" (1 Cor. 11:2–3).

Part of the sacred tradition he passed on to them is the teaching about wives and their submission to their husbands, and it is within this framework that the "power" symbolized by the veil enters into his exhortation. In other words, St. Paul is urging all who strive to "imitate Christ" (cf. 1 Cor. 11:1) to maintain the traditions that both *contain* and *confirm* sound doctrine and a holy life. "So then, brethren, stand firm and hold to the traditions which you were taught by us, either by word of mouth or by letter" (2 Thess. 2:15). This is indeed a teaching to which we must hold fast in the modern world. The present disintegration of family life is in some measure due to the fact that the apostolic tradition of family hierarchy has not been maintained either by the family or by the ecclesiastical hierarchy itself. For example, in spite of being inculcated six times in the New Testament by St. Paul, the duty of the wife to be subject to her husband as head of the family is altogether omitted from the *Catechism of the Catholic Church*, and it has fared no better in papal documents or in diocesan pastoral letters.[179]

---

[179] For two articles that show how dominant postconciliar trends contradict the teaching of Scripture as traditionally taught by the Church, see Josh Kusch, "'Mutual Submission' between Husbands and Wives in Ephesians 5?," *Crisis Magazine*, August 30, 2016; G.C. Dilsaver, "Karol Wojtyła and the Patriarchal

From the teaching of St. Paul, it seems clear that the wearing of a head-covering has its full "sacramental" meaning only for married or betrothed women (including nuns who are wedded to Christ and novices who are preparing for this mystical wedding).[180] Studied in context, St. Paul's recommendation that "the woman ought to have a veil over her head" as a symbol of the man's power (*exousia*) unquestionably refers not to man and woman as such, but to married women in relation to their own husbands.[181] For this reason, the traditional custom of *all* females wearing a veil in church finds justification in the natural and supernatural ordering of each woman to be a spouse — be it as a bride of Christ in religious life or as a wife in a Christian marriage.[182] Even before this ordering is actualized, and even when it is never actualized, it remains an ontological and spiritual reality that deserves to be recognized, honored, and placed within the great *mysterium fidei* celebrated in the Holy Mass.[183]

Hierarchy of the Family," *Christian Order*, June/July 2002 (online). Professor Adam Rasmussen, on the contrary, in a very revealing article, maintains that Scripture and the Fathers can be left aside wherever modernity has drastically changed our frame of reference: see "Are Christians Beholden to Ancient Writers' Cultural Assumptions?," *Where Peter Is*, March 23, 2021.

[180] See Anon., "Investiture as a Bridal Ceremony," *OnePeterFive*, October 28, 2020.

[181] One will also notice, however, that the same chapter gives instructions applicable to all women; St. Paul goes back and forth between women in general and those who are married, saying different things appropriate to each.

[182] See Mary Cuff, "There Is No Vocation to the 'Single Life,'" *Crisis Magazine*, August 7, 2020.

[183] A certain parallel can be found in the fact that only males can serve in the sanctuary because they are either ordained clerics or ordainable as clerics.

Practical reasons

There are also practical reasons for wearing a chapel veil, and since these reasons apply to the married as well as to the unmarried, they support the older convention of all females wearing veils in church.

First and foremost, wearing a veil can prevent distraction, both for oneself and for others. How many times have we caught ourselves looking around at others in church instead of concentrating on prayer? For women, the veil can help. Those who are protected by the veil, wrapped up in it, can focus better, as they are reminded of why they are in church to begin with: "This is a sacred time, and I am here to worship God."

Another motive for wearing a veil in church is a certain "privacy," a need to be alone with God instead of being chummy and sociable. At Mass, the divine Bridegroom visits the bridal Christian soul. We should be prepared for His visitation. The modern overemphasis on the social dimension of worship more often than not leads to a loss of contact with the one reality that makes everything else real: Jesus Christ, true God and true man, who should be received with the full and absolute attentiveness of the soul. The veil marks the woman as a person of prayer who knows why she has come and for whom she has come. People may say behind her back that she is too pious and old-fashioned, but in her heart, she is at peace. Her efforts are undertaken out of love, and this love is the only thing that matters. A woman who wears a veil says to her neighbors, "We are here together to worship God." In this way, she is performing a service to others as she helps them to remember what Mass is all about, and eventually, other women may follow suit.

There are many reasons, then, why the practice of wearing chapel veils is desirable. Most importantly, for wives, it has the same character that a habit has for a religious sister. It is a sign of her calling and consecration to the Lord, with and through her husband. Rather than being a stigma of women's oppression, it is a sign of a genuine committed love, as the Cross is the greatest sign of love ever given to mankind. Even this small custom of our ancestors is therefore part of a larger and more successful liturgical renewal that rightly embraces the past, understands the true needs of the present, and preserves the beauty and symbolism of Catholic worship for ages to come.

15

St. Thérèse of Lisieux on the
Sacristans of Her Convent

One of the most beloved and powerful of modern saints, St.
Thérèse of the Child Jesus and of the Holy Face, is a wonder-
fully attractive model of a Catholic fully engaged in the liturgy
without having to be a liturgical minister. She tells us why her
contribution, though different from the priest's, is no less valuable, no less precious in God's sight.

Many readers will be familiar with a photograph of St. Thérèse
in which she is shown posing in her work of filling a ciborium
with hosts (among other typical functions of a sacristan) for the
daily conventual Mass. This is in keeping with the usual customs
of convents, where the sisters perform many of the tasks that
would otherwise be assigned to clerics, such as leading the entire
Divine Office, chanting its readings and prayers, and making the
responses at low Mass from outside the sanctuary in situations
when no servers are available.[184]

---

[184] See Shawn Tribe, "Carthusian Nuns and the Use of the Maniple
and Stole," *Liturgical Arts Journal*, July 24, 2018. He quotes the
old *Catholic Encyclopedia*: "The Carthusian nuns have retained
the privilege of the consecration of virgins, which they have

A photo that is much less known, and which I myself saw only for the first time recently, shows Thérèse with (if I may say so) her liturgical assistants in November 1896. Three of them are her biological sisters Marie, Pauline, and Céline: Sr. Marie of the Sacred Heart, Mother Agnes of Jesus, and St. Geneviève of the Holy Face. One is her aunt Marie Guérin, known to us as Sr. Marie of the Eucharist. Sr. Marie of the Eucharist, Sr. Marie of the Angels (not in the photo), and St. Thérèse were the sacristans, while her three biological sisters were altar bread bakers.[185]

St. Thérèse was a gifted amateur poet and playwright who composed a surprising number of literary works in her spare moments during her nine years as a Carmelite nun. Some of her work was intended for communal occasions such as recreations, birthdays, and feast days, while other pieces were more private, sent to one or a few of her religious sisters. In the same month

inherited from the nuns of Prébayon. The consecration, which is given four years after the vows are taken, can only be conferred by the diocesan. The rite differs but slightly from that given in the *Pontifical*. The nun is invested with a crown, ring, stole, and maniple, the last being worn on the right arm. These ornaments the nun only wears again on the day of her monastic jubilee, and after her death on her bier. It is a consecrated nun who sings the Epistle at the conventual Mass, though without wearing the maniple" (and, it goes without saying, outside of the Choir or presbytery). It is not surprising that this unusual custom, which stands in tension with the norms of the liturgy as explained in the present book, remained confined to one of the smallest and most reclusive of religious orders.

[185] For this and other details, I am indebted to the excellent commentary in *The Poetry of Saint Thérèse of Lisieux*, trans. Donald Kinney, O.C.D. (Washington, DC: ICS Publications, 1996), 169–70.

of November 1896, she wrote a poem called "The Sacristans of Carmel" in rhyming, octosyllabic verse. The poem was written for Sr. Marie Philomena, who had asked Thérèse for something she could sing while baking, but it was first *read* by her aunt. Later, all of the sacristans and altar bread bakers got to know the poem and apparently sang it regularly in their work, to whatever familiar tune they chose that would match the meter. In this, we see a splendid example of the genre of a "work song" that has nearly disappeared from the world of mass-marketed and passively consumed entertainment. One may hope such work songs still survive in the Carmels.

The religious and theological content of the song is quite worthy of attention:

Ici-bas notre doux office
Est de préparer pour l'autel,
Le pain, le vin du Sacrifice
Qui donne à la terre: «Le Ciel!»

> Here below our sweet office
> Is to prepare for the altar
> The bread and wine of the Sacrifice
> Which brings to earth—"Heaven!"

Le Ciel, ô mystère suprême!
Se cache sous un humble pain;
Car le Ciel, c'est Jésus Lui-Même,
Venant à nous chaque matin.

> Heaven, O supreme mystery!
> Hides itself under humble bread;
> For Heaven is Jesus Himself,
> Coming to us each morning.

Ministers of Christ

Il n'est pas de reines sur terre
Qui soient plus heureuses que nous.
Notre office est une prière
Qui nous unit à notre Epoux.

> There are no queens on earth
> Who are happier than we.
> Our office is a prayer
> Which unites us to our Spouse.

Les plus grands honneurs de ce monde
Ne peuvent pas se comparer
A la paix céleste et profonde
Que Jésus nous fait savourer.

> The greatest honors of this world
> Cannot compare
> To the peace, profound and heavenly,
> Which Jesus lets us savor.

Nous portons une sainte envie
A l'ouvrage de notre main,
A la petite et blanche hostie
Qui doit voiler l'Agneau divin.

> We bring a holy envy
> For the work of our hands,
> For the little white host
> Which is to veil our divine Lamb.

Mais son amour nous a choisies.
Il est notre Epoux, notre Ami.
Nous sommes aussi des hosties
Que Jésus veut changer en Lui.

But His love has chosen us.
He is our Spouse, our Friend.
We are also hosts,
Which Jesus wants to change into Himself.

Mission sublime du Prêtre,
Tu deviens la nôtre ici-bas.
Transformées par le Divin Maître,
C'est Lui qui dirige nos pas.

Sublime mission of the Priest,
You become our mission here below.
Transformed by the Divine Master,
It is He who guides our steps.

Nous devons aider les apôtres
Par nos prières, notre amour.
Leurs champs de combats sont les nôtres.
Pour eux nous luttons chaque jour.

We must help the apostles
By our prayers, our love.
Their battlefields are ours.
For them we fight each day.

Le Dieu caché du tabernacle
Qui se cache aussi dans nos coeurs,
A notre voix, ô quel miracle!
Daigne pardonner aux pécheurs!

The hidden God of the tabernacle
Who also hides in our hearts,
O what a miracle! at our voice
Deigns to pardon sinners!

Notre bonheur et notre gloire,
C'est de travailler pour Jésus.
Son beau Ciel voilà le ciboire
Que nous voulons combler d'élus!

> Our happiness and our glory
> Is to work for Jesus.
> His beautiful Heaven is the ciborium
> We want to fill with souls![186]

The Carmelite commentators find this poem both charming and insightful:

> The sacristans are the untiring agents of this mysterious exchange [between heaven and earth]. In this poem, they readily call to mind something like Jacob's ladder. These stanzas are full of "gentleness." There is the discreet gentleness of the "housewife," if we dare call it that: of the spouse "happier than a queen" whose heart remains attentive to her Husband, while her hands are diligently working for Him. There is also the discreet gentleness of the Carmelite nun, who is associated with the apostle at the altar in the role that is hers, that of the hidden companion. In both cases, the assistant becomes like the one she assists.
>
> Here she [Thérèse] sings of her concrete way of sharing immediately in the "sublime mission of the Priest."

---

[186] The original French (PN 40, "Les Sacristines du Carmel") may be found in Kinney, *Poetry*, 301–2, as well as at the website of the Archives of the Carmel of Lisieux (https://www.archives-carmel-lisieux.fr/carmel/index.php/pn-40). Kinney's translation (ibid., 170–71) has been slightly modified to make it more literal.

"Transformed" into Jesus by the Eucharist, "changed" into
Him, does she not then also become an "alter Christus"
[another Christ]...? She cannot leave her cloister to
"preach the Gospel," but Jesus, the first Missionary, walks
in her and through her. He "guides her steps," as He does
those of the apostles she prays for, loves, and struggles for.
She cannot absolve from sins. But Jesus present in her
through the Eucharist gives her a share in his ministry of
reconciling sinners. She will never fill the ciborium with
consecrated hosts. But she is spending her life "filling
Heaven with souls"—living hosts in which Christ lives
alone from then on.... So Thérèse has no inferiority
complex toward "men" or priests. She has no presumption
either. For her, it is Jesus who acts in collaboration with
men—and women. Even in 1892, she wrote to Céline:
"I find that our share is really beautiful; what have we to
envy in priests?"[187]

In fact, though the expression "holy envy" is awkward, it conveys
a truth: it will always be the case that each Christian vocation
has reason to admire the goods of every other, since these goods
are not, simply speaking, compatible with one another. The
priest may well "envy" the female religious her total and silent
dedication to prayer, which he will almost never attain in his
active ministry. The married man or woman may "envy" the
consecrated soul its undivided attentiveness or availability for
the things of the Lord (cf. 1 Cor. 7). The consecrated man or
woman may "envy" the married their sacramental realization
of the faithful, fruitful union of Christ and the Church, which

---

[187] Kinney, *Poetry*, 169–70.

brings new immortal souls into the world to complete the number of the elect.

In the Mother of God alone do we find united that which nature cannot unite, combining and exceeding all Christian states of life: she is the "bride unwedded,"[188] the child-bearing virgin, mother inviolate, and Mediatrix of all grace as the inseparable helpmate of the High Priest. In her, all vocations are at one, like white light before it splinters into a spectrum of colors. For the rest of us, the individual colors are distinct, complementary, and beautiful, as they are intended to be for our individual benefit and for the common good of the Church.

St. Thérèse's poem serves as a profitable meditation on several intertwined mysteries: the unique, exalted, and irreplaceable nature of the ministerial priesthood; the lofty participation in Christ the High Priest enjoyed by all who are baptized into His sacerdotal and royal dignity; the special position of consecrated religious, who follow the priestly and sacrificial Lamb whithersoever He goeth; and the value in God's sight of the quiet, humble work done by sacristans whenever they reverently prepare the materials and environs required for worthily offering the sacrifice of praise.

---

[188] I borrow this expression from the popular Byzantine hymn "Agni Parthene," written by St. Nectarios of Aegina, in which the refrain reads: "Agní Parthéne Déspina, Áhrante Theotóke, ℟: Hére Nímfi Anímfefte" (O pure and virgin Lady, O spotless Theotokos. ℟: Rejoice, O unwedded Bride).

16

Confronting the Heresy of Activism
with the Primacy of Prayer

Having discussed the metaphysical and sacramental foundations
of all-male ministry in the liturgy, the history and tradition of
minor and major orders, the complementary roles of men and
women as taught in the traditional liturgy, the correct understanding of active participation in worship, and the richly fulfilling
vocation to which the laity are called as ambassadors of Christ
in the world, we turn now in the final chapters of this book to
broader views. For we must realize that in Catholicism, as in the
Mystical Body of Christ, even the smallest part bears a relation
to the whole—and when we step back to look at the whole, we
see where the part fits in, and why.

Chapter nine argued that the primary engine for pushing lay
ministries was a superficial notion of "active participation," to
which might be added claims that a shortage in clergy required
the drafting of laity, even though the same "solution" was not
chosen at other times of clerical deprivation in Church history.
The deeper root of this problem, however, lies in a preoccupation with or overemphasis on activity as the primary mode of
Christian life, a distortion that calls for a comprehensive spiritual

remedy. Three Josephs, among others, will assist us: St. Joseph of Nazareth, Josef Pieper, and Joseph Ratzinger.

St. Joseph is rightly exalted as the model of the humble, diligent laborer. But we must beware of subtly transforming him into a symbol of the proletariat—of the "world of total work" that Josef Pieper considers one of the most disturbing aspects of modern society, in which the goods that are most worthwhile and most holy in human life are swallowed up and smothered by goods that are instrumental, ancillary, temporary, and in urgent need of moderation and subordination.[189]

When in 1955 Pius XII established May 1 as the feast of "St. Joseph the Worker," he surely had no intention of isolating work from its natural and supernatural context, as both communism and capitalism had done, and placing it on a pillar for veneration. The feast was intended as a "counter-feast" to the communists' Labor Day. It served as a reminder of the virtues of St. Joseph the craftsman, who pleased God and sanctified his soul through, in part, bearing well the burdens of his livelihood.[190] Yet he pleased God still more through his prayer and contemplation, his intimate domestic communion with Jesus and Mary, and his joyful observance of the Sabbath and the liturgical calendar of ancient Israel. When we celebrate the saints in glory, we rejoice that they lived this life with their hearts in Heaven and reached at last *eternal rest* in God, which

---

[189] See Josef Pieper, *Leisure, the Basis of Culture*, trans. Alexander Dru (San Francisco: Ignatius Press, 2009), 19–74.

[190] There is a growing desire to restore the Roman calendar for May to its pristine form prior to 1955, such that the original feast of the patronage of St. Joseph during Eastertide would be observed instead of St. Joseph the Worker, and the apostles Philip and James could once again occupy their place on May 1.

is the most intense activity of all: the face-to-face vision of the Most Holy Trinity, in which the saints, without ceasing to be enraptured in the First and Last and All, see our needs and intercede for us in union with the High Priest of our confession. As even the pagan philosopher Aristotle saw, the highest contemplation cannot be described as work, or as a merely human occupation.[191] That which is highest in man, that toward which we are striving, is the sabbath of resting in God. The Christian faith is not primarily about *work*; it is primarily about *resting*. "Come unto me, all ye that labour and are heavy laden, and I will give you rest. Take my yoke upon you, and learn of me; for I am meek and lowly in heart: and ye shall find rest unto your souls" (Matt. 11:28–29). All of us are far too consumed with the idea of "working for God." We have to learn to *rest in God*. What is eternal life? It is the most intense activity: perfectly resting in the Father. God is pure act, He is *acting*, everything He does is identical to who He is. God can be compared to a fire that burns eternally — and yet there is no motion in Him, no moving around, no bustle, no hurry. He is a fire that never burns itself out. He is pure act, endless life, infinite rejoicing; He is stillness, peace, rest. Our acting, our living, our rejoicing and our suffering, if they are to be fruitful, must be soaked through on the inside with his stillness and peace.

This is no pagan exaltation of leisure or Jewish legalism about avoiding labor: it is the clear teaching of the Epistle to the Hebrews, which sums up the newness of Christian revelation better than any other single text in the New Testament. The surmounting of our finite labors in beatific leisure, in which God is all in all and we are immersed in His peace, is the end we believe in,

---

[191] See *Nicomachean Ethics*, bk. 10, ch. 7.

hope for, pray for, long for. In a magnificent sermon on Sirach 24:11, *In omnibus requiem quaesivi*, Meister Eckhart beautifully unfolded this truth:

> Eternal Wisdom says to the soul: "In all things I have sought rest," and the soul replies: "He who created me rested in my tent." And thirdly Eternal Wisdom says: "My rest is in the holy city." If I were asked to say to what end the Creator has created all creatures, I would say: rest. If I were asked secondly what the Holy Trinity sought altogether in all its works, I would answer: rest. If I were asked thirdly what the soul sought in all her agitations, I would answer: rest. If I were asked fourthly what all creatures sought in their natural desires and motions, I would answer: rest....
>
> The divine nature makes all the soul's desires mad and crazy for Him, so as to draw her to Him. For the divine nature tastes so well to God and pleases Him so much — that is: rest — that He has projected it out of Himself to stir up and draw into Himself the natural desires of all creatures. Not only does the Creator seek His own rest by projecting it and informing all creatures with it, but He seeks to draw all creatures back with Him into their first beginning, which is rest.... The Father seeks rest in His Son, in whom He has poured out and formed all creatures, and they both seek rest in the Holy Ghost, who has proceeded from them both as eternal and immeasurable love.... The soul seeks rest in all her powers and motions, whether a man knows it or not. He never opens or shuts an eye without seeking rest by doing so: either he seeks to reject something

that hinders him, or he seeks to draw in something on which to rest.[192]

If this ultimate and eternal divine rest is not the aim of human work—and it cannot be denied that our culture is programmatically against this transcendent orientation—our work becomes counterproductive and pernicious, a distraction, a snare, an apprenticeship to the industrious father of lies rather than a discipline by which to ascend above the stars.

The modern period has witnessed several waves of greedy iconoclasm against the monastic life, as we see in Henry VIII's dissolution of religious houses in sixteenth-century England or the "secularizations" imposed by anticlerical regimes of more recent vintage. Stratford Caldecott saw in this fact an X-ray of modernity's bone structure: "The destruction of the monasteries is particularly poignant as a symbol of what was taking place. It is as though our modern world was actually built on and presupposed the destruction of contemplation—or at least the destruction of that (largely Benedictine) ideal, the synthesis of contemplation and action that lay at the heart of Christendom."[193]

The separation of active life from contemplative life, a separation that had been proceeding slowly for centuries and suddenly took a giant leap forward after the Second Vatican Council, is a fatal separation, like that of nature from grace, reason from faith, science from piety. It has superficialized the Church's activity, making it a kind of "busy work" rather than the extension of Christ's

---

[192] *Sermon 45*. The full text may be found in *Meister Eckhart, Sermons and Treatises*, volume II, trans. and ed. by M. O'C. Walshe (Shaftesbury: Element Books, 1987), 13–17.

[193] *Not as the World Gives: The Way of Creative Justice* (Kettering, OH: Angelico Press, 2014), 231.

saving presence into the world around us. The reductionism of "relevance" and a preoccupation with productivity finally found their nesting place in the liturgy, which they colonized and dominated.

With the clear-eyed intensity of an Old Testament prophet, Cardinal Robert Sarah has warned the modern Church about what must happen to the human spirit and to religion itself when silence no longer surrounds and saturates us, when meditation dries up, when busyness replaces the contemplative surrender of adoration. In such a world, getting a taste of (and for) contemplation is difficult. Not surprisingly, we hear everywhere the glib sentiment (originating, perhaps, in an uneasy conscience) that "*everything* can be a form of contemplation."

Now, it may well be the case that for a man or woman already deeply immersed in the Trinitarian life — say, a Catherine of Siena or a Teresa of Ávila — anything they do will be an extension of that burning fire of interior prayer, and they will *actually* find God in everything. But that is not where we begin. We must take what the Psalmist calls the *vias duras*, the hard and narrow roads of disciplined personal and liturgical prayer, if we wish to reach the high plateau, the city of peace, the kingdom of contemplation (cf. Ps. 16). Being able to see God in everything and everything in God is the *destination*, not the point of departure. It is, moreover, a *gift*, something for which we must beg, not something we can instantly produce.

This, I believe, is the primary lesson that St. Joseph, the man of silence, the man of prompt obedience to the divine Word for which he was intently listening, would wish to teach us today. Perhaps he would say: "Given a choice between another hour at the human office and the recitation of part of the Divine Office, choose the latter. It will be better for you, for your work, for the Church, and for the world."

Combating the "heresy of activism"

In Henri de Lubac's *Vatican Council Notebooks*, we find the following summary of a speech in the *aula* given by Cardinal William Godfrey, archbishop of Westminster, on Friday, November 9, 1962, during the debate over the Divine Office:

> Some people exaggerate the *onus sacerdotum in opere pastorali* [the burden of priests in pastoral work]. I have been a parish priest; I see a large number of priests; I have never met any who have told me that they no longer have time for the breviary. Do not legislate universally for a few exceptional cases. Be careful of the *haeresis bonorum operum* [the heresy of good works]. Work must be subordinate to prayer. The breviary has already been made lighter. It must remain the *essentiale nutrimentum nostri laboris* [the essential nourishment of our work].... In our cathedral, the office is recited or chanted every day; our work is not neglected because of that.[194]

The following day, Bishop Martin Jaime Flores of Barbastro, Spain, made the rather obvious but important point that *Oratio est labor pastoralis* — prayer *is*, in a way, a pastoral work. It is something that benefits the people more than any other work.[195] Later that day, Bishop Luigi Carli of Segni spoke out against what he called *activismus exaggeratus* and said that the reduction of the breviary would be "shocking, a scandal to the whole Christian people."[196]

---

[194] Henri de Lubac, *Vatican Council Notebooks* (San Francisco: Ignatius Press, 2015), 1:258–59.

[195] Ibid., 266.

[196] Ibid., 268–69.

Ministers of Christ

To find the roots of this "exaggerated activism"—which Fr. Jordan Aumann, O.P. went so far as to call a "heresy"[197]—we need to go back to a controversy sparked in the late nineteenth century by Fr. Walter Elliott's 1891 biography of the founder of the Paulists, Fr. Isaac Hecker, which appeared in a French translation in 1897 with a controversial introduction by Bishop John Ireland of St. Paul, Minnesota. Bishop Ireland's support of doctrinal and moral concessions in the face of modernity, his claim that we are entering a new age of the Spirit, and his exaltation of "active" virtues and life in the world over the supposedly "passive" virtues of the cloister met with a severe rebuff in Leo XIII's letter *Testem Benevolentiae* of 1899, addressed to Cardinal Gibbons and the American bishops. As related in the 1976 book *Histoire des crises du clergé français contemporain* by Paul Vigneron, the biography of Hecker became a bestseller among the French clergy then under siege from an anticlerical government. Soon there was a turning away from the interior life toward activism, or, as we might nowadays call it, "being pastoral." Vocations to the diocesan priesthood plunged. Only the publication of Dom Jean-Baptiste Chautard's book on the primacy of the interior life, *The Soul of the Apostolate*, would reverse the trend. Vocations flourished until 1946, by which time over 250,000 copies of Chautard's book had been sold. Then, Fr. Marie-Dominique Chenu, national chaplain of the worker priests, publicly attacked *The Soul of the Apostolate* as outdated: the conditions under which Dom Chautard wrote no longer exist, he said. Vocations to the diocesan priesthood plunged, never to recover.[198]

[197] Jordan Aumann, O.P., "The Heresy of Action," in *Cross and Crown* 3 (1951): 25–45.
[198] I owe this information to Anthony Sistrom. Vigneron cites more than three hundred biographies and memoirs of French priests in establishing his narrative.

Thus, by the time of the meeting of the Second Vatican Council in 1962, the battle lines were fairly well drawn up between those who, in accord with Catholic tradition as enunciated by Chautard, saw the inherent priority of prayer and contemplation over works of the active life and those who, following the modern trend from Bishop Ireland to Fr. Chenu, wished to lessen the "*onus*" (burden) of prayer in favor of pastoral efficiency.[199] There is no doubt about which side won in practice: *all* of the liturgies of the Roman Catholic Church, from the sacramental rites to the Divine Office, from blessings to pontifical ceremonies, were greatly shortened, simplified, and streamlined;[200] the people

[199] One wonders if these authors had ever pondered Jeremiah 23:33–40: "When one of this people, or a prophet, or a priest asks you, 'What is the burden of the Lord?,' you shall say to them, 'You are the burden, and I will cast you off, says the Lord.' And as for the prophet, priest, or one of the people who says, 'The burden of the Lord,' I will punish that man and his household.... But 'the burden of the Lord' you shall mention no more, for the burden is every man's own word, and you pervert the words of the living God, the Lord of hosts, our God.... Thus says the Lord, 'Because you have said these words, "The burden of the LORD," when I sent to you, saying, "You shall not say, 'The burden of the LORD,'" therefore, behold, I will surely lift you up and cast you away from my presence, you and the city which I gave to you and your fathers. And I will bring upon you everlasting reproach and perpetual shame, which shall not be forgotten.'"

[200] This is true in most cases, but in the notoriously bad *Book of Blessings*, the full form of the quasi-blessing of holy water includes readings that turn it into a mini-Liturgy of the Word, which would take longer than the traditional blessing in the old *Rituale Romanum*. There are other examples of such bloating. Whether longer or shorter, the revised rites in general are lacking in the textual and ceremonial richness of the traditional rites.

were given much to "do," and the celebrant was given the more "active" roles of interlocutor, animator, commentator, improviser. Religious life was redefined in terms of social apostolate. Contemplatives, in particular, felt they had to justify their existence by pointing to concrete benefits they conferred on society. As vocations to the diocesan priesthood plummeted, so too, and for much the same reason, religious vocations plummeted, never to recover in the mainstream Church.[201]

Today, many decades into the weary aftermath, the costly "collateral damage" of all this frenzied activism, we are in a position to see more clearly than ever the wisdom of Godfrey, Flores, and Carli, the wisdom of Leo XIII, Chautard, and Aumann. No less a figure than Joseph Ratzinger has frequently and perceptively addressed the problem of activism, which he considers symptomatic of a loss of confidence in the reality of Jesus Christ and the primacy of His kingdom. In a poignant section of *The Ratzinger Report*, he speaks of the loss of the dimension of feminine receptivity in the Church:

> Activism, the will to be "productive," "relevant," come what may, is the constant temptation of the man, even of the male religious. And this is precisely the basic trend in the ecclesiologies ... that present the Church as a "People of God" committed to action, busily engaged in translating the Gospel into an action program with social, political, and cultural objectives. But it is no accident if the word "Church" is of feminine gender. In her, in fact, lives the mystery of motherhood, of gratitude, of

---

[201] See Hilary White's fine article "What Is the Catholic Religion Actually For? A Monastic Answer," *OnePeterFive*, October 26, 2017.

contemplation, of beauty, of values in short that appear useless in the eyes of the profane world. Without perhaps being fully conscious of the reason, the woman religious feels the deep disquiet of living in a Church where Christianity is reduced to an ideology of doing, according to that strictly masculine ecclesiology which nevertheless is presented—and perhaps believed—as being closer also to women and their "modern" needs. Instead it is the project of a Church in which there is no longer any room for mystical experience, for this pinnacle of religious life which not by chance has been, through the centuries, among the glories and riches offered to all in unbroken constancy and fullness, more by women than by men.[202]

In an address he gave to catechists and religion teachers in the Jubilee Year 2000, Ratzinger, like Chautard, pointed to the necessary foundation of apostolate in prayer:

"Jesus preached by day, by night He prayed." With these few words, he [Don Didimo] wished to say: Jesus had to acquire the disciples from God. The same is always true. We ourselves cannot gather men. We must acquire them by God for God. All methods are empty without the foundation of prayer. The word of the announcement must always be drenched in an intense life of prayer.... Theocentrism is fundamental in the message of Jesus and must also be at the heart of new evangelization.... To proclaim God is to introduce [others] to a relation with God: to teach how to pray. Prayer is faith in action. And

---

[202] *The Ratzinger Report* (San Francisco: Ignatius Press, 1987), 103.

only by experiencing life with God does the evidence of His existence appear.[203]

Pope Benedict XVI returns to this theme in his first encyclical, *Deus Caritas Est*, of 2005:

> Prayer, as a means of drawing ever new strength from Christ, is concretely and urgently needed. People who pray are not wasting their time, even though the situation appears desperate and seems to call for action alone. Piety does not undermine the struggle against the poverty of our neighbors, however extreme.... It is time to reaffirm the importance of prayer in the face of the activism and the growing secularism of many Christians engaged in charitable work. Clearly, the Christian who prays does not claim to be able to change God's plans or correct what He has foreseen. Rather, he seeks an encounter with the Father of Jesus Christ, asking God to be present with the consolation of the Spirit to him and his work.... Our crying out [to the Father] is, as it was for Jesus on the Cross, the deepest and most radical way of affirming our faith in His sovereign power.[204]

One of the most developed treatments of this theme is found in Benedict XVI's General Audience of April 25, 2012, in which he explains the apostles' decision to ordain deacons to assist them. The pope sees in the apostles' focus on the Word and the deacons' handling of the poor a reflection of the distinction between Mary

---

[203] The text of the lecture, entitled "The New Evangelization, Building the Civilization of Love," December 12, 2000, may be found a number of places online.

[204] *Deus Caritas Est* (December 25, 2005), §36–§38.

and Martha of Bethany, and notes that each aspect supports the other: prayerful meditation on the Word leads to its convincing proclamation, and, at the same time, the men to be chosen for works of mercy must be imbued with the Holy Spirit, not mere social workers. He then comes to his central point, which deserves to be read with the "burden" of the recitation or chanting of the Divine Office in mind:

> We must not lose ourselves in pure activism but always let ourselves also be penetrated in our activities by the light of the word of God and thereby learn true charity, true service to others, which does not need many things — it certainly needs the necessary things, but needs above all our heartfelt affection and the light of God.

In commenting on the episode of Martha and Mary, St. Ambrose urges his faithful and us too: "Let us too seek to have what cannot be taken from us, dedicating diligent, not distracted, attention to the Lord's word. The seeds of the heavenly word are blown away, if they are sown along the roadside. May the wish to know be an incentive to you too, as it was to Mary; this is the greatest and most perfect act." And he added that "attention to the ministry must not distract from knowledge of the heavenly word" through prayer (*Expositio Evangelii secundum Lucam*, VII, 85; PL 15:1720).

St. Bernard, who is a model of harmony between contemplation and hard work, in his book *De consideratione*, addressed to Pope Innocent II to offer him some reflections on his ministry, insists precisely on the importance of inner recollection, of prayer to defend oneself from the dangers of being hyper-active, whatever our condition and whatever the task to be carried out. St. Bernard says that all too often, too much work and a frenetic life-style end by hardening the heart and causing the spirit to suffer (cf. II, 3).

His words are a precious reminder to us today, used as we are to evaluating everything with the criterion of productivity and efficiency.... Without daily prayer lived with fidelity, our acts are empty, they lose their profound soul, and are reduced to being mere activism which in the end leaves us dissatisfied.... For pastors, this is the first and most valuable form of service for the flock entrusted to them. If the lungs of prayer and of the word of God do not nourish the breath of our spiritual life, we risk being overwhelmed by countless everyday things: prayer is the breath of the soul and of life.[205]

Looking back over these valuable texts from Ratzinger, we cannot avoid posing some uncomfortable questions for ourselves —for clergy, religious, and laity who are striving for holiness, which we know is not a product of our actions but a gift given to those who ask for it in prayer, who seek, who knock.

Do we actually *believe* in God? If we do, we will believe in His lordship, His primacy, His precedence over all created things, material or spiritual, visible or invisible—such that He always deserves priority in our daily life, the best of our time, energy, attention. That goes for liturgical prayer as well as private prayer.

Do we believe Our Lord's word when He openly says: "Seek ye first the kingdom of God and His righteousness, and all these

---

[205] Cited from http://www.vatican.va/content/benedict-xvi /en/audiences/2012/documents/hf_ben-xvi_aud_20120425 .html.

things shall be added unto you" (Matt. 6:33), or when He says: "Without Me, you can do nothing" (John 15:5)? If so, we will reject at its very root the secular Pelagian mentality that has crept into and corrupted so many "good works" sponsored by the Church or practiced in the name of Christianity.

Do we believe that Our Lord receives honor and glory when we put on our lips and fix in our hearts the words of the very Psalms He inspired for Himself to recite as man on earth, as the Church bids us do in the Divine Office? If we do, our thinking about the "burden" of the Office will change. We will consider taking up some form of the pre-Conciliar breviary, be it Roman or monastic. If we are praying in Latin already, we will not cut corners by a thoughtless rapidity of recitation. And we will not seek shortness, speed, and efficiency. As St. Francis de Sales observes, "haste kills all devotion."

Do we believe that the same Lord Jesus Christ is *really*, metaphysically, bodily, personally present to us at Mass, in the Most Holy Sacrament of the Altar? If we do, this belief should be obvious in the *way* we are worshiping and the place that worship occupies in our daily life.

Ultimately, do we believe in the power and mystery of *prayer*? That is the question Cardinal Godfrey's words, spoken sixty years ago, should prompt in us today.

17

Old Resources for a New Vocational Strategy

A clear picture of the priest's dignity and special work, the work that only he can do in the Church, attracts solid priestly vocations—it always has and always will. In contrast, the idea of the priest as a social worker aided by other social workers inspires almost no one. Something similar can be said for the contrast between the old and new profiles of the monk or nun, brother or sister. Indeed, the traditional understanding of the life of total dedication to God, with its hardships and rewards, elevates *all* callings in the Church: lay, religious, and clerical. As the last chapter probed the broad implications of the conflict between activism and the primacy of receptive or contemplative life, the present chapter will explore the effects of contrasting "vocational strategies" on the health and well-being of the People of God.

At the Fota XI conference in Ireland in July 2018, which had the Divine Office as its theme, participants commented on the way in which the recitation of the postconciliar Liturgy of the Hours has severely fallen off in practice—a problem that goes back some decades.[206] Anecdotal evidence suggests that many

---

[206] In the late 1960s, heyday of rebellious fermentation, the French bishops undertook a survey that disclosed how many French

clergy, apparently not seeing it as a serious obligation, either don't pray it at all or skip it all too readily "when busy." A priest of my acquaintance who has conducted studies on other areas of Catholic orthodoxy and orthopraxy related to me: "I have been assigned to parishes in five states and four countries. I would say within the Novus Ordo realm you have about twenty-five percent reading the breviary, while among the TLM priests, where the office is much more demanding, ninety-five percent or more." In the presentation he gave at the aforementioned conference, Cardinal Raymond Leo Burke stated:

> I recall a conversation with an older priest, shortly after I had taken up my first priestly assignment [in the mid-1970s]. Having been invited to the rectory of his parish for a gathering of priests, I noticed that his book of the Liturgy of the Hours was sitting on an end table, as we

---

clergy had abandoned the Divine Office, and they asked the Vatican for permission to adopt a simplified breviary to try to arrest this downward trend. A Church prelate wrote to me: "I recall discussions of priests [right after the Council] who characterized the obligation of praying the breviary as the inappropriate introduction of monastic discipline into the life of diocesan priests." Annibale Bugnini mentions this and similar cases in *The Reform of the Liturgy 1948–1975*, trans. Matthew J. O'Connell (Collegeville, MN: The Liturgical Press, 1990), 152 ("the abandonment of daily celebration of the Office by some priests"), 171 ("the increasingly worrisome abandonment of the Breviary by some of the clergy"), 496 ("clergy … were in danger of gradually abandoning the Church's official prayer"), and 514 ("a quickly spreading phenomenon—the abandonment of the Divine Office by some of the clergy"). On this last page are found a string of startling quotations from French clergy in 1967 indicating a more-or-less activist and experimental mindset.

say, "collecting dust." I asked him about the importance of the Liturgy of the Hours, to which he responded: "My work is my prayer." From my priestly experience in those years, I observed that some priests had lost the sense of the irreplaceable spiritual foundation of their priestly ministry to be found in the Liturgy of the Hours. The great danger in such an abstraction of the active priestly life from the contemplative spiritual life of the priest is priestly action undertaken, not as it should "in persona Christi Capitis" (see CCC 1548), but as work of the priest himself. In other words, if the priest is not in communion with Our Lord through prayer, especially the praying of the Liturgy of the Hours, he will not be able to bring Christ to others.[207]

One study done in Germany polled 1,371 priests: 831 of the respondents said they pray the Liturgy of the Hours never, seldom, or partially, while 540 said they pray it very often or completely.[208]

---

[207] "Canonical Questions regarding the Liturgy of the Hours," in Joseph Briody, ed., *Psallite Sapientier: The Liturgy of the Hours* (n.p.: Smenos Publications, 2019), 199–222, at 212–13.

[208] K. Baumann, C. Jacobs, A. Büssing, "Commitment to Celibacy in German Catholic Priests: Its Relation to Religious Practices, Psychosomatic Health and Psychosocial Resources," *Journal of Religion and Health* (2017). The study sought to find out if someone's opinion on celibacy is coordinated with the frequency of his celebration of Mass and praying of the Liturgy of the Hours. A notable majority of those who said they would or would likely choose celibacy again turned out to be the ones who offer Mass frequently and pray the Liturgy of the Hours very often or completely, while a notable majority of those who said they would not or might not choose celibacy again coincided with those who never, seldom, or partially do these things.

Ministers of Christ

Fr. Stephen J. Rossetti's book *Why Priests Are Happy: A Study of the Psychological and Spiritual Health of Priests*[209] testifies that the Liturgy of the Hours is not prayed in its entirety by a majority of priests. This is perhaps less a problem among the younger clergy than among older generations, who, in the confusion following the Council, threw off clerical clothing, daily Mass, daily Office, etc., as so many out-of-date "constraints" by which their "work in the world" was being hampered—or so they imagined. In reality, what finally killed their work in the world was the death of the spiritual life, the loss of the primacy of the cult of God over the "needs" (real or imagined) of mankind. This inversion and perversion is what is killing the Church in the West, wherever it is dying.

It is true that, as Matthew Hazell showed in his lecture at Fota XI,[210] there were a fair number of *vota* from bishops and superiors prior to the Council asking that the "burden" of the Divine Office be mitigated—sometimes considerably, as by the suppression of certain canonical hours or by the rendering optional of the little hours. As we know, in the end, the ancient office of Prime was suppressed without further ado,[211] and the entire breviary was stripped down and reorganized into what critics have called (not unreasonably) "the Liturgy of the Minutes."

Someone at the conference put forward a valuable observation: If a certain obligation is made too *easy*, it becomes more difficult to take it seriously and easier to hold it in contempt. One

---

[209] Notre Dame, IN: Ave Maria Press, 2011.
[210] "The Proposals for Reform of the Roman Breviary in the Antepreparatory Period of Vatican II (1959–1960)," in Briody, *Psallite Sapientier*, 64–103.
[211] See Wolfram Schrems, "The Council's Constitution on the Liturgy: Reform or Revolution?," *Rorate Caeli*, May 3, 2018.

feels that it is hardly worth the trouble. (A good example of a light burden readily shirked off is the current one-hour Eucharistic fast.[212]) A heavier burden, because it feels heavy, feels serious, and the absence of it is, oddly, uncomfortable. If one is used to bearing a yoke, and suddenly the yoke is lifted, one can feel off-balance, deprived of a companion, naked and exposed, at a loss.

The old Divine Office had weight or gravity to it, and the duty to pray it was emphasized strongly in canon law and priestly formation.[213] The sight of a Catholic priest praying his breviary in the sanctuary before Mass, in the pews after Mass, in the bus, on the train, in practically any spare moment, was a familiar sight. One of the participants in Fota told a story about how, before the Council, he knew an elderly priest who stopped his car at night, got out, and finished his breviary by the headlights in order not to fail in his responsibility.

Now, I have noticed that, as a general rule, there are two and only two ways of making an appeal to young men to discern the priesthood, and something similar can be said for appeals about religious life. The first way is to say through words, images, music, and the like: "This is going to be incredibly hard. It will demand everything you've got. Many won't be able to hack it. But with God's help, you just might. We're not desperate for you, though, so don't bother to come if you're not serious." The second way is to say: "The life of a Catholic priest is wonderful! You get to be so helpful to people every day. It's bright and cheerful, even

---

[212] See Kwasniewski, *Holy Bread of Eternal Life*, 75–78, 198.

[213] It makes little difference, for our present theme, whether we are speaking about the Benedictine monastic office, the Tridentine or pre–Pius X breviary, or the Pius X breviary; for each places comparable and considerable demands on the one who uses it.

fun at times. We need you. We'll make it work out for you and nothing will be too hard."

I was thinking about this contrast when my son showed me a vocations video, "Forged in Fire," made by a Russian Orthodox seminary. This "trailer" for the longer version (also worth watching) obviously and beautifully illustrates the first type of message, as it alternates footage of a blacksmith hammering the white-hot metal with scenes of flame-illuminated nocturnal divine worship and slowly unfolds the message: "Can you imagine what it would be like to be a seminarian in Jordanville?"[214] A priest says "it's like spiritual bootcamp." Another person adds: "They come into this willingly—they know they're going to suffer." A different priest says: "There is a training, a regimen, a discipline that is instilled, through hardship, self-deprivation, overcoming obstacles, and doing it as a group, as a team." The next voice says: "You are, in effect, a piece of metal that is being purified by a very intense fire. If you survive, then you will become the best version of yourself." And even though it makes cringeful use of the nowadays nearly obligatory "Gandalf slaying the Balrog" type of soundtrack, it is impressive in its earnestness. The imagery fills out the message by showing primarily the chapel and men at prayer.

Compare this virile message with the flaccid tone of too many Roman Catholic vocational videos, in which it is all smiles, handshakes, coffee hours, and the like. For example, a video from the Archdiocese of Washington, D.C.,[215] starts off with background music that can't decide whether it's jazz, classical, easy listening, or a movie soundtrack, then features a slick cardinal doing his

[214] To find this video, one must search YouTube for "forged in fire orthodox."

[215] Published on YouTube on April 23, 2013.

shtick, followed by jolly junior students—regular guys just like you and me! There isn't a hint of the earnest search for God through a life of liturgy, asceticism, and serious study: the only One who can possibly explain and justify the sacrificial gift of oneself to the Church, the only One who makes it sustainable and fruitful. Another video from the same diocese[216] is even worse, especially for the wild west liturgical life it gives us a sneak peak of. It would be hard to imagine most serious young Catholic men finding this appealing, and I'm afraid to say that those who *would* find it appealing are future beneficiaries of the clerical cabal that had its mask ripped off in August 2018 by Archbishop Carlo Maria Viganò.[217] Another off-putting vocation video is the one published in May 2012 by the Legionaries of Christ, which displays the same characteristics as the last two. In reality, the entire genre is choked with examples of this kind.

For an illuminating study in opposites, I recommend watching one of the Society of St. Pius X's vocational videos.[218] It's enough to watch a minute to see that this is going to be *very* different. Admittedly, the script could have been more interesting; it follows

---

[216] Published on YouTube on November 21, 2012.

[217] See *A Voice in the Wilderness: Archbishop Carlo Maria Viganò on the Church, America, and the World*, ed. Brian McCall (Brooklyn, NY: Angelico Press, 2021), 35–91.

[218] Published on YouTube on June 28, 2016, under the title "A Day in the Life of a Seminarian." My mention of a video from the SSPX should not be construed as a blanket endorsement of the Society but simply as a potent illustration of my argument—as was my mention of the Russian Orthodox video. Other traditional communities have also produced excellent vocational videos, e.g., the Priestly Fraternity of St. Peter (search YouTube for "fssp vocations") and the Institute of Christ the King Sovereign Priest ("icksp vocations").

the somewhat hackneyed "day in the life of" model. Nevertheless, what do we find here? The soundtrack is Renaissance polyphony. The narrator tells us about the symbolism of a liturgical vestment and shows the seminarians filing in for the office of Prime (believed by some beatniks to have been abolished—don't break it to them that it survived the purge!). Beautiful images of the Holy Sacrifice of the Mass offered *ad orientem* are followed by a panning shot that features a portrait of the Angelic Doctor, who is repeatedly referred to as a curricular reference point. Cassocked teachers lead seminarians in prayer on their knees before class begins. Athletics make a required but thankfully brief appearance. A man is shown repairing a chasuble, which I consider very forward-thinking. All in all, the SSPX video is far closer to the Eastern Orthodox one and would be similarly appealing to a man in search of a great cause to which to dedicate his life. Both the one and the other reflect the ancient wisdom found in the *Holy Rule* of St. Benedict, who describes in chapter 58 the "discipline of receiving brethren into religion":

> To him that newly cometh to change his life, let not an easy entrance be granted, but, as the Apostle saith, "Try the spirits if they be of God." If, therefore, he that cometh persevere in knocking, and after four or five days seem patiently to endure the wrongs done to him and the difficulty made about his coming in, and to persist in his petition, let entrance be granted him.... Let a senior, one who is skilled in gaining souls, be appointed over him to watch him with the utmost care, and to see whether he is truly seeking God, and is fervent in the Work of God, in obedience and in humiliations. Let all the hard and rugged paths by which we walk towards God be set before him. And if he promise

steadfastly to persevere, after the lapse of two months let this Rule be read through to him, with these words: "Behold the law, under which thou desirest to fight. If thou canst observe it, enter in; if thou canst not, freely depart."

This is the attitude that produces saints. It's the opposite of the pathetic "Please, oh please don't leave us! We'll do anything to keep you. We'll bend the rules, or even discard them!"

All this fits in well with the oft-observed phenomenon that the prospect of challenge or difficulty is what attracts intrepid spirits to make huge commitments. The U.S. Marines have capitalized on this strategy for years, with ad campaigns like: "We Look for a Few Good Men. And We Find Them," and "Battles Are Won Within." They seek to attract not just warm bodies but talented candidates looking for the best, prepared to endure hardship to win glory. In other words, they're looking for an *elite*. In fact, the strategy is as old as Our Lord, who says "take this teaching—if you can" (cf. Matt. 19:12), and St. Paul, who compares Christians to Olympic athletes in training (cf. 1 Cor. 9:24–27). Why, then, are we so afraid of this idea of an elite?

The apostles are often presented nowadays as a ragtag crew, but let us consider for a moment how false this picture is. Several were strong and dedicated fishermen who knew how to labor day and night. They were not lily-livered wimps. Another was a Jewish zealot, the desperate sort who would have been ready to ambush Roman soldiers and strangle them. Another was a tax collector, which meant someone who could dominate and intimidate people and keep a close eye on money in and money out. Two were nicknamed "sons of thunder," presumably because of their temperaments.

If you want to recruit good men, set them a towering challenge and then push them hard in its pursuit.

The psychology at work seems obviously true in the realm of the military and athletics, but it proves no less true in the realm of priestly and religious vocations. If a young man or a young woman is going to commit his or her entire life to the Lord, should it not look and feel serious and all-encompassing? Should it not only promise everything—but also demand everything? It will take all your mind, heart, soul, and strength, every waking minute, your voice, your lips, your senses, your imagination, your memory—"take it all, O Lord, I give it all to Thee," as St. Ignatius of Loyola prayed—but it promises to give you in return deification, eternal life, fruits a hundredfold now and forever.

For this admirable exchange to be believable—that is, for someone to be able to believe that *the Church* believes in the reality of this exchange—the way of life it entails must be radical and all-consuming. From the vantage of fallen human nature, *it will be burdensome*. But this is a necessary step along the path to that "freedom of the children of God" for which we long.

The traditional Latin liturgy is this way too: it *demands* more and *delivers* more.[219] It requires a *fuller* participation of the whole man, soul and body.[220] We are given more to do spiritually *and* physically. It makes nothing easy for us—except *praying*, the one thing we most need to do. All of the difficulty is for the sake of breaking open our minds and hearts for communion with God, which will not be won cheaply, lest it be held cheap.

There are a lot of people out there in media, public relations, and—dare I say it—the Church hierarchy who need to figure

---

[219] See "The Mass That Demands More, Delivers More," in Kwasniewski, *Reclaiming Our Roman Catholic Birthright*, 87–93.

[220] See "How the *Usus Antiquior* Elicits Superior Participation," in Kwasniewski, *Noble Beauty*, 191–213.

out this lesson. The "Youth Synod" of 2018 could have used a serious injection of the same realism and nobility, but it was rigged from the start to yield predetermined results, as can be seen in the proceedings of all autocratic regimes. Still, it never hurts to say what the Synod *might* have been, had it been run by sane people in touch with youth.[221]

Most vocational strategies are too wordy and too wimpy. What's needed are the powerful words of the saints, of the old liturgy, and of Scripture, and photos of a rich liturgical and cultural life. If you really want nuns, you need to send young ladies to a traditional monastery like that of the Benedictines of Mary, Queen of Apostles, in Gower, Missouri. They will either fall in love or run away screaming; indifference is not an option. Similarly, the connection between altar serving and vocations is more obvious with the serving of the traditional Latin Mass. More such Masses will mean more vocations. If churchmen wanted robust vocations, they would do the obvious thing. The fact that they do not is a sign that their real goals lie elsewhere.

The most obvious way we can recover the toughness, challenge, and lofty purpose we have lost is to take up again the old breviary and the Tridentine Mass and move on from there to a future full of promise.

The powerful and fruitful appeal of tradition

People who bring a well-developed life of faith to the Novus Ordo are equipped to derive spiritual benefit from it, while those who

---

[221] See Auguste Meyrat, "Why Youth Synods Drive Young People Away from the Catholic Church," *The Federalist*, October 18, 2018; John Monaco, "An Open Letter to Pope Francis from a 'Bold' Youth," *OnePeterFive*, March 29, 2018.

attend the traditional Latin Mass are confronted by a strong and definite spirituality that drives them deeper into the mysteries of faith and the exercise of the theological virtues. The new rite is a loosely demarcated playing field for liturgical intramurals, whereas the old rite is an ascetical-mystical bootcamp through which soldiers of the Lord are driven. The former presupposes virtue; the latter produces it.[222]

A sign of the truth of this analysis is how often one encounters young people who either converted to the Faith or discovered a religious vocation precisely *through the traditional liturgy*. It was the liturgy itself that powerfully drew them in. Conversion and vocation stories in the Novus Ordo sphere seem to have a lot more to do with "I met this wonderful person" or "I was reading the Bible" or "I found this great book from Ignatius Press" or "I got to know the sisters in my high school" or "their devotion to the poor was so moving." All these motives are truly good, and the Lord wants to use them all. But it is still noteworthy that the Novus Ordo is rarely the powerful magnet that draws them in. People who are *already* drawn to the Church for other reasons will go ahead and participate in the modern rite, as a means to an end. Young people today rely for help on the Novus Ordo; they fall in love with the traditional liturgy. We dutifully attend the Novus Ordo because it's seen as "good for us," like oatmeal; we get excited when the Latin Mass is available, because it's delicious to the spiritual palate. It has the character of an end, not just that of a means.

Perhaps readers may object that I am exaggerating the contrast. It may be that I am. But I can only speak from my own experience, as well as from conversations I've had as a teacher, a

---

[222] See my article "Divergent Political Models in the Two 'Forms' of the Roman Rite," *New Liturgical Movement*, May 14, 2018.

choirmaster, and a fellow pilgrim with hundreds of young people over the past twenty years. There seems to me to be a vast difference in the perception of the attractiveness or desirability of the old liturgy versus that of the new — so much so that if a Catholic college or university wished to increase daily Mass attendance, all they would have to do is to provide the Latin Mass, or to provide it more frequently, and the number of communicants would significantly increase. It might seem utterly counterintuitive, and yet it is borne out again and again at chaplaincies across the world. The appeal of traditional liturgy to youth was already well known when Pope Benedict XVI wrote, in his letter *Con Grande Fiducia* to all the bishops of the world on July 7, 2007: "It has clearly been demonstrated that young persons, too, have discovered this liturgical form, felt its attraction, and found in it a form of encounter with the Mystery of the Most Holy Eucharist particularly suited to them."

A psychologist or a sociologist would say that this can have many causes, but what concerns me at the moment is that there is a real *theological* explanation. One can see, in liturgical terms, why the old form of Mass (and Office and sacraments and blessings, etc.) would be powerfully attractive to today's youth who discover them. These age-old, pre-industrial, pre-democratic forms are so much richer and denser, more symbolic, involved, and mysterious, pointing both more obviously and more obscurely to the supernatural, the divine, the transcendent, the gratuitous, the unexpected. They are seductive, as only God can be seductive. *Seduxisti me, Domine, et seductus sum: fortior me fuisti, et invaluisti:* "You have seduced me, Yahweh, and I have let myself be seduced; you have overpowered me: you were the stronger" (Jer. 20:7). The reformed liturgy in all its Genevan simplicity, on the other hand, has never won any awards for seductiveness. It can barely be looked at head-on before people feel embarrassed about its nakedness and try to clothe it with every accoutrement they can find or invent. We have to bring to it a devotion or a seriousness of purpose that we ourselves possess so that we may be in a position to benefit from the divine sacrament it houses. Without love of the Lord presupposed, this would be a wearisome, unrewarding business, rather like having to convince an indifferent person to be friends with you. It's an uphill battle from the start. Why should young people be interested in something that is so boringly lecture-like, so logical and efficient, or so much in need of artificial sweeteners like sacro-pop music? Most of them would rather be anywhere else.

In attempting to understand how liturgy helps or hinders priestly and religious vocations, we should also take into account the demands of active life and contemplative life. Religious communities nowadays tend strongly in the direction of the active life, with apostolates in the world. As Dom Chautard and others have pointed out, modern people are sorely tempted to fall for the "heresy of activism," whereby we believe that by our hard work we will bring about the Kingdom of God on earth. Liberation theology is an extreme example of the same tendency, but it has been at work since at least the errors of the Americanism diagnosed by Leo XIII in his apostolic letter *Testem Benevolentiae* (1899), according to which the so-called "active virtues" of work in the world have surpassed in worth and relevance the so-called "passive virtues" of religious and contemplative life.[223]

---

[223] For commentary on Leo XIII's letter, see "Contemplation of Unchanging Truth," in Kwasniewski, *Resurgent in the Midst of Crisis*, 57–70.

Since the Novus Ordo valorizes the active and denigrates the passive, it seems to fit well with the activist or Americanist mentality. Thus, it seems that *active* religious orders could find it somehow amenable, as long as they could keep bringing to it an interior life cultivated largely through other means. But the *priesthood*, which must be rooted in the mysteries of the altar in order to remain strong and fruitful, and the *contemplative* religious life, which focuses on offering up the sacrifice of praise and not on an external apostolate, cannot flourish on a subsistence diet. What may seem "good enough" for the laborer in the vineyard is perilously inadequate for the priest and the contemplative, who need a truly sacerdotal and contemplative liturgy if they are fully to realize their great callings.

This is why we see everywhere across the world that serious priests and contemplatives will either "traditionalize" the Novus Ordo as much as they can, adopt the traditional Mass and Office, or do both. Examples of this variety of tradition-friendly approaches may be found in communities such as the Abbey of St. Joseph de Clairval and the Community of St. Martin in France, the Canons Regular of St. John Cantius in Chicago, and the monks of Norcia, Fontgombault, Clear Creek, and Heiligenkreuz.

Am I saying, then, that the (relatively few) healthy religious communities that use the Novus Ordo would be even better off with the Vetus Ordo? Yes, absolutely. The good they already have would be multiplied, their power of attraction and intercession greatly intensified. Unfortunately, however, even those who have come to recognize the superiority of tradition often feel discouraged by the hostility directed against it during the pontificate of Francis—especially since the publication of the motu proprio *Traditionis Custodes*—and they will refrain from returning to the Church's authentic *lex orandi* lest they suffer the fate of the

Franciscan Friars of the Immaculate or the Fraternity of the Holy Apostles.[224] In this official opposition to the desperately-needed restoration of Catholic tradition, we can see the telltale signs of the devil's implacable hatred for the celibate priesthood and the contemplative religious life.

But neither human nor angelic opposition should prevent any community, lay or religious, from quietly and judiciously incorporating the traditional liturgy into its daily life. "Here is a call for the endurance and faith of the saints" (Rev. 13:10). The ancient Latin liturgical rites and uses have nourished the saints of the Western Church for over 1,600 years. They have an imperishable power to do the same for all the saints Our Lord desires to raise up today. Traditional liturgy never failed to attract vocations of every kind or to support the Christian life of the laity; it continues to exercise the same fascination and fortification among us. The new-fangled liturgical rite of yesterday, like the Americanist world in which it was inculturated, is failing. A healthier Church, a healthier spiritual polity, is in the making.

[224] Owing to their embrace of Catholic tradition, these communities were suppressed or decimated by Vatican interference.

18

The Cult of Change and
Christian Changelessness

Much of this book has concerned itself with explicating and defending the bimillenial tradition of the universal Church in regard to the offices of liturgical ministry and the diverse but mutually reinforcing roles of the varied members of the Mystical Body of Christ. The ancient and venerable traditions of the Church have been long-lasting for good reason. Our "cult of change" has led us away from the core of the Christian message.

The modern age glamorizes constant change. It romanticizes variety, development, progress, newness. It exalts evolution as a paradigm of knowledge and of all reality. Those who hold tightly to perennial wisdom and permanent truths, traditional morals, inherited culture, artistic monuments, time-honored rites and customs, are criticized as backward, stunted, regressive, old-fashioned, stuck in their ways. They are not "going with the flow" and "moving with the times." They are "on the wrong side of history."

If, however, we look at the history of modern philosophy, modern science, and modern religion, we will see where the cult of change has led. This cult has tried to make us reject the principle of non-contradiction, according to which a thing cannot both be and not be at the same time, in the same respect. It has led to rejecting the unchanging essences of creatures, which are rooted in the eternal Logos of God. It has led to rejecting our very purpose so that, in spite of lip service to progress, nothing really has a direction toward fulfillment, and therefore nothing can have meaning or significance. It has led to rejecting the creaturely (and therefore dependent and receptive) status of the human being. And it has led to a rejection of the divine revelation addressed, through Christ, to mankind and to every individual man for his salvation.

In all these ways, the movement of modernity has ended in a deep chasm—a pit from which it cannot extract itself: a despairing, meaningless rat race for power, possessions, and pleasures, until people die with the empty comfort of painkillers. Modernity is like a cosmic *reductio ad absurdum*, a demonstration of the absurdity of life when God is forgotten—God, who gives meaning to all things, including suffering and death. We are seeing, firsthand, what happens when people try to live without reference to an eternal horizon, a truth not of our own making, a goodness we were made to love, and a beauty we were made to seek and rejoice in.

It is not surprising that "the world"—the world of separation from God, about which Our Lord and His apostles speak in such stark terms as if it were the rival of God—should think and behave in this manner: "the whole world is in the power of the evil one" (1 John 5:19). The world follows the prince of this world, who uttered the *non serviam* that first introduced egoism, discord, ugliness, hatred, and anarchy into the orderly universe God had made. But it *is* surprising, a scandal in the fullest sense of the word, when the Church's own rulers—men sacramentally entrusted with the office of teaching, ruling, and sanctifying the rational sheep of Christ—begin to follow the ways of the world.

The descent into the demonic is taking place today in the *non serviam* of those who reject the unequivocal teaching of Our Lord in the Gospels on the indissolubility of marriage and the necessity of not throwing the pearl of the Eucharist before the swine of the unrepentant. It is taking place in the *non serviam* of those who dare to invite non-Catholics to the sacrificial banquet that represents the unity of the Mystical Body. It is taking place in the *non serviam* of those who would abolish clerical celibacy in the West and extend clerical ministries to women. It is taking place in the *non serviam* of those who treat the liturgy as their own possession, to change and modify at whim, rather than treasuring it as the holy inheritance of the saints, handed down to us for the sanctifying of our souls.

Then again, we know that the devil never sleeps. Never being at rest in God, he restlessly seeks to induce restlessness in each of us, pulling us away from the immutable God who is our fortress, our stronghold, our rock of refuge, our savior, our protector, our invincible strength. The battle of the spiritual life takes place not "out there" in the world but right here in *my* heart, in *your* heart.

Will we lose our peace as the world goes up in flames? Will we drift from the only harbor in which safety lies, lured out to the open sea where we are bound to lose? Will we become so preoccupied with the fight that we forget the immortal victory already achieved and shared with us in the heavenly banquet of Holy Communion? Will we fall for the most subtle error of all—namely, that if the Church appears to be faltering and failing, then it must be that Christ is no longer able to save us—as if our finite and fallible gaze at the world can truly measure what is taking place in the vast invisible realm of angels and souls?

"The mystery of lawlessness is already at work," writes St. Paul to the Thessalonians (2 Thess. 2:7), to which St. John adds: "the dragon was angry with the woman, and went off to make war on the rest of her offspring, on those who keep the commandments of God and bear testimony to Jesus" (Rev. 12:17). The dragon of the *non serviam* makes war against her who said: "Behold, I am the handmaid of the Lord. Be it done unto me according to Thy Word" (Luke 1:38)—God's immortal, immutable, irrefutable, invincible Word.

The Christian faith sees change in a fundamentally different way from how modernity sees it. For the believer, the primary category is not change, but changelessness. For us, progress is measured not by access to running water, electricity, or wireless internet but by the three stages of the spiritual life: purgative, illuminative, unitive. The only newness that counts is the newness of Christ, the new Adam, into whom we have been baptized and unto whose "full stature" we are called to grow up by continual conversion (cf. Eph. 4:13). Change is good only when it serves the end of changing our vices into virtues, our alienation from God into friendship with Him. Any other change is incidental at best, distracting or destructive at worst.

The Christian faith, which is the continuation and completion of the faith of ancient Israel, is premised on three unchanging realities: the one, simple, ever-blessed God, Father, Son, and Holy Spirit; the hypostatic union of divinity and humanity in Jesus Christ, an ontological covenant that can never be broken; and the apostolic deposit of faith given by the same Christ to His apostles, and from them to their successors until the end of time. The deposit of faith never changes and never can change.

The Cult of Change and Christian Changelessness

St. Vincent of Lérins, in his great *Commonitory for the Antiquity and Universality of the Catholic Faith against the Profane Novelties of All Heresies*, written in the 430s, introduces two contrasting terms and explains their precise difference. The first word, *profectus*, refers to an advancement in our formulation of what we believe, an articulation of something already known to be true but not yet expressed with as much fullness as the human mind — under the guidance of faith and the prompting of the Holy Ghost — is capable of. The other word, *permutatio*, means a mutation, a distortion or deviation, from the original. St. Vincent insisted that the one true faith of the Church admits of *profectus* but never of *permutatio*. One may plumb deeper into the *nexus mysteriorum*, the tight network of mysteries, and see the glint of new facets of beauty, but one may never pull a rabbit out of a hat — or, one might say, a dove out of a mitre. The doctrine of the Immaculate Conception of the Blessed Virgin Mary has always been true and John Henry Newman argued that its truth could be gleaned simply from the book of Genesis as interpreted by the Church Fathers; yet there had been controversies over it throughout history, and it was not declared a dogma of the faith until 1854 when Blessed Pius IX defined it with his Bull *Ineffabilis Deus*. This is *profectus*, not *permutatio*.

Michael Pakaluk, a professor of ethics at the Catholic University of America, expresses this point well:

> Theories of development are meant to establish *identity* of doctrine, not difference.... Newman, when he put his argument into deductive form in Latin, for theologians in Rome after his conversion, stated that, objectively, doctrine is given all at once in the revelation of Christ and never changes. Our subjective reception of the doctrine

may change, but it must never do so in a way that makes the objective content appear to have changed.... Of course no *contradiction* is properly described as a development, any more than an axe to the root of a tree can "develop" the tree.[225]

What St. Vincent of Lérins states about doctrine also includes the principles of Christian morality, above all the reality of intrinsically evil actions—actions that can *never* be good, no matter what intention lies behind them, no matter what the circumstances may be. The Church has made her mind absolutely clear on such actions, faithfully following her divine Master. There has been *profectus*, as we see in the teaching of modern popes like Pius XII and John Paul II, but no *permutatio*, by which the commandments are turned upside-down and inside-out. The rule of charity, of good and God-pleasing action, like the rule of faith that governs our assent to the truth, is unchanging and unchangeable.

The crisis in the Church, as the Encyclical *Veritatis Splendor* so clearly laid out, is a crisis of faith and charity—a crisis of adherence to revealed truth and of the willingness to *live* the truth, suffer for it, die for it. This, in one form or another, is always the struggle between Satan's *non serviam* and Christ's declaration, "not my will but Thine be done"—between the self-destructive freedom of sin and the self-perfecting freedom of obedience, between the boring titillation of perpetual change and the fulfilling romance of divine love. The struggle has entered a new phase with a new intensity, but Christ our Lord is the same, His truth abides, and His victory is assured.

[225] "Four Ideas about Development," *First Things* online, November 17, 2017.

Aging novelty versus timeless tradition

The Instruction *Liturgiam Authenticam*[226] defended the principle that the substantial unity of the Roman rite must prevail, plainly and evidently, in and through the plurality of expressions of it allowed by Church authority. That is, the liturgy celebrated by Roman Catholics must contain and transmit a certain historical and theological identity. Here is not the place to argue about whether that substantial unity is actually possible within the framework of the Novus Ordo Missae and associated books — or the prior and more disturbing question of whether the substantial unity of the Roman rite as such has been shattered. The direction the Vatican has taken in the pontificate of Francis abandons the pretense of "substantial unity" by accelerating the process of inculturation and customization, while simultaneously seeking to impose the reformed liturgy as the only expression of the Roman rite. The progressive view of liturgy, whose partisans find support in the Apostolic Letter *Magnum Principium* of 2017 and in the pope's letter to Cardinal Sarah,[227] gives primacy to a pragmatic pluralism within an ideological drive for postconciliar uniformity. There is no concrete historical-theological identity of Catholicism: such a view is called "monolithic" and said to be outmoded in our times, having been dispensed with — or so it is claimed — by the Council.

---

[226] Subtitled "On the Use of Vernacular Languages in the Publication of the Books of the Roman Liturgy" and dated March 28, 2001.

[227] Issued October 15, 2017; full text at "Pope Francis Publicly Corrects Cardinal Sarah over New Liturgy Rules," *LifeSiteNews*, October 23, 2017. For commentary, see "Nostalgically Stuck in the Spirit of Vatican II," in Peter Kwasniewski, *Tradition and Sanity* (Brooklyn, NY: Angelico Press, 2018), 169–73.

For this reason, I was fascinated to find in the book *Athanasius and the Church of Our Time* by Dr. Rudolf Graber (1903–1992), Bishop of Regensburg, a summary of the work of the ex-canon Paul Roca (1830–1893), who, late in the nineteenth century, right around the time of the Americanist crisis, "prophesied" what the Church of the future must look like:

> The divine cult in the form directed by the liturgy, ceremonial, ritual, and regulations of the Roman Church will shortly undergo a transformation at an ecumenical council, which will restore to it the venerable simplicity of the golden age of the Apostles, in accordance with the dictates of conscience and modern civilisation.[228]

Bishop Graber continues:

> Roca's dominating idea is the word "new." He proclaims a "new religion," a "new dogma," a "new ritual," a "new priesthood." He calls the new priests "progressists," he speaks of the "suppression" of the soutane and the marriage of priests.[229]

Whatever may be said about Roca's imaginary council or the actual Council that took place, it is undeniable that the past sixty years or so have been characterized by an obsession with newness. We have painted ourselves into a corner by insisting that everything be "new" or "renewed," as if this adjective, all by itself, were the token and guarantee of the rightness of an enterprise. This places a subtle pressure on us to innovate, to change, to be

---

[228] Rudolf Graber, *Athanasius and the Church of Our Time*, trans. Susan Johnson (Palmdale, CA: Omni Publications), 35.
[229] Ibid., 36.

different—to privilege motion over stability, acting over suffering, doing over being, work over contemplation. It starts to look like a flaw that a doctrine has remained the same for centuries or that a discipline has not been "adapted" or "updated." Indeed, given the tendencies of fallen human nature together with the peculiar errors of the modern mentality, the insistence on new things goes in the direction of privileging ugliness over beauty, comfort over self-denial, efficiency over dignity.

Speaking of the cretinism of the liturgical reform, Stratford Caldecott wrote:

> Intimations of transcendence—indeed, references to the soul—were minimized. Within the churches, walls were whitewashed and relics dumped in the name of "noble simplicity." Unlike the much earlier Cistercian rebellion against the artistic extravagances at Cluny, this modern campaign for simplicity was not coupled with the asceticism and devotion that might alone have rendered it spiritually "noble." It fell easy victim to the prevailing culture of comfort and prosperity.[230]

All this "reform" has led not to renewal but to an inversion of means and ends, narcissism, anarchy, and, symbolic of all of them, dreadful art. As the Catholic poet Elizabeth Jennings once said, "Many people judge a religion by its art, and why indeed shouldn't they?" The old axiom "nature abhors a vacuum" has been exhaustively demonstrated in our midst: when spiritually

---

[230] *Not as the World Gives*, 180. On the removal from the Novus Ordo of references to the soul, see my article "How the Church Recognizes a Powerful Truth about Mankind in Traditional Requiem Mass," *LifeSiteNews*, November 4, 2020.

muscular, culturally dense religion vanishes, its place is quickly filled with feel-good sentimental claptrap, pop art, pseudo-mysticism, and bleeding-heart political advocacy. "When a man stops believing in God, he doesn't believe in nothing, he believes in anything," as Chesterton didn't say, but might as well have said. We are left with the embarrassing spectacle of some Church leaders, inheritors of millennia of wisdom and beauty, chasing after the miniskirts of modernity. One awakens in a Kafkaesque world where mitred ecclesiastics have metamorphosed into Beatles.

Why this feverish and irrational prejudice for the new? What has it got to do with the one true God who never changes; with the sacrifice of Christ, which is once-for-all; with divine revelation, which is complete at the death of the last apostle; with the principles of the spiritual life, which are perennially valid; with the greatness of the Christian tradition, which gives birth to new things conceived and nurtured by old things and cherishes them all? We might say, inspired by St. Vincent of Lérins, that the Christian religion is a permanent wellspring of truth and holiness from which endless ages can draw fresh water, but it is always the same source, the same substance, the same qualities of refreshment, light, and peace. "Jesus Christ is the same yesterday, today, and forever. Do not be led away by diverse and strange teachings" (Heb. 13:8–9). Christ died once for all. He is the only High Priest who offers the sacrifice of the New Covenant, with His ordained minister empowered to act on His behalf. He gives us the true religion whose dogmas never change, however much the theological understanding of them grows through the ages. The Christian religion is *inherently* new, permanently new, yet in essence unchanging and everlasting. That is why it is capable of never growing old.

Tradition, rightly understood, shares in this perpetual youthfulness; it is not something of the past, much less an object of nostalgia, but a vital energy in the Church that carries us forward, uniting us with the entire Church outside of our age and with the Church Triumphant and the Church Suffering. Indeed, Jews and Christians in the past viewed our ancestors as our *antecessores*, those who have run ahead of us to eternity and, therefore, the ones we are following behind. This is the very opposite of how we tend to think about time and history and culture: we think that *we* are ahead and our ancestors are behind. They are behind the times; we are on the cutting edge. But that makes no sense, because our ancestors went before us. They have already lived their lives. They know the mysteries of life and death, and we are dependent on them. We are *their* pupils, their followers.

The sacred liturgy, the *divine* liturgy as our Byzantine brethren so tellingly call it, must unmistakably reflect the immutable essence of the Faith. As man remains essentially the same, so does Christ and so does His Church, to whom He communicates a share in His stability. This is why the gates of Hell cannot prevail against her — an invincibility she enjoys to the extent that she is living in communion with Him, the immovable and unassailable Rock. Our worship no less than our theology should not only mention or expound the divine attribute of immutability (which grounds the unity of the history of salvation) but should *contain* and *convey* it. Even if, as a created reality unfolding in time and space, liturgy cannot be immutable in itself, it should *signify* all the divine attributes so that in its ceremonies, gestures, texts, and music it is always a bearer of truths about God and His Christ and is never guilty of lying to us or misleading us. The symbolic separation of sanctuary from nave; the Christological symbolism of the males who minister in the Holy of Holies; the *opus Dei* or worship of God that belongs to all in common, uniting us in charity and rising up to Heaven with the beauty of hierarchical order; the symphony made up of diverse Christian callings within the temple and out in the world — these are not arbitrary constructs or subjective preferences but lasting templates of wisdom handed down from our forefathers, Gospel lights to illuminate our minds, sharings in the Cross to save our souls. The liturgy we have inherited from our predecessors, the fruit of the slow growth of ages under the guiding hand of Providence, is admirably suited for this work of initiating us into the eternal mysteries of God and bringing us to perfect union with Him. Let the "ministers of Christ and stewards of the mysteries of God" (1 Cor. 4:1) play their proper role and do their proper work; let each and every one of us do all that belongs to him — and only what belongs to him — to give glory to the Father, and to the Son, and to the Holy Ghost, now and always and unto ages of ages. Amen.

Appendix

Litany for the Clergy

(for private use)

Lord, have mercy. *Lord, have mercy.*
Christ, have mercy. *Christ, have mercy.*
Lord, have mercy. *Lord, have mercy.*
Christ, hear us. *Christ, hear us.*
Christ, graciously hear us. *Christ, graciously hear us.*

God the Father, from whom all fatherhood in Heaven
    and on earth is named, *have mercy on us.*
God the Son, Eternal High Priest and
    Sovereign King, *have mercy on us.*
God the Holy Ghost, Source of sanctity and
    Guide of shepherds, *have mercy on us.*
Holy Trinity, one God, *have mercy on us.*

For the Pope, Vicar of Christ, *hear us, O Lord,*
    and have mercy.
For all the cardinals of God's Holy Church,
    hear us, O Lord, and have mercy.
For all the bishops of God's Holy Church,
    hear us, O Lord, and have mercy.

Ministers of Christ

For all the priests of God's Holy Church,
hear us, O Lord, and have mercy.
For all the deacons of God's Holy Church,
hear us, O Lord, and have mercy.
For all ministers of God's Holy Church,
hear us, O Lord, and have mercy.
For all the seminarians of God's Holy Church,
hear us, O Lord, and have mercy.

For clergy faithful to their promises, *fortify them,*
O precious Blood of Jesus.
For clergy striving to be holy, *fortify them,*
O precious Blood of Jesus.
For clergy reverent in liturgy, *fortify them,*
O precious Blood of Jesus.
For clergy orthodox in doctrine, *fortify them,*
O precious Blood of Jesus.
For clergy courageous in preaching, *fortify them,*
O precious Blood of Jesus.
For clergy generous with Confession, *fortify them,*
O precious Blood of Jesus.
For clergy devoted to works of mercy, *fortify them,*
O precious Blood of Jesus.

For disoriented clergy, *console them,*
O precious Blood of Jesus.
For demoralized clergy, *console them,*
O precious Blood of Jesus.
For exhausted clergy, *console them,*
O precious Blood of Jesus.
For unappreciated clergy, *console them,*
O precious Blood of Jesus.

Litany for the Clergy

For calumniated clergy, *console them,*
  O precious Blood of Jesus.
For persecuted clergy, *console them,*
  O precious Blood of Jesus.
For silenced clergy, *console them,*
  O precious Blood of Jesus.

For heretical clergy, *convert them,*
  O precious Blood of Jesus.
For irreverent clergy, *convert them,*
  O precious Blood of Jesus.
For ambitious clergy, *convert them,*
  O precious Blood of Jesus.
For vindictive clergy, *convert them,*
  O precious Blood of Jesus.
For abusive clergy, *convert them,*
  O precious Blood of Jesus.
For cowardly clergy, *convert them,*
  O precious Blood of Jesus.
For lukewarm clergy, *convert them,*
  O precious Blood of Jesus.

Lamb of God, who takest away the sins of
  the world, *spare and save Thy priests.*
Lamb of God, who takest away the sins of
  the world, *heal and purify Thy priests.*
Lamb of God, who takest away the sins of
  the world, *multiply Thy holy priests.*

℣. Arise, O Lord, into Thy resting place:
℟. Thou and the ark, which Thou hast sanctified.
℣. Let Thy priests be clothed with justice:
℟. And let Thy saints rejoice.

Let us pray. O Lord Jesus Christ, be merciful unto Thy Church and let the light of Thy countenance shine upon us, that we who dwell in the valley of the shadow of death may be delivered from the evils that afflict us and may receive many shepherds after Thy Sacred Heart, who will lead Thy flock in holiness to the pastures of grace and glory, where Thou livest and reignest with the Father in the unity of the Holy Ghost, God, world without end. *Amen.*

Our Lady, Queen of the Clergy, *pray for us.*
St. Joseph, chaste spouse of the Virgin, *pray for us.*
St. Michael the Archangel, *pray for us.*
St. John the Baptist, *pray for us.*
St. John, beloved disciple, *pray for us.*
St. John Chrysostom, *pray for us.*
St. John Vianney, *pray for us.*

Litany of Subdeacon Saints

(for private use)

Lord, have mercy on us. *Lord, have mercy on us.*
Christ, have mercy on us. *Christ, have mercy on us.*
Lord, have mercy on us. *Lord, have mercy on us.*
Christ, hear us. *Christ, hear us.*
Christ, graciously hear us. *Christ, graciously hear us.*

God the Father of Heaven, *have mercy on us.*
God the Son, Redeemer of the world, *have mercy on us.*
God the Holy Ghost, *have mercy on us.*
Holy Trinity, one God, *have mercy on us.*

Holy Mary, *pray for us.*
Holy Mother of God, *pray for us.*
Holy Virgin of virgins, *pray for us.*

St. Baldomer, devoted servant of God and
    worker of miracles, *pray for us.*
St. Andeolus, beaten with thorns and cut
    asunder with a sword, *pray for us.*
St. Leo, faithful companion of the
    priest St. Caius, *pray for us.*

Ministers of Christ

St. Januarius, companion of SS. Felicissimus
and Agapitus, *pray for us*.
St. Magnus, great in the eyes of the Lord, *pray for us*.
St. Vincent, conqueror over the fear
of death, *pray for us*.
St. Stephen, faithful imitator of the
Protomartyr, *pray for us*.
St. Servus, tortured, nailed, burnt,
and smitten, *pray for us*.
St. Rusticus, witness to Catholic truth
against the Arian heresy, *pray for us*.
St. Evortius, elevated from subdeaconhood
to the episcopacy, *pray for us*.
St. Martyrius, slain by heretics, *pray for us*.
St. Quadragesimus, who raised a dead
man to life, *pray for us*.

Lamb of God, who takest away the sins
of the world, *spare us, O Lord*.
Lamb of God, who takest away the sins of
the world, *graciously hear us, O Lord*.
Lamb of God, who takest away the sins
of the world, *have mercy on us*.

Let us pray. Grant, we beseech Thee, O almighty God,
that the intercession of holy Mary, Mother of God, and
of all the holy apostles, martyrs, confessors, and virgins,
and of all Thine elect, may everywhere gladden us, that,
while we commemorate their merits, we may experience
their protection. Through our Lord Jesus Christ Thy Son,
who livest and reignest with Thee in the unity of the Holy
Ghost, God for ever and ever. Amen.

Source of the Litany: Entries from the *Martyrology*[231]

• At Lyons, St. Baldomer, a subdeacon, devoted servant of God, whose tomb is glorified with many miracles. (February 27/28)

• In France, in the Vivarais, blessed Andeolus, subdeacon, whom with others St. Polycarp sent from the East into France to preach the Word of God. He was beaten with thorny rods under the Emperor Severus, and at last suffered martyrdom, his head being cut crosswise into four parts with a wooden sword. (May 1)

• The holy martyrs Caius, priest, and Leo, subdeacon. (June 30)

• Likewise, at Rome, SS. Felicissimus and Agapitus, Martyrs, deacons of the same blessed Sixtus, Januarius, Magnus, Vincent, and Stephen, subdeacons, who were all beheaded together with him and buried in the cemetery of Praetextatus. There suffered also with them blessed Quartus, as St. Cyprian relates. (August 6)

• At Carthage in Africa, the holy martyrs Liberatus, abbot, Boniface, deacon, Servus and Rusticus, subdeacons, Rogatus and Septimus, monks, and Maximus, a boy; in the Vandal persecution under King Hunneric they were assailed by various unheard-of tortures for confessing the Catholic faith and defending the non-repetition

---

[231] Taken from the 1956 edition of the *Roman Martyrology*. The English translation may be purchased in hardcover from Angelus Press and in a pocket-sized paperback from Os Justi Press. To learn more about the liturgical and devotional use of this book in connection with the office of Prime, see my article "How to Incorporate the Traditional *Roman Martyrology* into Daily Prayer," *New Liturgical Movement*, December 2, 2019.

of baptism. Last of all they were fastened with nails to pieces of wood wherewith they were to be burnt; but although the fire was kindled again and again, yet by the power of God it was each time extinguished, and by command of the king they were smitten with oars and their brains dashed out, so that they were slain, and thus, being crowned by the Lord, they fulfilled the splendid course of their battle. (August 17)

• At Orleans in France, the death of St. Evortius, bishop, who was at first a subdeacon of the Roman Church, and then by the divine grace was designated bishop of Orleans by means of a dove. (September 7)

• At Constantinople, the passion of SS. Martyrius, subdeacon, and Marcian, a chanter, who were slain by heretics under the Emperor Constantius. (October 25)

• Likewise, St. Quadragesimus, a subdeacon, who raised a dead man to life. (October 26)

Litany of Sacristan, Lector, Acolyte, and Exorcist Saints

(for private use)

Lord, have mercy on us. *Lord, have mercy on us.*
Christ, have mercy on us. *Christ, have mercy on us.*
Lord, have mercy on us. *Lord, have mercy on us.*
Christ, hear us. *Christ, hear us.*
Christ, graciously hear us. *Christ, graciously hear us.*

God the Father of Heaven, *have mercy on us.*
God the Son, Redeemer of the world, *have mercy on us.*
God the Holy Ghost, *have mercy on us.*
Holy Trinity, one God, *have mercy on us.*

Holy Mary, *pray for us.*
Holy Mother of God, *pray for us.*
Holy Virgin of virgins, *pray for us.*

(Sacristans)
St. Abundius, sacristan in Rome of the
    Church of St. Peter, *pray for us.*
St. Constantius, church guardian remarkable
    for the grace of miracles, *pray for us.*

Ministers of Christ

(*Acolyte*)

St. Tharsicius, martyr for the Real Presence,
pray for us.

(*Exorcists*)

St. Agatho, burnt up for God's glory, *pray for us*.

St. Theodore, notable for works of power
over demons, *pray for us*.

St. Philip, liberator of those possessed
by demons, *pray for us*.

St. Calogerus, freeing the devil's captives, *pray for us*.

St. Fortunatus, famous for putting unclean
spirits to flight, *pray for us*.

St. Paulinus, renowned for casting
out demons, *pray for us*.

St. Arsacius, adorned with virtue and
authority over demons, *pray for us*.

(*Lectors*)

St. Eutropius, falsely accused of arsony, *pray for us*.

St. Bassian, put to death by fire, *pray for us*.

Sts. Serapion and Ammonius, witnesses
for Christ, *pray for us*.

St. Theodulus, drowned in the sea, *pray for us*.

African lector killed while singing
the Alleluia, *pray for us*.

St. Marian, strengthened in torment
by revelations, *pray for us*.

St. Jovinian, victim for Christ, *pray for us*.

St. Dioscorus, favored with a shining
light from Heaven, *pray for us*.

St. Desiderius, fettered for the Word of God, *pray for us*.

St. Viator, faithful companion in years
of desert exile, *pray for us*.
Sts. Fortunatus and Septimus, who refused to
yield up the sacred books, *pray for us*.
St. Synesius, who converted many
souls to Christ, *pray for us*.

Lamb of God, who takest away the sins
of the world, *spare us, O Lord*.
Lamb of God, who takest away the sins of
the world, *graciously hear us, O Lord*.
Lamb of God, who takest away the sins
of the world, *have mercy on us*.

Let us pray. Grant, we beseech Thee, O almighty God,
that the intercession of holy Mary, Mother of God, and
of all the holy apostles, martyrs, confessors, and virgins,
and of all Thine elect, may everywhere gladden us, that,
while we commemorate their merits, we may experience
their protection. Through our Lord Jesus Christ Thy Son,
who livest and reignest with Thee in the unity of the Holy
Ghost, God for ever and ever. Amen.

Source of the Litany: Entries from the *Martyrology*[232]

Sacristans
• At Rome, St. Abundius, sacristan of the Church of St.
Peter. (April 14)
• At Ancona, St. Constantius, guardian of the church,
remarkable for the grace of miracles. (September 23)

---

[232] It would appear that no porters or doorkeepers are named, at
least under that specific title, in the *Martyrology*.

Ministers of Christ

Acolytes

At Rome, on the Appian Way, St. Tharsicius, an acolyte, whom the heathen found bearing the Sacrament of the Body of Christ, and asked what it was that he bore; but he deemed it unbecoming to cast pearls before swine, and was therefore attacked by them for a long time with sticks and stones, until he gave up the ghost. When his body was moved, the sacrilegious assailants could find nothing of Christ's Sacrament in his hands or among his clothing; but the Christians gathered up the body of the martyr and buried it with honour in the cemetery of Callistus. (August 15)

Exorcists[233]

- At Alexandria, the holy martyrs Cyrion, a priest, Bassian, a lector, Agatho, an exorcist, and Moses, who were all burnt and winged their flight to Heaven. (February 14)
- At Constantinople, St. Theodore, Confessor, surnamed Trichinas from the rough habit of sackcloth which he wore, who was noteworthy for many works of power, especially against demons. From his body flows an oil which gives health to the sick. (April 20)
- At Agirone in Sicily, St. Philip, priest, who was sent to that island by the Roman pontiff, and converted a great

---

[233] Anyone listed in the *Martyrology* as having exercised power over demons has been included in this category, since the men ordained as exorcists are entrusted with the spiritual work of praying for the demonically possessed and obsessed, for those who are appointed official exorcists by their bishops, and for all who are engaged in spiritual warfare against our unseen enemies.

part of it to Christ. His holiness was chiefly manifested in freeing those possessed with devils. (May 12)

• At Sciacca in Sicily, St. Calogerus, hermit, whose holiness was shown especially in liberating those possessed by devils. (June 18)

• At Todi in Umbria, St. Fortunatus, bishop, who (as blessed Pope Gregory relates) was remarkable for his great power in putting unclean spirits to flight. (October 14)

• At Nola, a town in Campania, birthday of blessed Paulinus, bishop and Confessor, who, though a man of great riches and nobility, for Christ's sake became poor and humble, and what was more, even gave himself up into slavery to redeem a widow's son, whom the Vandals had taken captive into Africa after the devastation of Campania. He was renowned, not only for learning and for great holiness of life, but also for his power over demons. SS. Ambrose, Jerome, Augustine, and Pope Gregory set forth his praises in their writings. His body was afterwards translated to Benevento, and thence to Rome, but was eventually restored to Nola by command of Pope St. Pius X. (June 22)

• At Nicomedia, St. Arsacius, Confessor, who in the persecution of Licinius forsook the life of a soldier and lived as a solitary. He was adorned with so great virtues that he is said to have cast out demons, and by prayer to have slain a huge dragon; at last, after foretelling the future destruction of the city, he yielded up his spirit in prayer to God. (August 16)

Lectors

• At Constantinople, SS. Tigrius, priest, and Eutropius, lector, who in time of the Emperor Arcadius were falsely accused of the fire which destroyed the chief church and the Senate House; it was alleged that they had caused the fire to avenge the exile of St. John Chrysostom. They suffered under Optatus, the prefect of the city, a man attached to the worship of false gods and a hater of the Christian religion. (January 12)

- At Alexandria, the holy martyrs Cyrion, a priest, Bassian, a lector, Agatho, an exorcist, and Moses, who were all burnt and winged their flight to Heaven. (February 14)
- At Pentapolis in Libya, the birthday of the holy martyrs Theodore, bishop, Irenaeus, deacon, Serapion and Ammonius, lectors. (March 26)
- At Thessalonica, the holy martyrs Agathopodes, deacon, and Theodulus, lector, who, under the Emperor Maximian and the governor Faustinus, were for their confession of the Christian faith drowned in the sea, with stones tied to their necks. (April 4)
- In Africa, the passion of the holy martyrs who, in the persecution of Genseric, the Arian king, were slain in the church on Easter Day; and among them a lector, who, while he was singing the Alleluia in the pulpit, was pierced through the throat by an arrow. (April 5)
- At Lambesa in Numidia, the birthday of the holy martyrs Marian, lector, and James, deacon; the former, when he had overcome the assaults of the Decius persecution in his confession of Christ, was again taken with his renowned companion, and both suffered dire and cruel torments, during which they were twice miraculously strengthened by divine revelations. Finally with many others they were martyred by the sword. (April 30)
- At Auxerre, the passion of St. Jovinian, a lector. (May 5)

- At Heracles in Egypt, St. Dioscorus, lector, against whom the governor practiced many different torments, such as pulling out his nails, and burning his sides with torches. But those who were torturing him fell down, terrified by the shining of a light from Heaven: and at last, burnt with hot plates, he completed his martyrdom. (May 18)
- At Pozzuoli in Campania, the holy martyrs Januarius, bishop of the city of Benevento; Festus, his deacon; and Desiderius, a lector; Sosius, a deacon of the church of Miseno; Proculus, a deacon of Pozzuoli; Eutychius and Acutius. All these being fettered and imprisoned were beheaded, under the Emperor Diocletian. (September 19)
- At Lyons in France, St. Justus, bishop and Confessor, a man of wondrous sanctity and endowed with the spirit of prophecy. He gave up his bishopric and departed with Viator, his lector, into an Egyptian desert and, after leading an almost angelic life for many years, and the fitting end of his labors drawing nigh, he passed to the Lord to receive a just reward. His holy body, and the bones of blessed Viator, his minister, were afterwards translated to Lyons on September 2. (October 14)
- At Venosa in Apulia, the birthday of the holy martyrs Felix, an African bishop; Audactus and Januarius, priests; Fortunatus and Septimus, lectors, who in the time of Diocletian were by the procurator Magdellian put into irons and for a long time enfeebled in prison in Africa and Sicily. Since Felix would not, in accordance with the emperor's edict, deliver up the sacred books, they were at last slain with the sword. (October 24)

Ministers of Christ

• At Rome, St. Synesius, Martyr, who was ordained lector in the time of blessed Pope Sixtus II. After he had converted many folk to Christ, he was accused before the Emperor Aurelian and, being smitten with the sword, obtained the crown of martyrdom. (December 12)

Acknowledgments

Chapter 1 owes its genesis and much of its content to my dear friend Dr. Jeremy Holmes, whom I thank for yet another fruitful collaboration. I thank His Excellency Bishop Athanasius Schneider for permission to include two articles of his own (chapter 4 and chapter 11). All of the chapters began as articles published online at various places: *OnePeterFive* (chapter 1, chapter 2, chapter 7, chapter 14, part of chapter 18), *New Liturgical Movement* (chapters 3 and 4, part of chapter 6, chapters 8, 10, 12, 15, 16, and 17, part of chapter 18, and the appendices), *LifeSiteNews* (chapter 5, part of chapter 9), *Crisis* (part of chapter 6, chapter 11), *The Remnant* (chapter 13), and *Views at the Choir Loft* (part of chapter 9). Their content has been rewritten in the process of developing them into a book. Chapter 2 was originally published in *Homiletic & Pastoral Review* 100.7 (April 2000).

I would like to thank several readers of the manuscript who prefer their names to go unmentioned but whose excellent comments improved the text. The Lord knows who you are and will reward your kindness. Nor are my editors at Sophia Institute Press, Michael Warren Davis and Laura Bement, deserving of any less gratitude for their painstaking work on the manuscript, which certainly improved it in many ways.

Ministers of Christ

The "Definitions" that follow the Preface are adapted from booklets produced for ordination rites by the Priestly Fraternity of St. Peter, to which I extend my thanks for their admirable pastoral work in general and, in particular, for having reintroduced minor orders and the subdiaconate to an ever-broader segment of Catholics. Finally, I thank Lisa Bergman of St. Augustine Academy Press for sharing with me the illustration of the steps of the priesthood from Morrow's *My Catholic Faith*.

Select Bibliography

The purpose of this bibliography is not to list all the works cited in the foregoing pages but, rather, to make focused recommendations for further reading on the major topics discussed herein.

Liturgy in General

Fiedrowicz, Michael. *The Traditional Mass: History, Form, and Theology of the Classical Roman Rite*. Brooklyn, NY: Angelico Press, 2020.

Kwasniewski, Peter A. *The Holy Bread of Eternal Life: Restoring Eucharistic Reverence in an Age of Impiety*. Manchester, NH: Sophia Institute Press, 2020.

———. *Noble Beauty, Transcendent Holiness: Why the Modern Age Needs the Mass of Ages*. Kettering, OH: Angelico Press, 2017.

———. *Reclaiming Our Roman Catholic Birthright: The Genius and Timeliness of the Traditional Latin Mass*. Brooklyn, NY: Angelico Press, 2020.

———. *Resurgent in the Midst of Crisis: Sacred Liturgy, the Traditional Latin Mass, and Renewal in the Church*. Kettering, OH: Angelico Press, 2014.

Shaw, Joseph, ed. *The Case for Liturgical Restoration*. Brooklyn, NY: Angelico Press, 2019.

Priesthood and Other Orders/Ministries

Andrieu, Michel. "Les ordres mineurs dans l'ancien rit romain." *Revue des Sciences Religieuses* 5.2 (1925): 232–74.

Anon. [a Benedictine Monk]. *In Sinu Jesu. When Heart Speaks to Heart: The Journal of a Priest at Prayer*. Kettering, OH: Angelico Press, 2016.

Bacuez, Louis, S. S. *Major Orders*. St. Louis: Herder, 1913.

———. *Minor Orders*. St. Louis: Herder, 1912.

———. *Priestly Vocation and Tonsure*. St. Louis: Herder, 1908.

Biskupek, Aloysius, S.V.D. *Deaconship*. St. Louis: Herder, 1944.

———. *Priesthood*. St. Louis: Herder, 1945.

———. *Subdeaconship*. St. Louis: Herder, 1944.

Cole, Basil. *The Hidden Enemies of the Priesthood*. Staten Island, NY: Alba House, 2007.

Davies, Michael. *The Order of Melchisedech: A Defence of the Catholic Priesthood*. Fort Collins, CO: Books for Catholics, n.d.; reprint of 1993 edition.

de Malleray, Armand, F.S.S.P. *X-ray of the Priest in a Field Hospital: Reflections on the Sacred Priesthood*. Waterloo, ON: Arouca Press, 2020.

Durand, William. *On the Clergy and Their Vestments*. [*Rationale divinorum officiorum*, Books 2–3.] Translated by Timothy M. Thibodeau. Scranton, PA: University of Scranton Press, 2010.

Foley, Michael P. "Male Subjection and the Case for an All-Male Liturgical Ministry." *Antiphon* 15.3 (2011): 262–98.

Hauke, Manfred. *God or Goddess? Feminist Theology: What Is It? Where Does It Lead?* Translated by David Kipp. San Francisco: Ignatius Press, 1995.

———. *Women and the Priesthood: A Systematic Analysis in Light of the Order of Creation and Redemption.* Translated by David Kipp. San Francisco: Ignatius Press, 1988.

Martimort, Aimé Georges. *Deaconesses: An Historical Study.* San Francisco: Ignatius Press, 1986.

Pieper, Josef. "What Makes a Priest?" In J. Pieper, *In Search of the Sacred*, 51–81. San Francisco: Ignatius Press, 1988.

Ratzinger, Joseph. *The Spirit of the Liturgy.* Translated by John Saward. Commemorative Edition with Romano Guardini's *The Spirit of the Liturgy* (1918). San Francisco: Ignatius Press, 2018.

Saward, John. "The Priest as Icon of Christ." *The Priest* 50.11 (November 1994): 37–48.

———. "Thanks for the Feminine." In *The Enemy Within: Radical Feminism in the Christian Churches*, ed. Christine Kelly, 124–35. Milton Keynes: Family Publications, 1992.

Solá, Francis P., S.J., and Joseph F. Sagüés, S.J. *Sacrae Theologiae Summa, IVb: On Holy Orders and Matrimony; On the Last Things.* Third edition. Translated by Kenneth Baker, S.J. N.p.: Keep the Faith, 2016.

Thomas Aquinas. *Scriptum super Sententiis*, Book IV, Distinction 24. In *Commentary on the Sentences, Book IV, 14–25.* Translated by Beth Mortensen. Steubenville, OH: Emmaus Academic, 2017.

———. *Summa theologiae*, Supplement, Question 37. In *Summa theologiae, Supplementum 1–68.* Translated by Laurence Shapcote, O.P. Steubenville, OH: Emmaus Academic, 2017.

Van Slyke, Daniel G. "Consecration to the Office of Acolyte: An Historical Perspective." *Usus Antiquior* 2.2 (July 2011): 89–128. Available online at www.academia.edu/2100146/Consecration_to_the_Office_of_Acolyte_in_Historical_Perspective.

Catholic Life, the Laity, and Renewal

Bullivant, Stephen. *Mass Exodus: Catholic Disaffiliation in Britain and America since Vatican II*. Oxford: Oxford University Press, 2019.

Chautard, Jean-Baptiste, O.C.S.O. *The Soul of the Apostolate*. Translated by a Monk of Our Lady of Gethsemani. Charlotte, NC: TAN Books, 2008.

Chesterton, G. K. *Brave New Family: G. K. Chesterton on Men and Women, Children, Sex, Divorce, Marriage, and the Family*. Edited by Alvaro de Silva. San Francisco: Ignatius Press, 1990.

Davies, Michael. *For Altar and Throne: The Rising in the Vendée (1793–1796)*. St. Paul, MN: The Remnant Press, 1997.

de Mattei, Roberto. *Love for the Papacy and Filial Resistance to the Pope in the History of the Church*. Brooklyn, NY: Angelico Press, 2019.

Houghton, Bryan. *Judith's Marriage*. Brooklyn, NY: Angelico Press, 2020.

———. *Mitre and Crook*. Brooklyn, NY: Angelico Press, 2019.

Kwasniewski, Peter A., ed. *A Reader in Catholic Social Teaching, from Syllabus Errorum to Deus Caritas Est*. Tacoma, WA: Cluny Media, 2017.

Lamont, John R. T., and Claudio Pierantoni. *Defending the Faith Against Present Heresies*. Waterloo, ON: Arouca Press, n.d.

Lawler, Leila Marie. *God Has No Grandchildren: A Guided Reading of Pope Pius XI's Encyclical* Casti Connubii *(On Chaste Marriage)*. Second expanded edition. Waterloo, ON: Arouca Press, 2021.

———. *The Summa Domestica: Order and Wonder in the Home*. In three volumes. Manchester, NH: Sophia Institute Press, 2021.

McGinley, Brandon. *The Prodigal Church: Restoring Catholic Tradition in an Age of Deception*. Manchester, NH: Sophia Institute Press, 2020.

Mectilde of the Blessed Sacrament. *The Mystery of Incomprehensible Love*. Translated by a Benedictine Oblate. Brooklyn, NY: Angelico Press, 2020.

Murr, Charles Theodore. *The Godmother: Madre Pascalina, a Feminine Tour de Force*. N.p.: CreateSpace, 2017.

Sammons, Eric. *Be Watchful: Resist the Adversary, Firm in Your Faith*. Cincinnati, OH: Saragossa Press, 2016.

Schneider, Bishop Athanasius, and Diane Montagna. *Christus Vincit: Christ's Triumph Over the Darkness of the Age*. Brooklyn, NY: Angelico Press, 2019.

Steichen, Donna. *Ungodly Rage: The Hidden Face of Catholic Feminism*. San Francisco: Ignatius Press, 1992.

Vasconcelos, Bernardo, O.S.B. *The Mass and the Interior Life*. Waterloo, ON: Arouca Press, 2021.

von Trapp, Maria. *Around the Year with the von Trapp Family*. Manchester, NH: Sophia Institute Press, 2018.

Waldstein, Michael. Introduction to John Paul II, *Man and Woman He Created Them: A Theology of the Body*, 1–128. Boston, MA: Pauline Books & Media, 2006. [This introduction situates the work of John Paul II in the context of his response to, *inter alia*, the Cartesian-Baconian reduction of the person to consciousness of power and the human body to raw matter for exploitation. This has ramifications for how we understand states of life, liturgical prayer, and hierarchy.]

Walshe, Sebastian, O.Praem. *Understanding Marriage and Family: A Catholic Perspective*. Waterloo, ON: Arouca Press, 2020.

Tradition

de Mattei, Roberto. *Apologia for Tradition. A Defense of Tradition Grounded in the Historical Context of the Faith*. Translated by Michael J. Miller. Kansas City, MO: Angelus Press, 2019.

Ferrara, Christopher, and Thomas E. Woods, Jr. *The Great Façade: The Regime of Novelty in the Catholic Church from Vatican II to the Francis Revolution*. Second edition. Kettering, OH: Angelico Press, 2015.

Ripperger, Chad. *The Binding Force of Tradition*. N.p.: Sensus Traditionis Press, 2013.

———. *Topics on Tradition*. N.p.: Sensus Traditionis Press, 2013.

Sire, H. J. A. *Phoenix from the Ashes: The Making, Unmaking, and Restoration of Catholic Tradition*. Kettering, OH: Angelico Press, 2015.

The Wearing of Veils

Anon. FAQs at "Veils by Lily." www.veilsbylily.com/frequently-asked-questions.

Blanski, Tyler. "Your Wife Is Wearing What? Men, Veils, and the Mystery of Femininity." *Catholic Gentleman*, October 31, 2014.

DeVendra, Rebecca. "The Chapel Veil and a Woman's Rights." *OnePeterFive*, February 4, 2015.

Elissa, Anna. *Mantilla: The Veil of the Bride of Christ*. Malang: Penerbit Dioma, 2016.

Kwasniewski, Peter A. "*Mantilla: The Veil of the Bride of Christ*— A New Book on the Practice of Veiling." *New Liturgical Movement*, August 31, 2016.

Shaw, Joseph, ed. *The Case for Liturgical Restoration*, ch. 7, "Headcoverings in Church," 45–52. Brooklyn, NY: Angelico Press, 2019.

Index of Names

Index of Names

Index of Scripture

Genesis
general ◆ 239
1:26–27 ◆ 6
1:27 ◆ 122
1:28 ◆ 5
2:18 ◆ 5, 187
2:23 ◆ 5
2:23–24 ◆ xxxiv
3:16 ◆ 188

Exodus
general ◆ 42
4:22 ◆ 119
20:3–5 ◆ 42

Leviticus
general ◆ 42

Numbers
18 ◆ xxxix

1 Kings
10:4–5 ◆ 171

1 Chronicles
23 ◆ xxxix

Tobit
8:8 ◆ xxxiv
12:15 ◆ xlii

Psalms
general ◆ 217
2:7 ◆ 119
16:4 ◆ 208
44:15–16 ◆ 174
83 ◆ 146
84 ◆ 146
85 ◆ 146
88:21–22 ◆ 174
109:4 ◆ 62
115 ◆ 146
127 ◆ 118
129 ◆ 147

Proverbs
31:10–31 ◆ 175–77

Ministers of Christ

Wisdom
1:7 ✦ 84

Sirach
24:11 ✦ 206
45:3–20 ✦ 174

Isaiah
general ✦ 183
6:2 ✦ 183–84
6:3 ✦ 42
43:6–7 ✦ 119
54:5 ✦ 8
62:4–5 ✦ xxxiv
66:1 ✦ 71

Jeremiah
20:7 ✦ 231
23:33–40 ✦ 211
31:9 ✦ 119

Ezekiel
general ✦ 183
16:8 ✦ xxxiv

Hosea
2:19–20 ✦ 6

Matthew
3:16–17 ✦ 120
4:4 ✦ 66
5:17–18 ✦ 42
6:33 ✦ 217
11:28–29 ✦ 205
12 ✦ 112
13:24–30 ✦ 80

Matthew (continued)
17:5 ✦ 120
19:12 ✦ 8, 227
20:25–28 ✦ 187
24:30 ✦ xlii
25:1–13 ✦ 174
26:38 ✦ 187

Mark
1:11 ✦ 120
9:7 ✦ 120
11:22–24 ✦ 174

Luke
1:38 ✦ 27, 96, 186, 187, 238
2:51 ✦ 161
3:22 ✦ 120
4:16 ✦ 61
12:42 ✦ 174
20:35 ✦ 8
22:19 ✦ 6
22:27 ✦ 43, 49
22:42 ✦ 187

John
1:8 ✦ 11
1:14 ✦ 6
2:1–11 ✦ 100
2:15 ✦ 61
2:19–21 ✦ 140
3:16 ✦ 29
12:32 ✦ 20
15:5 ✦ 217
19:26–27 ✦ xxiii, 27

Index of Scripture

Ministers of Christ

2 Timothy
2:20 ◆ 171

Titus
general ◆ 135

Hebrews
2:10 ◆ 119
2:13 ◆ 127
5:1–10 ◆ 62
7:20–22, 26–28 ◆ xxx
7:27 ◆ 187
9:12 & 26 ◆ 187
10:10 ◆ 187
10:14 & 21 ◆ xxx
13:8–9 ◆ 244

2 Peter
1:4 ◆ 117
1:17 ◆ 120

1 John
1:8 ◆ 11
3:1–2 ◆ 127
4:1 ◆ 226
5:19 ◆ 236

Revelation
general ◆ 183
5:6 ◆ xlii
8:2 ◆ xlii
12:17 ◆ 238
13:10 ◆ 234
19:7 ◆ ix, 8
19:9 ◆ ix
21:2 ◆ xxxiv
21:2–5 ◆ 174
21:7 ◆ 119
21:22–23 ◆ 96

About the Author

Peter Kwasniewski holds a B.A. in Liberal Arts from Thomas Aquinas College and an M.A. and Ph.D. in Philosophy from the Catholic University of America. After teaching at the International Theological Institute in Austria, he joined the founding team of Wyoming Catholic College, where he taught theology, philosophy, music, and art history and directed the choir and schola until 2018. Today, he is a full-time author and speaker whose work is seen at websites and in periodicals such as *The New Liturgical Movement*, *LifeSiteNews*, *Rorate Caeli*, *OnePeterFive*, *The Remnant*, *Catholic Family News*, and *Latin Mass Magazine*. Dr. Kwasniewski has published extensively on Thomistic thought, sacramental and liturgical theology, the history and aesthetics of music, Catholic Social Teaching, and issues in the contemporary Church. He has written or edited thirteen books, the most recent being *The Ecstasy of Love in the Thought of Thomas Aquinas* (Emmaus Academic, 2021) and *Are Canonizations Infallible?* (Arouca Press, 2021). His work has been translated into at least eighteen languages. For more information, visit his website: www.peterkwasniewski.com.

A special thanks to our *Ministers of Christ* launch team, who read this book before publication and helped us with promotion. Thank you for your time and enthusiasm.

Patti Blahut, Mark Anchor Albert, Mark Allen, Sarah Armstrong, Theresa Ascanio, Adolfo Ayala, Marian Bacik, Matthew Balan, Alexandros Barbas, Brian Barker, Margo Basso, Graham Beduze, Adriana Beaumont, Phillip Bellini, Kyle Bennett, Fr. Ambrose Bennett, Jane Bicandi, Chuck Bienvenu, Fr. Brandon Bigam, Will Bloomfield, Lisa Bonocore, Cristina Borges, Robert Brajkovich, Jim Brehany, Dan Burke, Rachel Bush, Florencia Cabrera, Phillip Campbell, Dave Capan, Fr. Gregory Charnock, Rinju Chenet, Becky Cloetta, Dominic Colucy, Terry Conway, Jean-Patrice Coulon, Tracy Cruz, Emanuele Daddi, Gene D'Agostino, Dave D'Alessandro, Gerry Davila, Peter De Loca, Christie Raleigh DeTrude, Daniel Devine, Zachary Dong, Ninian Allan Doohan, Kendra Dowlatshahi, Anna Elissa, Fr. Cliff Ermatinger, Amanda Evinger, Ivan Fadeyev, Fr. Patrick Fenton, Rebecca Fidero, Jacob Flaherty, Timothy Flanders, Stephen Fleischer, Maksim Fomich, Angela Fontenot, Fr. Athanasius Fornwalt, Brock Fowler, Steve Fredriksson, Ian Gallagher, Kristi A.S. Gomez, Carlos Gort, Andrew Greenwell, Mark Gross, Most Rev. Thomas Gullickson, Irene Hacke, Christoph Matthias Hagen, Daniel Harrigan, Matthew Hazell, Aaron Henderson, Hugh Henry, Maike Hickson, Alexander Hilton, Amy Hintzman, Gregory Hogan, Herman F. Holbrook, Ed Hurlbutt, Gregorius Ioannis, Shannon Marie Jones, Anthony Jones, Joachim Ardiles Jukie, Fr. Hrvoje Juko, Juventutem DC, Sharon Kabel, Anna Kalinowski, Fr. Matthew K. Kauth, Charlie Kerscher, Aaron P. Kessler, Fr. Jeffrey Keyes, Amy Kline, Fr. Thomas Kocik, Stephen Kokx, Patrick Kornmeyer, Evan Le Doux, Nicholas Lemme, Timothy S. LeRoyer, Kenneth Lieblich, Samuel Livingston, Kristopher Manghera, Emily Mangiaracina, Brad Markham, Maurisa Mayerle, Brian McCall,

CRISIS Publications

Sophia Institute Press awards the privileged title "CRISIS Publications" to a select few of our books that address contemporary issues at the intersection of politics, culture, and the Church with clarity, cogency, and force and that are also destined to become all-time classics.

CRISIS Publications are *direct*, explaining their principles briefly, simply, and clearly to Catholics in the pews, on whom the future of the Church depends. The time for ambiguity or confusion is long past.

CRISIS Publications are *contemporary*, born of our own time and circumstances and intended to become significant statements in current debates, statements that serious Catholics cannot ignore, regardless of their prior views.

CRISIS Publications are *classical*, addressing themes and enunciating principles that are valid for all ages and cultures. Readers will turn to them time and again for guidance in other days and different circumstances.

CRISIS Publications are *spirited*, entering contemporary debates with gusto to clarify issues and demonstrate how those issues can be resolved in a way that enlivens souls and the Church.

We welcome engagement with our readers on current and future CRISIS Publications. Please pray that this imprint may help to resolve the crises embroiling our Church and society today.

Sophia Institute Press® is a registered trademark of Sophia Institute.
Sophia Institute is a tax-exempt institution as defined by the
Internal Revenue Code, Section 501(c)(3). Tax I.D. 22-2548708.